DANCING
WITH DOGS

MARY ANN NESTER

DANCING
WITH DOGS

INTERPET PUBLISHING

Published by
Interpet Publishing,
Vincent Lane,
Dorking,
Surrey RH4 3YX,
England

ISBN 978 1 84286 216 2

The recommendations in this book are given without any guarantees on the part of the author and publisher. If in doubt, seek the advice of a vet or pet-care specialist.

Credits
Editor:
Philip de Ste. Croix
Designer:
Philip Clucas MSIAD
Cartoons:
Kim Blundell
Photography:
Mark Burch
Index:
Richard O'Neill
Production management:
Consortium, Suffolk
Print production:
1010 Printing International Ltd, Hong Kong
Printed and bound in China

The Author

Mary Ann Nester arrived in England from New York in the 1970s and never went home. In 1977 she set up Aslan Dog Training offering classes and workshops in obedience, agility and doggy dancing at home and abroad.

Her credentials are impressive. Mary Ann is a member of the Association of Pet Dog Trainers and, as an accredited trainer in the DAQ® method, she is qualified to design functional training programmes for handlers and their dogs in any canine sport.

Mary Ann's miniature poodles have been Crufts agility finalists and represented Great Britain at the World Agility Championships three years in a row. Performing tricks was always part of their warm-up routine, not only to stretch muscles but also to increase their mental flexibility. To keep herself mobile, Mary Ann relied on her background as a keep-fit instructor and gymnastics coach. It was inevitable that she would put the two together, add some music and start doggy dancing. And it wasn't long before one of her poodles gained excellent qualifications by winning classes in canine freestyle and heelwork to music. What started as a bit of fun is now a full-time addiction and Mary Ann is not only an enthusiastic competitor but has passed the Kennel Club examination on "Requirements of a Heelwork to Music Judge".

Committed to promoting canine sports, Mary Ann combines training her own dogs with writing. The publication of her first book, *Agility Dog Training*, is one of her proudest landmark moments.

When not dancing with her own dogs or teaching other people how to dance with theirs, Mary Ann works as the part-time Clinic Administrator for an out-of-hours veterinary emergency service.

1
2
3
4
5
6

Contents

I love to dance. If there is music playing, I'm tapping my foot. It doesn't matter if I'm in the supermarket or in my kitchen. I love bouncing around to a good tune and I've always had dogs who have loved to bounce around with me, either jumping over my head or knocking me to the floor. Fun, but is that doggy dancing?

Then came Tam, my Border Collie. Everyone has had a dog that they wish they could have again. Tam never heard the phrase "click and treat" but that didn't stop him from being a stylish obedience dog. If I boogied across the floor, he would hold himself in the heel position and travel with me. I swear he could read my mind. We had great fun performing dance routines to raise funds for local charities, but we never competed at a heelwork to music show. It wasn't a competitive sport back then but, if Tam were alive today, I'm sure we would have a cupboard full of trophies. It's too late for Tam, but not for your dogs.

So don't delay. This book aims to get you started and keep you going. It's time to make the leap from bouncing around in the kitchen to doggy dancing. If you have always wondered how to teach your dog to wave a paw or walk backwards, read on. Each trick has been road tested on my own dogs, young and old. They've loved all the extra attention and treats and so will yours. And there is nothing like success to make you feel good. The first time my pup did a "peek-a-boo", I cried because he looked so cute. If you have already taught your dog some stunts, but don't know how to string them together into a routine, help is at hand. And if you make mistakes or encounter problems along the way, don't give up.

Introducing The Sport

Despite the best intentions, things can and do go wrong. What are you going to do if your dog spooks at the judges, the zip breaks on your costume or your music won't play on the sound system?

These are typical of the questions that this book tries to answer. As an instructor, I'm asked all sorts of things by first-time pet owners as well as experienced handlers on their second or third dog. I can guarantee that there will be a student in class whose dog barks non-stop and someone else whose dog turns his nose up at treats. But no matter how well prepared I am, I can still be stumped and surprised. I will never forget the man who asked what to do with his false teeth. And the questions never stop, especially in doggy dancing where each dog and handler partnership is unique and the creative possibilities for moves and routines endless.

So, I may not have answered all of your questions, but I've certainly tried! I can pat myself on the back if you've had fun teaching your dog something new. I can breathe a sigh of relief if I've helped you to solve a training problem and you understand your dog a little better. And I can celebrate with my own dogs by turning on the radio and dancing.

LEARN TO TALK DOGGY DANCING

A

ABC An ABC (Anything But Collies) is any breed or type of dog except a collie or collie cross. The term comes from dog agility where there are ABC classes at shows limiting entry to non-collies.

Accuracy and execution of movement Accuracy and execution of movement is one element of the judging criteria used at Kennel Club shows with a maximum number of ten points. Judges are looking for a quick response to cues and commands as well as a smooth and slick performance.

Across The across position *(right)* in heelwork is when the dog is placed across the front or the back of the handler. The dog's head should be reasonably close to the handler's leg and the dog should be able to maintain this position moving in any direction at any speed – slow pace, walk or a run!

Additional categories These are the classes that appear on show schedules in addition to the Official classes. They include Dressage and Dances with Dogs.

Advanced Advanced classes are open to dogs that have gained 20 points or more in Intermediate classes at a Kennel Club-licensed Heelwork to Music show.

Anticipation When your dog second guesses you. You may not have given the command to "Sit" but the dog has made a guess and acted on his own prediction. In the past, you gave him a biscuit for sitting so why not now? Although anticipation is a vital learning component, it can ruin a dance routine if your dog anticipates a move before you have given the cue.

Anything goes This is an unofficial class. Routines starring singles, pairs, braces or groups of dogs are acceptable. You can go wild as long you are sensible.

Attention Attention is selective concentration. The dog must focus on the handler and cues and ignore distractions in the environment (no matter how tempting the treats left on a spectator's chair). You can't teach a dog anything if his mind is wandering and he is thinking about the bitch next door.

Attitude The characteristics of a dog with attitude are all positive. A dog with attitude wants to please, wants to learn and wants to make the world smile (even if he is being naughty). Many trainers believe that you need a dog with attitude if you want to stand out on the dance floor.

Audio cassette You can record your music onto an audio cassette. The majority of shows will have both CD and cassette players.

Away This command is used in obedience competitions to send a dog away from the handler to a box or marker. In agility, it is used to send the dog ahead of the handler over fences. In doggy dancing, the command "Away" is used to send the dog to a prop or target.

B

Back The command used when the dog walks backwards. A dog can be heeled backwards or he can be backed away from his handler, creating distance between them.

Balance Many moves in doggy dancing require good balance. A pose, such as "Sit pretty", has to be held for a few seconds without wobbling. In addition, a dog should have balanced movement and be comfortable at doing things to the right and left, forwards or backwards.

Banana This term refers to the shape of a dog's back. If a dog's back is curved behind the handler's leg instead of straight when the dog is in the heel position, it is "bananaed".

Bear Teach your dog to be a bear and sit on his haunches *(right)* and lift his paws in the air. Big dogs look best as bears! You

could choose to use "Sit pretty", or "Beg" instead if you have a more petite breed!

Beat You need to listen and count the beats in your music. Each note of the music will have a value; for example, a whole note has four beats or a half note has two beats. The metre or time signature at the beginning of a piece of music tells you how many beats in each measure or bar.

Beg – see **Bear**

Booking in All competitors must book in on the morning of the show and hand in either CDs or cassette tapes of their music to the organisers.

Bounce When your dog acts like a rubber ball and jumps up and down on the spot *(left)*. Alternative commands include "Bong" or "Pop".

Bow This command cues the dog to rest his elbows on the ground and keep his bottom in the air. His head can be either up or resting on his paws. I have also heard the command "Bend".

Bridge This is an operant conditioning term. More simply, the clicker noise "click" is the bridge between a dog's behaviour and the reward (treat, toy or hug) that will be coming his way. A handler uses a verbal bridge when he marks a behaviour with an exclamation like "Yes!" or "Super!" and delivers a goody to his dog.

Busking This is unplanned choreography. Handlers will have to busk and make up moves it they have forgotten what comes next in their routine. In addition, some fun classes challenge entrants to busk to music that they have never heard before.

C

Caller The caller makes sure every competitor is present and ready to go into the ring in the order that has been drawn.

Cane A cane is one of the most common props in dog dancing because it can be used during a performance just like a target stick to lure and direct the dog as in training.

Canter A canter is a little faster than a walk or a trot, but not as fast as a gallop. A canter consists of three evenly spaced beats.

Catch Like people, some dogs are naturals at catching balls, and others aren't. Practice helps and catching a prop on the beat can be an impressive part of a dance routine. But some objects are more difficult to catch than others; for example a walking stick or a hula hoop.

Tennis balls are relatively easy to catch if thrown in a gentle arc, like this. Catching a hat will be a bit harder!

Carry This term is used when a dog carries an article in a routine; for example, carrying a bowler hat while trotting with his handler at the heel position.

CD You can buy CDs (compact discs) of your favourite music or download tunes onto disc from your computer. Portable CD players allow you to practise your dance moves with your dog anywhere.

Choreography A dance is made up of steps put together in a specific order to match the beat and mood of the music. Doggy dancing is not just about training your dog to do tricks but learning how to put them all together to match your music.

Chorus A collection of words set to music that are repeated after each verse of a song.

Circle The dog moves in a 360 degree circle either around his handler *(right)* or an object. He may go forwards or backwards. The circle may be large or small, clockwise or anti-clockwise. Also called "rounds".

Clicker A small device that makes a "click" sound to mark the dog's behaviour that will be rewarded. It is small enough to hold in your hand and can be operated by pressing directly onto a piece of metal or a button. Some clickers have volume settings so that the click noise can be softened for noise-sensitive dogs.

Come This is the recall command. The dog should instantly return to his handler when he hears the command "Come".

Content The content of a routine is one of three sections that judges will mark at Kennel Club competitions. The routine must have a number of moves of varying difficulty. You just can't walk your dog around the floor in the hope of high marks!

Costume The handler's dress should aid the musical interpretation. Choose the theme tune to *Laredo* and you can shop for a cowboy outfit. But make sure your costume is appropriate to your moves. It's no good donning a ball gown for a waltz if the skirt keeps wafting your dog in the face.

Crawl The dog is in the Down position and moves forward *(right)* keeping his elbows and tummy as close to the ground as possible. It is also known as the "Creep".

Cue The cue is the signal that elicits the behaviour you have taught your dog. The cue may be a word like "Sit" or an action from the handler; for example, you could cue your dog to "roll over" when you raised your hat or to "twist" when you opened an umbrella.

D

Dances with dogs This is an additional class that requires the handler's moves to be recognisable as a dance; for example, a highland fling, while the dog works in dressage or freestyle or a combination of the two.

Debut The first time you step out in costume with your dog in front of judges and an audience will be your debut. You will never forget your first public performance!

Deportment Deportment is how the dancer carries her body and uses her limbs to interpret the music. The appropriate posture for a military piece would be very upright and a complementary gesture would be a salute.

Design A routine that has good design will be planned to balance space and direction. The handler and dog won't have their back to the judges nor will they have choreographed all the action in one corner of the floor.

Dig This command will cue the dog to paw, scratch and dig the floor.

Direction Direction refers to any point on the compass on your floor plan. Where is your dog moving in relation to you? Is he travelling towards you or away from you? Can he perform his moves to the right and to the left?

Distance Distance refers to the space between you and your dog. Your dog may be able to do a "spin" in the heel position, but will he "spin" if you are in one corner of the room and he is some distance away in the other?

Down This is the command that is used to cue your dog to lie down on the ground *(right)*. The dog may lie with his elbows and tummy touching the floor or he may lie on his side. The Down can be jazzed up if he has been taught to rest his head on his paws or cross one paw over the other while in this position.

Dressage Many shows hold classes in dressage and concentrate on a dog's gait. Whether the dog is walking, trotting, cantering or galloping, his foot falls must maintain the continuous rhythm of the music in the heel or free position throughout the routine.

Drive Drive is another word for motivation. A dog with lots of drive performs with gusto and wants to do it all again when he hears the last note of music.

Duration Duration refers to the length of time a note or silence lasts in a piece of music.

Dynamics This term refers to the interaction of dog and the handler. There should be a strong flow of energy and communication between them. It can also refer to the loudness or softness of the music.

No hesitation and a dynamic leap through the handler's arms.

The timing and execution of such a move takes practice, trust and teamwork.

E

Elimination No points for you! You will be eliminated if your dog leaves the ring.

Excellent qualification If your dog wins a class and you have the required number of points, then you may use the "Ex" title after your dog's name. If you see "Dancing Diva HTM St Ex" then you know that this dog is now competing in novice heelwork to music (HTM) classes and won a starters heelwork to music class.

Expressive A routine may communicate ideas and emotions through dance movements of handler and dog.

F

Fetch This is the command used to tell the dog to retrieve an object.

Flat Many handlers use this command to distinguish between two down positions. They say "Down" for the dog lying on his tummy in a sphinx position or with one hip folded over and "Flat" for lying on his side with his legs outstretched and head on the floor.

Freestyle Freestyle is an official category or class – the dog is allowed to work in a variety of positions and speeds relative to his handler. No more than a third of the routine can be heelwork.

Front When your dog is at your feet and facing you, he is in the front position *(right)*. Many moves start from this position.

Fudging Not really cheating, but close! Pretending that the swooping swing you did with your dog was really a crisp, sharp turn!

Fun classes These are the fun classes that can be scheduled in conjunction with the official classes at a show, for example, "Dancing Virgins" or "Lucky Dip". These classes can be judged, but are often not marked, and food or toys may be allowed in the ring.

G

Gait This refers to how the dog moves and can be a walk, trot, canter or gallop.

Gallop Any animal with four feet can gallop and it will be their fastest pace. All four feet are off the ground at the same time in a single stride.

Genre Genre is a type of music. To name a few – country music, the blues, rock and roll or folk.

H

Harmony Just as two different notes when played together at the same time can result in a pleasing and beautiful harmony, the handler and the dog must demonstrate the same unity of purpose to achieve a good effect.

Head This command is often used to cue the dog to place his chin on his paws or on the floor.

Heel position In obedience the heel position *(left)* for the dog is on the handler's left side. The definition has been broadened in heelwork to music classes to include both the left and right hand side of the handler, facing forwards or backwards to the handler, and across the front or the back of the handler. There are eight official positions.

Heelwork Heelwork is when the dog moves with the handler in the heel position. .

Heelwork To Music Heelwork To Music is an official category or class of competition. In this discipline the dog must work in the heel position in any direction or at any pace. A minimum of two thirds of the routine must consist of heelwork.

High This command tells the dog to stand upright on his hind legs with his front paws in the air.

I

Improvisation Making it up as you go along. Your cane has broken in half. What do you do? Use the two pieces like drum sticks? Creating a dance without prior practice or rehearsal.

Intermediate This class is for dogs that have gained 16 points or more in novice classes at Kennel Club-licensed heelwork to music shows.

Interpretation Musical interpretation is one section of the judging criteria used at Kennel Club shows with a maximum number of ten points being awarded. The handler and his dog will translate the music into a choreographed dance which should be flowing and balanced.

J

Judge This is the person who will mark your routine if you enter a competition. At Kennel Club shows there will be three of them marking programme content, accuracy and execution of movement, and musical interpretation.

Jump When your dog is airborne, he is jumping *(above)*. He can stand on four or two legs and jump off the floor or he may jump over a cane or through a hoop to land on the other side. And he can jump and land on things like your back!

K

KC Registration In the United Kingdom, dogs must be registered with the Kennel Club in order to compete at Kennel Club-licensed shows. There is an activity register for non-pedigree dogs.

Kiss You can teach your dog to lick your cheek on command and call it giving you a kiss. Beware – this trick is not always very hygienic!

L

Links These are the moves that keep your routine flowing and travelling across the dance floor. They help you change direction or re-position without stopping; for example, if you are heeling your dog on the left you could send him under your right leg and heel him on the right hand side without a break in continuity.

Teach your dog to give a paw when you introduce him to friends.

M

Metre This is another name for the time signature of a piece of music.

Music man The man in charge of the sound system at a show, display or demonstration.

Musical interpretation Musical interpretation is one element of the different judging criteria used at Kennel Club shows with a maximum number of ten points available. The handler and his dog will translate the music into a choreographed dance which should be flowing and balanced.

N

NFC This stands for Not For Competition. Dogs should be entered at a Kennel Club-licensed show even if they are not going to compete.

Notes The musical symbols that denote the pitch and duration of a sound.

Novice Novice classes are open to dogs or handlers which have gained 14 points or more in Starters classes at Kennel Club-licensed heelwork to music shows.

O

Official classes Official classes at Kennel Club shows include heelwork to music and freestyle. Handlers can progress from Starters to Novice, to Intermediate and then to Advanced through a points system and gain titles for their dogs in the process.

Out This command can be used to send the dog away from the handler.

P

Paw This is the shortened version of "Give a paw" *(above)*. Some handlers use this command to cue the dog to tap an object with his paw.

Peek-a-boo If you teach your dog to cover his face with a paw, you could choose this as a command.

Performance Going live with your dance routine. When you practise with your dog at home, you can stop and start over if you make a mistake, but with an audience (even if it is only your grandmother), you have to give it your all from beginning to end and keep smiling.

Piggyback Asking your dog to hop up onto your back so he can have a ride *(right)*.

This piggybacking dog isn't afraid of heights!

Pop This command is used to cue the dog to jump straight up into the air like a jack in the box.

Pray Tell your dog to pray and he should put his head down between his paws.

Programme content Programme content is one element of the different judging criteria used at Kennel Club shows with a maximum number of ten points available. The handler and his dog will present a series of varied moves that showcase the dog's strengths. The judges will have a higher expectation of difficult moves in Advanced classes than in Starters.

Progress awards These awards are run by the Paws 'n' Music Association and aim to help handlers achieve the fundamentals in heelwork to music. Handlers can progress through four divisions.

Props Anything you can carry into the ring with you to use during your dance is a prop. It could be a chair, a broom, a basket *(left)* or a ladder but it must be relevant to your routine.

Q

Quiet Dogs that woof hear this command a lot! Barking during a routine will be penalised by the judges.

R

Release Common release words include "OK", "Finished" or "Done". They indicate that the exercise is over.

Reverse This is used to cue the dog to walk backwards.

Rewind This command tells the dog to walk backwards around the handler's legs as if he is rewinding a cassette tape.

Rhythm This is the organisation of notes and rests that create a beat in the time signature. Count them; for example: one, two, three AND four.

Ring This is the space available to you for your routine. The ring shape is usually square or rectangular and may be laid out in a marquee on grass, a leisure centre gymnasium or a village hall. The ring size will be stated on the competition schedule. The judges usually sit on one side and the audience on the other three.

Roll over When a dog is lying down on his tummy and rolls right over *(right)* from one side to the other to end up once again lying down on his tummy.

Rounds A dog does "rounds" when he circles your legs or an object.

Runners These are the show volunteers that collect the judges' marks and take them to the scorekeepers.

Running order Each dog will receive a numerical running order randomly drawn for each class you have entered at a show.

S

Schedule This is the printed notice of a heelwork to music show and will contain information such as the host club, venue, classes, entry fees and so on.

Scorekeeper The scorekeeper is responsible for collating and recording the marks from the judges. Many shows these days have customised computer programmes that calculate rankings and places.

Shake This is another command for "Give a paw".

Shy This is another command for "Peek-a-boo".

Sit A dog is sitting when he has his bottom on the ground, but not his chest, and his forelegs are straight. The "Sit" is another one of the three fundamental positions – Sit, Down and Stand – and the starting point for many tricks.

Speak Dogs can be taught to bark on this command.

Spin This command is often used to cue the dog to turn in a tight circle to the left.

Stand A dog is standing when he has four feet on the ground – not his tummy or bottom.

Starters These classes are for dogs and handlers that have not yet gained more than 14 points at a Kennel Club-licensed heelwork to music show.

Stay If you tell your dog to "Stay", he shouldn't move a muscle until you release him.

Steward This is the show official who helps competitors in or out of the show ring. They are often asked to help carry props or hold dogs.

T

Table When a handler is on his hands and knees on the floor, he is like a table and this is the command used to prompt the dog to jump on his back.

Target Popular choices for targets include plastic lids, mouse pads or squares of carpet. A target may be big enough for the dog to lie down on or so small that he can only touch it with his nose.

Tempo Tempo is characterised by the speed (adagio is slow and allegro is fast, for instance) and rhythm of the music. For example, waltzes are usually in 3/4 time meaning there are three crotchet beats to each bar of music.

Through This command is frequently chosen to cue the dog to go underneath and through the handler's legs *(left)*.

Touch Touch means make physical contact. Your dog can touch the end of a cane with his nose or place his paw on a stool.

Trot When your dog is lifting each diagonal pair of legs at the same time, he is trotting. This gait is faster than a walk and there is usually a moment of suspension in the air. If not, your dog is pacing like Spotty Dog.

Twist Twist is the opposite of spin. The dog turns to the right and ends up back where he started as if he has been chasing his tail.

U

Up This command usually signals the dog to lift his front feet in the air into a "Beg" or "High" position. Or it may be the command to jump up and over a cane or outstretched arm.

V

Verse A set of words performed to music. Some handlers listen to the vocals and if the singer says "clap your hands", that's what they teach their dog.

W

Walk This is the slowest gait for your dog.

Wave When your dog lifts a paw and moves it up and down in the air – it looks like he is waving hello or goodbye!

Weave You can teach your dog to wiggle in and out of your legs *(left)* as you walk forwards or backwards. Use this command to initiate the weaving movement. If you have a big dog, can you lift your leg high enough for him to fit through?

XYZ

Zoomies When a dog has lost the plot and the handler has lost control of him. Instead of following his handler's lead, he zooms around the ring at one hundred miles an hour. The dog has the zoomies!

PART ONE

WHAT IS DOGGY DANCING?

Throughout history, there have been many famous
dance partnerships gracing the stage and screen.
But how many stars have teamed up with a dog that
has stolen the show? What is doggy dancing?
Is it a recreation or a sport? Is it really dog training?
No matter how you define doggy dancing,
everyone agrees – it's lots of fun!

The History Of Dancing With Dogs

People have been dancing with their dogs through the centuries. I am willing to bet that the first time a cave man jigged round the camp fire waving a knuckle bone, he was not alone. His faithful wolf-dog tried to keep in step! As long as there's been music and people training dogs, there has been doggy dancing.

Birth of the sport However, until the late 20th century dancing dogs were limited to the vaudeville stage and the circus ring. It was not until the 1990s that doggy dancing really blossomed as a competitive sport and it has been growing in popularity ever since. In 1991, The Musical Canine Sports International (MCSI) was created in Canada in order to monitor the growth of the sport, develop a system of guidelines for judges and formulate regulations to govern classes. Similar organisations sprouted in the United States, such as the Canine Freestyle Federation (CFF) and the World Canine Freestyle

Left An eye-catching pose that's sure to please an audience.

Right As dog dancing has grown in popularity, more and more handlers have decided to enter shows to test their routines with the judges and some have gone on to become international stars.

Organisation (WCFO) whose founder Patie Ventre, would like to see canine freestyle become an Olympic sport. These organisations do their best to promote doggy dancing through newsletters, shows and club listings. In England we have the Paws 'n' Music Society and Canine Freestyle GB. National and regional emphasis may vary, but all insist that dog and handler perform with enthusiasm and style

Queen of style And no one has more style that Mary Ray. She has been the greatest proponent of heelwork to music in the UK and, for many years, she has repeatedly wowed the crowds by performed breathtaking routines on the closing day of the Crufts Dog Show. In addition, her demonstrations and training events have helped spread the word to many European countries as well as Australia and South Africa. They have helped kick start competitive doggy dancing here and abroad. It is no wonder that Mary is the president of Paws 'n' Music, the UK's first dedicated heelwork to music club and the first club to become Kennel Club-registered in 2003.

trainer and choreographer as the performers I was admiring.

If the music on the radio gets you up on your feet and your dog joins in, that's doggy dancing. You may choose to keep dancing in the privacy of your own home or go public and attend classes.

The nuts and bolts Doggy dancing is a choreographed programme of canine tricks, transitional moves and obedience exercises set to music. It is a test of your inventive and expressive skills. A good routine will showcase a dog's abilities and athleticism while keeping to the beat of the music. Interpretation of a tune can be subtle or eye-catching as long as your four-legged friend is the star of the show – don't try to outshine him!

Whether at your village fete, a variety show or a Kennel Club competition, doggy dancing is always entertaining and fun to watch. Some will argue that the term "doggy dancing" is a derogatory label conjuring up images of demeaning circus acts and poodles jumping through hoops.

Not me. I know that the routine I saw on a television talent show took just as much planning and practice as the one I watched winning the international freestyle final at Crufts. Both routines have the originality and style that I admire so much. Both got me wishing I could be as good a dog

It is up to you. Does your husband love to stay in and watch football on the television? Then you might find that your canine friend is a more enthusiastic partner and keener to follow your feet than he is!

Left Your dog will love doing tricks with you. Make learning fun and he'll always want you as a dance partner.

Look at that tail wag in time to the music!

Above Such a clever trick, but how are you going to get your dog's feet back on the ground by the next beat of the music?

Competition Classes

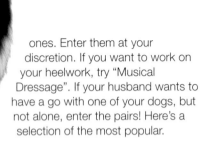

Like all forms of dance, doggy dancing comes in a range of styles and levels, with something to suit all tastes and abilities. Before you start teaching your dog new moves or choosing music, do have a look at all your options. If you are thinking of competing, here are some of the classes that will be available to you at shows or fun days.

Kennel Club official classes These classes are held at shows licensed by the Kennel Club and if you do well, you can gain points to win not only a trophy but a title. And don't worry. You won't be up against the big guns at your debut. Begin at Starters and work your way up through Novice, Intermediate to Advanced.

Heelwork to music Your dog must work in the heel position with your dog's shoulder close to your leg. Unlike competitive obedience, in heelwork to music the Kennel Club permit this position to be either on the right or left of the handler, facing forward or backward to the handler or across the front or back of the handler. And the dog must stay in the heel position whatever the pace or direction that the handler is moving. At least two thirds of your routine must be heelwork if you enter this class.

Freestyle You will see heelwork in Freestyle too, but it must not exceed a third of the routine. Obedience moves and eye-catching tricks are all acceptable provided you are not asking your pet to do anything dangerous. Jumping through hoops of fire is a big No!

Additional Classes and Fun Days You might see these classes on the schedule alongside the official ones. Enter them at your discretion. If you want to work on your heelwork, try "Musical Dressage". If your husband wants to have a go with one of your dogs, but not alone, enter the pairs! Here's a selection of the most popular.

Musical dressage Your routine must showcase your dog's paces – a walk, trot or canter – and show rhythm and regularity in time to the music.

Dances with dogs This is your chance to show you know a few steps, too. The judges must be able to identify your choice of dance. If you decide on a Highland Fling, you'll have to hold your arms in the air like antlers and point your toes while your dog performs dressage or freestyle moves.

Dancing virgins Thankfully not you – the dog! This class is open to dogs and handlers who have never entered a dancing competition before and is the ideal opportunity to give your routine a public airing before the judges start marking in earnest.

Puppy stuff If you have a dog in training that is not quite old enough to enter a show (12 calendar months), this is the class for you. You can introduce him to the ring and try out your moves. A great opportunity to get an idea of what needs more practice or changing and developing.

Pairs Grab a partner and start planning your moves. You don't have to have the same size or breed of dog, but it helps if your moves are synchronised.

You don't need to compete to do doggy dancing. Many handlers let off steam by creating dance routines to perform just for fun at village fetes or to audiences at nursing homes. And you need not dance alone. Consider joining a canine line-dancing team. It's a great way to make new friends, exchange training tips and share some laughter.

Looking At Other Options

If doggy dancing appeals, you may also be attracted to obedience work, agility or flyball – all challenging and stimulating activities. It may seem difficult to choose the best option for you and your dog. Luckily, there is no need to choose. Try it all! If you have a suitable dog, his capacity for work will know no bounds, provided it's fun.

Every time I get a puppy, I have a go at all the different canine sports available in my neighbourhood. Each has something different to offer and dog training basics, like the "Sit", "Down" and "Wait" are fundamental exercises for any canine sport. I relish the chance to practise them while doing different things and meeting new dogs and people. I end up with a well-rounded dog that can do everything which gives me a great deal of flexibility when planning my doggy diary! If agility is cancelled because of the wet weather, I can go to the obedience classes held in the dry village hall. If there isn't a heelwork to music show at the weekend, I'm free to go to the flyball match.

What's so special? So what makes doggy dancing different from all the other canine sports? What I love about dancing with a dog is that it gives me the opportunity to be unique and think creatively. Even if using the same music, no two dance routines will ever be the same. How could they be? One dog was a Newfoundland and the other was a

Above Dancing with dogs encourages you to think creatively. Take off your ringmaster's hat and teach your dog to carry it in his mouth, sit inside it or stand on top of it!

Yorkshire Terrier! How many ways can you use an umbrella? It will depend if you are dancing as Gene Kelly or Mary Poppins! My dog will hold a stick in his mouth. Can I teach him to beat a drum? Yes! If I build a routine around a drum, should I pick a marching tune or something with a wild Ginger Baker drum solo? What else can I teach him to do with a drum? And once I've settled on my music, how am I going to link all my dog's new moves together? Training challenges keep my brain and my dogs in top form.

A creative partnership Working at any discipline – dancing, obedience, flyball or agility – makes life more interesting for your dog and helps to build up your relationship with him. What is special about doggy dancing is that you are acting together in a creative process and this adds a whole new dimension to your partnership. It's something I wouldn't want to miss out on. So, have a go. Attend a few classes. You may opt to take it no further or you may decide that you would like to see how your routine measures up against others and enter a show. You may concentrate on agility and then when your dog is too old to jump the fences decide to return to dancing because in this discipline you can decide how much physical effort your individual dog has to put into routines. For now, don't limit the fun you can have with your young dog. He is only too willing and able to excel at them all and he could be the next freestyle champion!

Coping With Challenge

You may feel sure that your dog would love to take up doggy dancing, but worry about your own abilities. Don't think that doggy dancing is ruled out for you just because you have two left feet.

If you want to try doggy dancing, it is far more important that you are a good dog trainer. The star of the show is your dog, not you. Your challenge is not to display your dancing prowess but to make your dog the centre of attention and develop his talents so that he catches the judge's eye. Help him show everyone what a wow he is by teaching him a variety of tricks and linking them together in a routine. To do that you will need his favourite treats and a clicker, not a pair of ballet shoes!

And it's a funny thing. The prouder you become of your pet's accomplishments, the more you will want to show them off. In the process you will gain self-confidence and lose some of your inhibitions. Teach your dog to wave a paw. What an accomplishment! You'll want to show everyone in your family. And although you might find teaching your dog to weave between your legs difficult at first, when you get the knack I bet you will be practising on the way to the shops and won't care a hoot who is looking! And every time you practise, your coordination and timing will improve.

Your forgiving partner Good dog training makes every exercise a great game that is fun and rewarding for you both. If there is washing to hang on the line, wouldn't you rather be doing the cha-cha with your dog? Get out the treats and toys. You'll never want to stop dancing once you start and you couldn't ask for a better partner. He will never shout at

Right A bow is a great way to introduce your dog to the judges.

Right Weaving your dog takes good co-ordination and timing, so it can take a while to get the knack. Keep practising and you will find that this trick becomes one of your favourites.

you, laugh at your mistakes or call you names. If you get a step wrong, he won't hold it against you. He'll always be ready to try it again. Dogs don't hold grudges and he will love you no matter how many times you step on his paws because he knows that you'll learn and improve too.

Making time for practice If you already have a busy lifestyle, you may wonder how you can fit in the time for learning and teaching a new routine. Whatever your schedule, your dog deserves some quality time with you and the great thing about doggy dancing is that you can spend as much or as little time practising new moves or competing as you want. And training sessions are easy to fit into a busy timetable because you don't need any specialist equipment. It's just you and the dog!

Here are some of my favourite training opportunities:

Commercial breaks
If you are watching television, instead of making yourself a cup of coffee during the adverts, get off your arm chair and ask your dog to find the heel position on the left and the right side.

Visitors Whenever anyone comes to your house, even if it's the television repair man, take a minute to show off a few canine tricks. I've taught my dog to wave a paw which I can work into the conversation as a "Hello" or a "Goodbye", whichever is more appropriate.

Gardening Finished planting the bulbs? Stick your spade in the ground and ask your dog to circle around it. I have seen a dance routine choreographed to *"An English Country Garden"* using flowerpots, fork and trough as props. It was excellent and I bet the handler's garden is beautiful.

Left He's cute and capable. Incorporate a little training into everyday life and he'll be a dancing star in no time.

artist's name and write it down at the next red traffic light. You've taken the first step to choreographing a dance routine and the dog was at home!

Left Dogs are natural show-offs! Once your dog learns to wave hello, he'll be keen to greet each visitor to your house with an appealing wave.

Waiting for the kettle It will never boil if you watch it, so take the opportunity to do a few leg weaves. Make it a game. How many can you do before the kettle whistles? Your score should improve with each cup of tea!

Establish your goals You will never achieve anything if you try and squeeze ten minutes into five and your dog will hate training if you make it a chore. In doggy dancing you can set your own personal goals and take your time reaching them. But beware. Any kind of dog training is addictive. You will want to repeat the buzz you get after teaching a new trick. Yes! That was a perfect bow! Good dog! You will start thinking of more new things to teach him and the washing up will get left in the sink and the laundry piles will grow bigger. But you will be having lots of fun!

Tidying away the kids' toys Instead of bending over to pick up the teddy bear or gym shoe, ask your dog to pick them up and bring them to you. Retrieve training is always useful!

Driving to work Turn on your radio. Did you like that tune? Would it suit a routine? Keep listening to get the

Finding A Class

Finding a class with a good instructor is the first step. Don't just enrol on the first class you discover in your area, but make enquiries about any alternatives. Choosing the right class means you will learn more, be inspired to take up new challenges, and acquire new friends, both human and canine.

Classes There are a number of places to look for classes which may be called "doggy dancing", "heelwork to music" or "canine freestyle". The Kennel Club will have a registry of Dog Training Clubs and Societies that hold classes in a range of canine disciplines including heelwork to music. In addition, the Paws 'n' Music and Canine Freestyle GB websites have lists of independent clubs, self-help groups and trainers who may hold sessions or seminars near you. Check out the notice board at your veterinary surgery or pet store. And don't forget to ask your dog-walking buddies. Word of mouth is often the best recommendation.

What to ask Classes can be held in village halls, scout huts, leisure centres or on playing fields. Ring up and ask. Find out how many students are in each class and how much a session will cost. Will you have to pay for one class at a time or for a course of six? Find out if there is parking, somewhere to exercise your dog and whether there are toilets for you. You would be surprised at the number of village halls that provide kitchen facilities for tea and coffee but lock the Ladies at night! And ask if you can watch a class before you join up. This is the best way to get a feel of things. Do you like what you see? Is the instructor funny and sympathetic? Are the dogs wagging their tails?

Instructors Instructors vary in backgrounds and ability. What they have in common is a love of their chosen sport and dogs. Some come from obedience backgrounds and others from agility. Some are successful heelwork to music competitors and others are great trainers but have never entered a show ring. Your instructor could be a member of the Association of Pet Dog Trainers or the British Institute of Professional Dog Trainers. She may have a teaching background in dance or she may have no qualifications whatsoever. What is important is that you like and respect your instructor. Your instructor shouldn't arrive 15 minutes late for class every week. You shouldn't have to watch your fellow classmate's collie get all the attention from the teacher while your own dog gets bored and ignored in a corner. And, if you can't stand the way your instructor bullies her own dog, look elsewhere for a class.

Shop around until you find something that suits you. If you find a class with a teacher and students you like, you'll be back week after week. Your doggy dancing knowledge base will grow and grow and your dog will start having so much fun that he will exceed all your expectations on the dance floor!

Below Find a teacher you like and respect who will make dog training fun.

Picking A Puppy

There's no certain way, when choosing a puppy out of a litter, to select the one who will be the best future partner for you on the dance floor. Baby puppies are not sufficiently developed mentally or physically for you to assess their future performance accurately, so you can only concentrate on picking the one you like best.

Who barks at it? Who chases it? Who tugs on it? You can learn a lot through observation. I like dogs that are up for a good time. I use toys as lures and rewards during training so if a puppy is curious and interacting with balls and tuggies now, he is a good candidate. Remember, you are the one that will be leading on the dance floor and life will be easier if you choose not to partner a dog who is either a wimp or a bully.

Household The pup you choose must be able to flourish in your home. Will he be the only dog or do you already have an adult pooch who is the boss? Perhaps he would prefer a pup that wasn't going to challenge his authority! If you have a bitch, a dog will suit you better than another girlie. And vice versa. If you have children, you will have other considerations. Pick the pup with the strong eye and he might herd the kids into their bedroom and keep them there until it's time to turn off the light!

Picking a puppy is always pretty much a lottery. No one has a crystal ball to look into and see a future of red rosettes. But you can stack the odds in your favour by considering a few of these four points.

Health Your pup should have the mandatory four legs – one on each corner. Has he been wormed? Are his eyes bright or are they discharging goop? Is he bouncing and ready for action or is he flat and lethargic? Pick a healthy puppy now and you will have fewer trips to the vet in later life and more time to train him to weave between your legs.

Temperament Watch the puppies play together. Does one sit in the corner? Who runs away when you sneeze? Who investigates the new toy first?

You And finally you. Which one do you like? You will never be able to train your dog if you can't start bonding with him as soon as you get him home. Is there any chemistry between you and one of the puppies? If you want to turn him into a dancing aficionado you will have to spend a lot of time with him. Your partnership will be like marriage is supposed to be – for life.

The bottom line? If you love your puppy, you can do anything on the dance floor!

Puppy Preparation

If you are starting with a puppy, you can't just dive straight into dance lessons. Your new baby has a lot of growing to do, both physically and mentally, before he will be ready for such demanding work. He will not yet have the strength and coordination to perform many of the more complex moves. Nor will he yet have the stamina for long training sessions, and too much exercise will only damage his growing bones and muscles. So let's not get ahead of ourselves. Leave the fancy stuff alone for now and concentrate on laying the foundations for future schooling. For now, go BATS!

B is for Bond Bond with your puppy. There's more to him than cuteness. Get to know his personality, sensitivities, likes and dislikes. Be active together. Go for walks and let him help you clean the kitchen cupboards – there might be an old tennis ball lurking there! Interact. Throw a ball – who will get there first? Hide a treat under the chair and help him find it. Have some fun, play some games and don't forget to have a cuddle. You'll find all of your puppy's tickle spots!

A is for Apple Become the apple of your dog's eye – so tasty he'll want to eat you! He should not only look to you for life's necessities like a full water bowl, but for a good time. Wow! Mum opened the post, screwed the envelope into a ball and threw it for me to chase! But he should also respect you and learn the household rules. No chewing on Mum's fingers, no barking at the postman and definitely no peeing in the kitchen.

T is for Tools Every dog trainer will have a variety of tools in their training bag. This is a good time to introduce your pup to the clicker and different toys and treats. Teach a hand touch or a send to a target. Ensure that he doesn't object to being handled in case you ever need to hold his collar. Practise using different training techniques so that you are an expert. Teach your puppy his name, and how to sit and to lie down.

S is for Socialise You don't need to turn your pup into a party animal, but he does need some social skills. Give him the opportunity to meet new dogs and people. Take him to the shops, schools and different training venues. It's all new territory for him and he should be confident and happy for adventure. But there are rules here, too. Don't jump up on strangers, don't bite that dog's tail and don't pee on your best friend's handbag. It doesn't matter how cute he is. No one likes a dog that pees on their handbag.

Your new pup may be gorgeous but he will need more than good looks to get top marks from the judges. Don't delay learning how to enjoy one another's company.

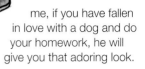

Breed Of Choice

Any breed of dog can enjoy and, with the right training, excel at doggy dancing. If you attend any doggy dancing show, you will almost certainly notice that collies are the most popular breed. This doesn't mean, however, that you have to have a collie to do well in this sport. Collies are a popular choice, but many of the traits that make them so liked and admired can also be their downfall on the dance floor.

If a non-working breed such as a Chihuahua or a Tibetan Spaniel suits your lifestyle better than a working breed, it will also be a better choice for your dancing partner. Consider:

Physique Collies are the ideal size. They are tall enough for you to feel their shoulder against your thigh in heelwork and their legs are long enough to show off any fancy foot work. They are agile creatures that can turn on a pin or jump over your shoulders. However, a toy breed can do something that no collie can, like sitting in a flower pot! And what a crowd pleaser that would be!

Left This collie can easily rest his nose on his handler's hip pocket – is there perhaps a tasty titbit inside?

Adoration Collies gaze adoringly at their dance partners regardless of how crookedly they have applied lipstick. Such attention! But collies are not pre-set to do so. It's hard work and they can just as easily become infatuated with a tennis ball. Believe me, if you have fallen in love with a dog and do your homework, he will give you that adoring look.

Tireless Collies are tireless workers and aim to please. When their handlers have blisters and need a coffee break, collies will still want to do the whole routine one more time. "More!" they bark. Pity is that they keep making the same mistake over and over again. Be grateful if you have a dog you can turn off as easily as you can turn him on. And have a biscuit with your coffee. Little dogs may need a rest as much as you do.

Aim to please Collies want to get it right. They are clever dogs and learn very quickly – often the wrong things. The onus is on their handlers to ensure their instructions are clear so that they don't make mistakes. Communication is important in dog training and if you and your dog already have an understanding, build on that and you will be surprised what he can do for you.

At home Lastly, remember that you have to take your dance partner home with you. Not all collies fit easily into family life. They are herding dogs and you don't want them to chase the cat out of the door. How big is your garden and how much time do you have to exercise your pet?

Collies are the breed of choice and excel in all the canine disciplines but owning one is not a guarantee of success. Indeed, collies can be demanding pets that take time and patience to train. You need to be up for the task. Otherwise you may that find your pet becomes a burden rather than the pleasure you had anticipated. Be a trend setter. Don't get yourself a collie just because everyone else has one.

Choosing The Sex Of Your Dance Partner

The choice of a girl or a boy is yours alone. There are a number of things to consider when making your decision but at the end of the day, it is a matter of personal preference. When all is said and done, the new dog must suit you.

Personality Girls are reputed to be biddable and loyal while boys are labelled laid back and easygoing. Some argue that bitches are easier to train than male dogs while others insist that it is the boys who shine in competition. I have heard the adjectives, "territorial", "affectionate", "stubborn" and "independent" applied to both sexes when someone has tried to list the differences! Generalise as much as you like but there will always be a puppy that refuses to conform – a little boy with girlie attributes or a little bitch that is macho.

Biology Female dogs will usually come into season twice a year. This not only demands extra vigilance from you if you don't want unwanted puppies but it means a break from the show circuit and club training. While she is in season (a period of three to four weeks), your bitch cannot attend classes or shows – not just to prevent the risk of pregnancy, but because her scent will put all the male dogs off their work and may even set them fighting.

On the other hand, entire males can't help being attracted to the ladies. If aroused, they can leave the dance floor to find one and may behave aggressively if a rival gets in their way. And they cock their leg and mark territory and possessions. There is nothing worse than picking up your prop and discovering that your dog has left the message "MINE"!

The good news is that dogs that are neutered will often not have gender specific problems such as these, so it is worth discussing spaying and castration with your vet. Both involve surgery, although less expensive and invasive for the boys, and your pet will need some time to recuperate before returning to training.

Pack The only time I would advise specifically in favour of a dog or a bitch is if there is already another canine in the household. Adding another dog to the pack will often destabilise it and fights can break out if positions in the hierarchy are unclear. However, girls tend to be more accepting of boys and the boys more accepting of girls. For example, it's easy to be top bitch if the rest of your pack are male dogs! Again, this is a generalisation and many dogs coexist in all bitch or all male dog households without any aggravation.

Personal preference My personal preference is for boys but I have friends that swear by girl power. I don't think that one sex is better for training than another, but you may find some gender traits are more attractive and easier to live with than others. And if your pup is a welcome addition to your household and heart, you will enjoy training him or her.

Working With An Older Dog

Don't think that you have to go out and buy a puppy in order to take up doggy dancing. If you already have a canine companion, even if he is already middle-aged, give him a chance. Unless your dog is heading for retirement age, starting a new hobby won't do him any harm at all. As long as he is fit and healthy, there is no reason why he shouldn't take his first steps towards a dancing career.

A Bit Of Support
If your dog's back isn't as strong as it used to be and he is having trouble balancing on his haunches or standing on his hind legs...

...let him place his front paws on a chair for support – how cute!

Health check If you are worried that your dog is not up to the task, make an appointment at your vet's surgery for a health check. The vet will look for signs of ageing like arthritis, deafness or cataracts in the eyes *(left)*. If there is any physical reason why he should sit the next dance out, he will tell you. But if he gives you the go-ahead, you can happily dance the night away.

Exercise Dancing is a nice way to stay fit. You can choose the tricks and moves that won't be too demanding but will keep your dog strong and supple. He may be a bit slower and tire more quickly than when he was a pup so if he runs out of puff, shorten training sessions to what he finds comfortable. By tailoring a routine to your dog's age and abilities, you could surprise yourself by entering a show and winning the class!

Mental stimulation You can teach old dogs new tricks! Exercising your dog's brain with a few brain games and mental gymnastics will keep him fun-loving and alert. He will be trying to figure out all sorts of things. What do you want him to do with a target stick? How many times does he have to wave a paw to get a cube of cheese? And why are you dressed like Dorothy from *The Wizard of Oz*? And, if you make training fun, he'll work hard to find the answers.

Attention Your dog will love the attention – a night out training with you every week! As a mature fellow, he is less likely to act the juvenile delinquent in class and will arrive ready to learn. The bond you already have will continue to strengthen and grow as you face new challenges together. Why call a halt to that really satisfying process just because your dog is getting old?

Go on and get out of the house. Make new friends and have some fun. Just because he is getting on in years doesn't mean he wants to sit at home every night in front of the television. If he is ready, willing and able, sign up for the class. You won't regret it.

How To Handle Difficult Dogs

Don't imagine that you have to start with the perfect dog! You may have a rescue dog who has not been properly socialised or who carries emotional baggage from his past life. It's not uncommon for such a dog to be suspicious of strangers or nervous and unpredictable with other dogs. This doesn't mean that he can't learn to overcome his difficulties and become a great dancing partner – in fact dance lessons may help to improve his confidence.

Above *What nice clean teeth you have. Please put them away!*

To the rescue! Why do dogs end up in rescue centres? The break-up of a marriage, long term hospitalisation or work commitments are all reasons for a pet to need a new home. Behavioural problems like chasing cats or nipping the children can be serious issues that

Left *This dog may be behind bars through no fault of his own. Why not give him a second chance? He could be your perfect partner.*

some people are unable to deal with and so give up their pet for adoption. Many are strays. When nothing is known about a dog's background, you don't know what baggage he will bring with him to his new home. There might be some pleasant surprises and there could be some nasty ones. I have a friend who fostered a dog that could touch his nose with his paw on command but he also had a vacuum cleaner phobia!

The good and the bad You have to look at the whole dog. Many rescue dogs need some positive socialisation work to get them comfortable and happy around other dogs and people – it will help if they are keen on treats or toys. Join an obedience club that has an instructor who can assess your dog's problems. She may feel they are something that she can tackle in class or she may refer you to a behaviourist for a consultation. Either way, you will be getting the guidance you need.

Dance, dance, dance! There is no reason why you and your dog can't dance together. Many of the things you will learn at your obedience class, like heelwork, are fundamentals to doggy dancing. And you might find that just spending time together on walks or learning new tricks will help your dog be more relaxed when he is confronted with unfamiliar faces and places. Over time, you will become more adept at reading him and he will be more predictable. You will have strategies in place for dealing with any displays of bad manners.

Dancing stars There are some dance divas out there who are real grumble-guts around other canines. Their owners are aware of the problem and recognise that, despite their best efforts, their dogs will always be poor mixers in crowds. However, this doesn't stop them from loving their pets or having fun training them to shine on the dance floor. One or two have become top handlers. When the music plays, it doesn't matter who else is in the room – it's just dog and handler. At the end of the day it is only you and your dog centre stage.

What Size Of Dog?

In one way, size doesn't matter in doggy dancing. Big or small, any dog is a potential dance partner. A dainty Papillon can be just as much a star as a tall, elegant Belgian Shepherd. However, it does matter in another way, simply because big dogs and small dogs dance differently, and you need to decide which style you prefer.

Lifestyle However, not every dog will fit into your home. If you live in a flat without a garden, perhaps one of the larger breeds that needs lots of exercise is not for you. Do you travel and want to take your dog with you? Many airlines accept dogs that weigh under 6kg (13lb) into the passenger cabin and they are certainly easier to sneak into hotel rooms or hide under tables in restaurants. But, if you want to impress, go large. Few burglars are frightened by miniature poodles snapping at their ankles.

Heelwork And that's exactly it. Being ankle height, small dogs find it more difficult to settle into a comfortable heel position against your leg. Big dogs can rest their heads on your thigh without too much disturbance while you walk. And all you need do to tickle their ears is drop your hand. In contrast, it is a long way down to small dogs and you have to keep bending over to give them a treat or pat on the head. If you want to avoid back ache, a small dog may not be for you!

Choice of moves

There are many things you can do with a small dog that you can't do with a big one and vice versa. You wouldn't want to give a large breed a piggyback on your shoulders, but you could balance a little dog there easily. Walk with a big dog between your legs and you look like you are riding a horse in a cowboy film. It's just not the same move done with a small dog – you might look as if you were trying to sit on a flea! Whatever size dog you choose, you will have to pick tricks and moves that suit your dog's conformation when you choreograph a routine.

Safety And when you choose props, size and weight will come into the equation. You can fit a miniature poodle in a flower pot and he'll look cute but good luck trying the same thing with a standard poodle! And it's really hard for a small dog to retrieve your bowler hat – it's as big as he is! A handkerchief would be more manageable for a little dog. Do you want your dog to dance on the table? Make sure it is sturdy enough to hold his weight. How embarrassing and dangerous if it collapsed in a pile of splinters! Again, it is a question of choosing a prop to fit your dog's height and weight.

There are two sides to the story regarding every size of dog and choice is largely a matter of personal preference. Invent new moves that reflect a dog's personality and size.

***Left** Dogs come in all sizes. Pick one that suits your lifestyle and choose moves that complement his conformation.*

Getting Children Involved

Doggy dancing, like obedience and agility, is just as suitable for dog-loving children as it is for adults. Children (with appropriate adult supervision) can form very close relationships with their pets, and aren't hampered by any preconceptions about what a dog can or can't achieve.

Learning how to look after and train a dog is often a child's first lesson in responsibility and their canine friend can be relied on to pay them back with love and devotion. Doggy dancing can be a great way for a child to learn what makes a dog tick. In addition, getting a child hooked on any canine activity from an early age means she is likely to continue dog training as an adult.

Fun Get your child a good book or video on doggy dancing. Take her to a show or demonstration so she can see what goes on. Join a dog training club with heelwork to music classes. I suspect that in no time at all she will be teaching her dog to twist and spin, walk backwards or stand on his hind legs. Be on hand if she needs help downloading music for routines or gets stuck with choreography. But don't be offended if she does it all without you!

Competition A child can have a lot fun training her own dog and she may like to take it a step further and compete. If you feel she is emotionally mature enough to handle the highs and lows of public performance at a show, fill in an entry form. I have seen children pull off some really dazzling routines, but others have been disasters and I hate to see a kid crying after a disappointing display. Getting up in front of an audience is not easy, especially if the dog decides he would rather scratch a few fleas as soon as his music starts playing.

Young Kennel Club Your child could enter the standard classes at a show and potentially put the adults to shame or she might find it more fun to compete against her peers. The Young Kennel Club (YKC) hold competition classes for handlers from ages six to 12 and between 12 and 18 years old. There are two official categories: heelwork to music and freestyle and three subdivisions in each – elementary, primary and open. If the child wins one of the top two places in one of these, she'll find herself competing at the Crufts YKC final.

Pet hates I love seeing a child handler with talent, but I hate:
- Dogs running to "Mummy" leaving a crying child alone in ring.
- Young kids made up as if they were adults, especially little girls who look like they have been standing on a street corner all night.
- Pregnant teenagers or mothers competing in under 18 classes.

Remember that your child is only young so it is important to keep dog training fun. Get it right and who knows? She might grow up to be one of Britain's top freestyle competitors.

Left This junior handler has got talent – she may one day be a heelwork to music champion.

And Senior Citizens

Even if you're drawing your old age pension, you're not too old to start doggy dancing so long as you have a suitable dog. In fact, both you and your dog will benefit from the mental stimulus, physical exercise (as demanding or undemanding as suits you both) and companionship.

So, if your dog would love to do some doggy dancing with you, go ahead and give it your best shot. You may not be as lithe and limber as a 20 year old, but I bet you have other attributes that will be an advantage on the dance floor. You may not have the stamina you used to, but your dog won't mind if you have a sit down now and again. Don't let your age stop you from having fun with your dog.

But you may want to give mini skirts a miss!

Above *Anything you can do, I can do better! You are never too old to have fun training your dog to dance.*

Warm-up A warm-up will be even more important for you than it is for the younger dancers. The older you are, the longer it takes to get your body ready for action so take some extra time to loosen up. You don't want to strain a muscle or pull a hamstring. And even if your dog is still young, she'd like a warm-up too so why not do it together.

Disco dancing Go to a club or disco and it's hard to know who is dancing with whom. Did your dancing days call for a bit more structure and communication between you and your partner? If so, you are already accustomed to dancing as a team and this is what you will be ultimately doing with your dog.

Musical horizons You may not realise it but your musical world is vast. You have heard far more number one hits than your grandchildren. And think of all the theme tunes from films you have watched over the years. You are the lucky one when it comes to trying to pick your piece of music. You just have to remember the title!

Maturity With age comes grace and elegance. It is not necessary to gyrate all over the dance floor like a teenager. You don't need to wear a mini skirt (unless you still have great legs). Express the wisdom of your years through your posture and movements. You can achieve a stateliness and maturity that young people will envy.

Individuality You may not be able to cover the whole dance floor in the course of one bar of music, but you can traverse it with style and dignity. Remember that many young people are still searching for their own identity. Your individuality comes from life experience and if you can express that with confidence, you and your dog will be a great dancing duo. Don't copy what that 16 year old is doing. Create something that is you and be a role model for the young.

Dog dancing is not about the young competing against the old. Each has something different to offer the other. So don't delay. Go and sign up for a course of lessons at your local dog training club. I'm sure that you both will thoroughly enjoy yourselves.

GETTING STARTED

It's never too late to start dancing with your dog.
Dogs that already have some obedience skills and good
manners will have a head start, but anyone can catch
up. Start with the basics and have fun teaching your
dog new tricks and moves. Old or young, little
or large – your pet could turn out to be a star!

Teaching A Puppy Basic Skills

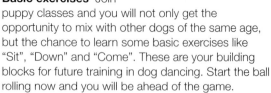

A young dog won't be able to compete in heelwork until he is a year old, but there is plenty of preparation work you can do for his dancing debut. He doesn't yet have the coordination or stamina of an adult, but he has lots of learning capacity and will benefit from constructive mental stimulation. The more work you put into teaching him the basics now, the readier he will be for grown-up work when the time comes.

The perfect dancing partner is a well adjusted canine companion that can cope with the pressures of life and stress of competition. Start here.

Play-mate Puppies are for playing. Introduce your puppy to games of fetch, tug and hide and seek. Acquaint him with a variety of toys. Which is his favourite? The orange rubber hedgehog or the plush blue rugby ball. The more laughter you share with him, the quicker you will bond and become the centre of his universe. He will always look to you first for fun. And that's what training is – fun!

Socialisation Take him out and about. Has he been to your Post Office? Has he met the lollipop lady? What did he think of the cattle in the field? Make each experience pleasant and he will grow up to face new challenges with confidence and an open mind. When he sees the palm tree you want to use as a prop in "Ships of the Desert", he will not be nonplussed. He won't even think of barking at it!

Manners Manners are necessary, especially as if your pup will grow into a big dog. Start early and teach him not to push through doorways ahead of you. Don't let him jump up at strangers. Remember, he will be a big boy and able to put his paws on people's shoulders. And the household rules you choose to enforce now will last a lifetime. It's no good telling him when he is a year old that he is now too big to sleep on the bed with you.

Basic exercises Join puppy classes and you will not only get the opportunity to mix with other dogs of the same age, but the chance to learn some basic exercises like "Sit", "Down" and "Come". These are your building blocks for future training in dog dancing. Start the ball rolling now and you will be ahead of the game.

Training tools Try out different training tools in class and at home. Both clicker and target sticks can be used with puppies. The sooner you "charge" your clicker (see page 39 for an explanation of charging a clicker), the sooner you can use it as a conditioned reinforcer to help your dog learn new things now and when he is older.

Fun classes Although your dog won't be able to compete until he is older, he can enter fun classes. These classes are usually restricted to dogs between six and 12 months and allow toys and treats in the ring. They are a great way for a dog to make a show debut. Good luck!

Make sure your dog is looking where you throw the toy.

And tell him to "Get it!"

Game of Fetch

1 *Toys are fun and a great way to reward your dog. You can throw them for your dog to chase, but he has to bring them back.*

1

Sit

A dog in the Sit is half way to the Down.

Down

Basic Exercises

The Sit and the Down are valuable positions for your dog to learn. Integrate them into your daily routine – e.g. by sitting your dog before attaching the lead.

Game Of Tug

You can reward your dog with a game of tug, but make sure that he knows how to let go of the toy on your "Leave" command.

Toys on ropes keep some distance between the toy in the dog's mouth and your fingers!

2 *Give your dog a few words of encouragement to help him on his way.*

3 *When he has picked up her toy, call him to you in a happy voice. He'll look in your direction and come running.*

You can take the toy in exchange for a treat and another throw.

2

3

Understanding Your Clicker

When you start your doggy dancing classes, you will probably be given a list of things to bring with you, such as your dog's favourite treats and toys and, very often, a clicker. Clicker training is a very effective means of teaching a dog complicated routines, and therefore ideal for dance lessons.

What is a clicker? A clicker is a hand-held device with a button or lever that, when pressed, will make a "click" noise. The clicker has been used to train a variety of animals including dolphins, horses and chickens. Once the trainer has married the expectation of a reward with the "click", the noise is used to mark the behaviour that the trainer will reward with a treat – a piece of cheese, a carrot or a fish depending on the animal being trained! Every good dog trainer has a clicker in their training tool kit.

Advantages

- The "click" noise is a constant and therefore an unambiguous and easily understandable signal. We humans can be hard to fathom. You can say "Good boy" softly, loudly, with a high or low pitch, or a rising or falling intonation. It is sometimes hard for your dog to know if you are scolding or praising him with so many vocal cues. No wonder he looks confused.
- Because the "click" noise is short, it is a precise marker. By the time you say "Fantastic, super dog" to your dog, he will have forgotten what he was doing to make you so rapturous.
- The "click" noise can be heard when a dog is on one side of the room and you are on the other. In doggy dancing, you will want to teach him distance; to be able to perform a trick with two, three or ten feet of floor between you.

Disadvantages

- The "click" noise must be delivered at the right moment. A trainer's timing is important. If you are teaching you dog to "bow", that is when you must click – not when he has collapsed into the "Down" and this precise timing is not always as easy as it looks initially .
- The "click" noise must be faded. You will not be able to take your clicker into the ring with you if you compete in heelwork to music or canine freestyle. This process is often rushed or ignored by handlers and then they wonder why their dogs are looking at them blankly as the music begins and the judges pick up their pencils.

Clicker types Clickers come in all shapes, colours and sizes. You can buy loud clickers, soft clickers and clickers with adjustable volumes. Some have levers and some have buttons. You can wear them on your wrist or hanging from your neck. Buy one that you are comfortable holding in your hand. Choose one with a volume that your dog can hear without jumping on the ceiling. Some dogs find a loud "click" scary.

Personal choice I like red clickers because if I drop them in the grass and lose them, they are easy to see and find again. I like button clickers because I can put them under my foot and still make them go "click" which leaves my hands free to lure or treat. Buy a clicker and experiment. Can you make it go click if you sit on it? And buy more than one. I have a clicker in my jacket, another one in the car, and one even by the back door. Once you start clicking, you'll want to keep a clicker handy at all times.

How To Introduce A Clicker

Charging A Clicker
This exercise makes your dog associate the sound of a click with the expectation of a reward. Don't start until you have his attention.

Repeat the click and treat sequence up to 20 times.

When your dog looks back to you, repeat the exercise.

1 Hold your clicker in one hand and some yummy treats in the other.

2 Go click and immediately treat. Not ten seconds or twenty seconds later.

3 Alternatively, click and throw your treat on the floor for him to enjoy.

The purpose of a clicker is to give your dog a clear, unmistakable signal that he is on the right track. It isn't the equivalent of a "Good dog" when he has completed a task, but confirmation that he has achieved a distinct step. This enables you to teach complex routines by breaking them down into tiny stages. However, before you can achieve any of this, you need to teach your dog the meaning of the click.

You can do that by "charging" your clicker. You are aiming at building an association between the "click" noise and a piece of food.

1 Prepare a bowl of your dog's favourite treats, chopped into bite-size pieces that he will be able to eat quickly one after the other. You don't want him to choke! Slices of frankfurter, cubes of cheese or anything that is easy to swallow and gets your dog salivating will do the job.

2 Click and immediately give him a treat. Do this 20 times. Your dog doesn't have to do a thing except eat his titbit and while he is doing that he will be learning that "click" means that something yummy will be coming his way.

3 Has the message got through? If it has, your dog should be looking for a treat every time he hears a click. Wait for him to look away and click. Is he looking back at you for his treat? If so, you have successfully loaded your clicker with meaning.

Click for good behaviour Now that your clicker is charged, you are ready to use it to mark behaviour. In class, you will learn how to click your dog for watching you, sitting, lying down or chasing his tail! Don't devalue your clicker with aimless clicking. Always click with a purpose and always for a reward. And never click in his ear. Once you have built up the expectation of a juicy sliver of sausage with the click noise, he will be listening very carefully and trying to figure out how to make you go "click" again.

Effective Ways Of Using A Clicker

Once your dog has learned that a click means he gets a dog biscuit, it's time to progress to teaching him that he has to earn the click and treat. You will often hear people talking about waiting for your dog to perform an action spontaneously, and then clicking to show him that this is a desired action. In practice, you will often have to be more proactive – if your dog is a beginner he is unlikely to do more than look at you expectantly! There are three main approaches you can take: capturing, luring and shaping.

Capturing You can wait for your dog to do something you like and then capture it with a click and treat. If he has had a long day and is a bit weary, he'll sit. Click and treat. Every time he sits, click and treat. He will figure out that if he wants to make you click and treat, he has to have his bottom on the floor. Dogs do offer a variety of unprompted behaviours that you can catch with your clicker, like sitting, lying down, lifting a paw or picking up a ball. You made need more patience to capture your dog spinning, digging or sitting on his haunches. And you may wait a lifetime for your dog to suddenly turn on the washing machine. Make sure your expectations are realistic.

Luring Hold a treat in front of a dog's nose and he will follow you

anywhere! Try it. Hold a piece of cheese just above your dog's nose, not too high or he will jump up. Slowly move it backwards behind his head and he will sit. If he doesn't sit, he will fall over trying to follow the treat. As soon as his bottom hits the ground, click and give him his treat. You are not waiting for the sit, but making it likely to happen. Your are offering help and guidance by using a lure, but only clicking and treating the desired behaviour – sit.

Shaping So, you want your dog to sit? Some dogs are adamant that they can only stand. Try taking little steps to reach your target behaviour. As soon as he bends his back legs a little, click and treat. Next time he will bend them a little more. Click and treat. And then a little more. Click and treat. His bottom will get lower and lower and when it hits the ground, he will be in the Sit. Click and give him a huge handful of treats. It has taken a little while to get there, but you have successfully shaped a "Sit" so go on and celebrate!

You do not have to use one of these methods in isolation; for example, you can combine luring with shaping to get the result that you want. I think you'll find the more clicker training you do with your dog, the more active he will become in the hope that you will click and treat him. He will begin to offer you more and more complex behaviours. Is that a dog I see emptying the dishwasher?

Left Hold a treat close to your dog's nose. Move it behind his head and click and treat when he sits.

How To Use Toys

Toys are also useful tools when training your dog. Remember, the more fun you make his training sessions, the more enthusiastic he will be and the faster he will learn. Some dogs work better for a toy than for a treat, most dogs appreciate a variety of stimuli – and, while a titbit disappears in a few seconds, a toy can last for years.

Toys are for you and your dog to play with together. Don't expect him to be a solitary player – you need to join in. You'll have fun and learn a lot about each other so don't keep them locked in a cupboard.

My favourite toys I like toys that are easy to see. I want to be able to find them in the long grass. I also like toys that are multi-purpose and can be used to play either fetch or tuggy games. And I tend to go for the ones that are small enough to fit in a pocket without making me look a misshapen mass of lumps. I look for robustness – I don't want it falling apart the first time I play tug or put it in the washing machine. A small pink ball on a rope is perfect! However, a toy has to be your dog's favourite plaything too and he might think that the dust pan and brush are ideal. Try and compromise.

Bond Play can deepen the bond between you and your dog, especially if it is fun and you play by the book. You throw the ball and the dog brings it back to you rather than parading it around the park. You have a game of tug and he lets go when you tell him to "Leave". He doesn't growl and hang on for grim death.

Arouse and stimulate Playing games with a toy will arouse and stimulate your dog and make training exciting. If he is a bit of a plodder, a ball can be the

Play Power

Get down on your hands and knees and ignite your dog's imagination and drive with his favourite toy.

key to his mental ignition. Chasing or tugging a toy will raise his adrenalin levels and he will be ready for action and raring to go.

Filters There are many things that can catch a dog's eye and put him off his work – strange people, new dogs, unfamiliar objects. Having a game with a tug toy can filter out many of these distractions and help your dog to focus his attention on you. He'll be too engrossed trying to win his toy to worry about the lady with the funny hat selling raffle tickets by the side of the ring.

Fetch It

A dog needs a reason to leave his handler's side. Throw a toy and watch him go, go, go!

And chasing a toy is good exercise too.

Distance work Whenever you want your dog to accelerate away from you, throw his toy and he'll give chase. You will always be able to throw a toy further than you will a treat. So if he is on the other side of the room and that is where you want to reward him for doing a spin, throw his ball for him to catch.

Toy manufacturers make some mighty cute play things for dogs these days. Use them as training aids and don't be afraid of getting them dirty!

How To Use Target Training

Another useful technique at dog dancing classes is target training. It may help to think of the target used in dog training as being very similar to the bullseye on a dart board. If your dog hits it, he gets maximum points and a jackpot of his favourite treats. And targets can be used to teach many, many different things. Learning to go to a target and touch it, with nose or paw, is the first step towards undertaking a whole range of clever tricks.

What is a target? A target is anything that you teach your dog to hone in on just like the darts player who squints his eyes until he can see nothing but the bullseye or the treble and then throws his dart. And once your dog is focused on the target, he must perform an action, like touching the target with his nose.

Some examples You could place a target three, five or ten feet away from you and teach your dog to run to it – a send away! Or you could teach him to target the back of your hand and follow it as you walk – heelwork! Place a target on the lever of your pedal bin and teach your dog to open it. But beware – if he is a scavenger, your rubbish will never be safe again!

Types of target I like targets that are easy to replace and that can be reduced in size. My favourite is the top of a snack biscuit tube. Such a good excuse to eat lots of crisps! The lid of a margarine tub, piece of carpet or a mouse pad are also good targets. You can use the tip of your finger or the bottom of your toe as a target or you can attach something to your clothes like a plaster to act as a target. Put a target on the end of an extending aerial and you have a target stick (see also next entry). Anything that your dog is unlikely to pick up in his mouth or break if he stands on it is an ideal target.

Target behaviours So your dog has found and focused on the target. What's next? You can teach him to touch his nose to it, touch it with his paw, or lie down and rest his chin on it. Hold the target above his head and you can teach him to jump or stand on his hind legs when cued.

Fading targets Some targets will always be there – like the pedal on the bin – but others need to vanish.

Send Away To A Target

1 Put a mat on the ground and I bet your dog will want to investigate. Let him satisfy his curiosity and go and have a closer look. You are aiming to click and treat when he touches it.

If he shows no interest, place a titbit on top.

1

2

Adding A Down

1 Use your target to help teach your dog to perform tricks, like the Down, at a distance from you.

2 Throw the treat so it lands between his feet. There's no need for him to get up from the Down or move off his target to eat it.

You don't always want to wear a target plaster on your trousers! Fade targets gradually. You can trim a plastic margarine lid to make it smaller. You can shorten your target stick. Instead of your hand, use a few fingers. The smaller and less important the target, the more important the target behaviour becomes and the bigger rewards and titbits.

Have fun target training. You will find targets an invaluable training tool and if you are anything like me, you will soon have pot lids stuffed into your training bag, lying on the window sills at home and crammed into the glove compartment of your car. I am sure that your class teacher will be impressed with your collection!

2 Watch carefully. As soon as your dog gives you the desired target behaviour, like two front feet on the mat, praise, click and treat.

3 Make it a game. Your dog has to run back and forth between you and the target for a click and treat.

Raise the difficulty level by gradually increasing the distance between you and the target.

And tell him he's a clever boy!

How To Use A Target Stick

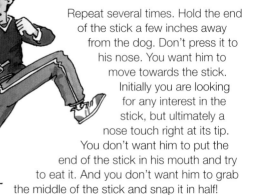

Another key tool to help get your dog started (and later to introduce him to increasingly complicated routines) is a target stick. If you can get your dog to focus on following the end of the target stick, you will have added a powerful new training tool to your armoury.

Repeat several times. Hold the end of the stick a few inches away from the dog. Don't press it to his nose. You want him to move towards the stick. Initially you are looking for any interest in the stick, but ultimately a nose touch right at its tip. You don't want him to put the end of the stick in his mouth and try to eat it. And you don't want him to grab the middle of the stick and snap it in half!

What is a target stick?
A target stick is just what it says – a long stick with a target on the end. You can buy ready-made target sticks. They are usually manufactured in lightweight aluminium and have a small ball on the end to shield the point and attract a dog's attention. A collapsible target stick can be either long or short. You can make a target stick from a car aerial and stick a small ball on its tip. Or tape a tea strainer to the end of it and put a piece of cheese inside. Turn it upside down to deliver a treat.

What a target stick is not! I'm sure you would never dream of tapping your dog on the head with the target stick or poking him in the eye. The target stick is not for pushing, shoving or reprimanding your dog. If you teach him to follow the tip of the stick with a clicker, he will freely follow it wherever it leads him.

Magic wand Target sticks are valuable training aids in doggy dancing, especially for handlers with small dogs who want to avoid bending over! Teach your dog to touch the end of the stick and follow it. You will then be able to train a number of tricks so get out your clicker and make a start.

1 Show your dog the ball on the end of the target stick and if he shows any interest – a look, sniff or lick – click and treat. If balls aren't his thing, rub a bit of cheese on it to set his olfactory senses alight!

2 Will your dog touch the end of the stick when it is on his left and on his right? Will he touch it if you hold it on the ground or above his head? Always click and treat if your dog dives on the end of your stick enthusiastically. If he looks vacant, don't hold the stick out to him waiting for a response that isn't about to come. Withdraw the target and try again in a few seconds.

3 Will your dog follow the target when it is moving? Will he run after it? Start with one step and gradually build up the pace. Make it a game. Will he go round in a circle or between your legs to touch the stick? Have fun.

4 Keep training sessions short. If you go on for too long, he will get bored and switch off. Don't ask for too much initially or he may think your demands are way beyond what he can deliver. You do want to build on success and you want him to look forward to your next training session.

Where to next? Once your dog has got the mechanics of the target stick under his belt, there will be no stopping him. You will be able to teach him to walk by your side without cricking your back. You will be able use the target stick to lure him to objects. Direct him to the laundry basket and get him to jump in with the towels. Get him to follow the target stick over jumps or under chairs. Teach him to trot around you like a Maypole dancer. You may discover that your target stick is your favourite training aid and start thinking of one hundred and one different ways of using it.

Tool box A tool box is a great idea for a training bag. There will be plenty of room for a target stick plus your dog's favourite toys, clickers, treats, small props. And he will not be able to get inside to help himself to titbits if you remember to lock it. Don't forget to add a training diary so you can make notes and keep a chart of his progress.

Follow Your Nose
Where your training stick leads, your dog will follow – to the right or left, up or down.

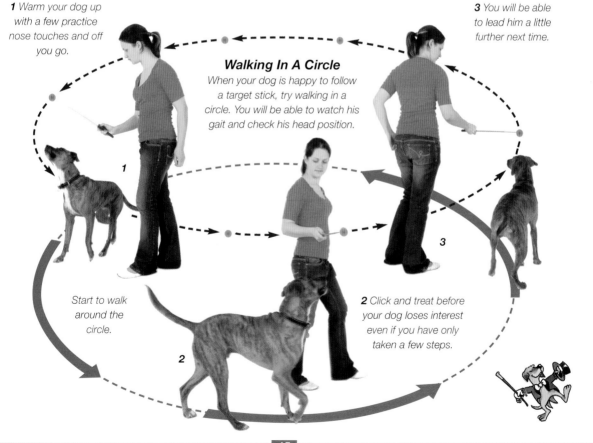

1 Warm your dog up with a few practice nose touches and off you go.

3 You will be able to lead him a little further next time.

Walking In A Circle
When your dog is happy to follow a target stick, try walking in a circle. You will be able to watch his gait and check his head position.

Start to walk around the circle.

2 Click and treat before your dog loses interest even if you have only taken a few steps.

Starting Simple

When you're starting out, don't be put off by the intricate and complicated moves you see experienced competitors performing at shows. Remember that all these skilled performers had to start from the beginning with foundation exercises. Your first step is to teach your dog the basic building blocks which are explained in the following 16 pages.

There are no required movements in doggy dancing. A minimum amount of heelwork may be prescribed in certain classes, but on the whole handlers are free to be as inventive as they like and to create movements and poses that suit their dogs. However, there are certain exercises that form the beginnings of more complex manoeuvres on the dance floor.

I've chosen seven exercises that I believe are worth teaching your dog whether he is a puppy or adult. If you do, you will have a strong, agile and well-balanced dog who can locate his own centre of gravity without your help. He will be more than a step ahead of the competition. Here are the hows and whys for those handlers who already have some of the simpler obedience exercises under their belt and are familiar with clicker, toys and treats.

1 Heel position

Defined loosely, the "heel position" is when your dog is walking at your side, not ten feet in front of you scouting for rabbits as he might do on a walk in the country. You have probably seen obedience dogs working in the heel position. The dog is always on the handler's left side. His shoulder is in line with the handler's thigh or hip and this position is maintained when the handler is stationary or moving through different paces or turns. If you are going to enter heelwork to music classes in the UK, there are a few more permutations. Heel position can be on the left or right side of the handler, facing forwards or backwards, or across the back or front of the handler moving in any direction and at

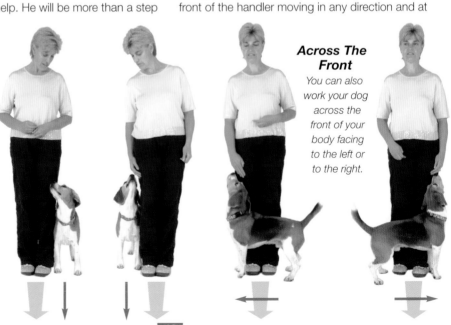

Heel Positions
Working the dog on the left side is the traditional heel position in obedience, but in heelwork to music, the right side is also acceptable.
Try to resist the temptation of looking down at your dog and remember to fade your hand target.

Across The Front
You can also work your dog across the front of your body facing to the left or to the right.

any pace provided the dog's shoulder is reasonably close to the handler's leg. The photographs below illustrate the various permutations that are possible. But first things first.

The heel position is a fundamental in the majority of canine disciplines and there are many different ways to teach it. This is my favourite and works on the principle that where the dog's nose goes, the rest of his body will naturally follow!

1 Touch. Teach your dog a hand touch. Have your clicker ready and hold a treat with your thumb against the palm of your hand. Offer the back of your hand. Most dogs will sniff out of curiosity. What's hidden behind there? When your dog's nose touches the back of your hand, click and turn your hand over so that he can eat the treat. Try it a few times. Do you think he will touch your hand without a hidden treat to tempt him there? Have a go – and click and treat if he does. If you offer your hand and he looks blank, don't be tempted to leave it there in the belief that he just needs a minute or two to remember what the rules of the

Hand Touch
Teach your dog to touch or follow your hand by marking the action with a click and rewarding with a treat.

But take care you don't press your hand into his nose.

game are. Nope. He's lost his chance. Withdraw your hand. Go back a stage and try again with a treat in your hand. When your dog is touch perfect, give the action a command – "Touch".

Across The Back
Working your dog across your back is a little more difficult as you can't see him unless you twist your upper body.

Facing Backwards
But it is easy to check if his tail is wagging when he is by your side, facing in the opposite direction to you.

Starting Simple

2 Position. Stand with your dog in front of you. Take a step back with your left leg and bring your left hand past your side and behind you. The dog should follow the back of your hand. When he has travelled at least a body length straight behind you, bring your arm back to your side. Your dog should turn into you and follow your hand which you bring back to your side and rest against your thigh. Ideally he should swing his bottom around as he turns so that he will arrive in the heel position with a straight body. Now that your hand has stopped moving, he can catch up with it and press his nose into the back of it. He's in the heel position. Click and treat! This exercise takes a bit of coordination from the handler and dog, but once he gets the idea it will look smooth and effortless. Then you can think about using a command like "Close" for this position. With practice your dog will hear you say "Close" and pivot round and straighten himself into the heel position without the aids of your leg, arm or treat. But don't fade them out too soon! It is your responsibility to ensure that he arrives neatly and is in position for a hand touch. Have you got that off pat? Then now try it all on the right-hand side!

3 Follow. When your dog is enthusiastically targeting the back of your hand, see if he will follow it. With the dog on your left, stretch out your left hand and take a few steps in a right-hand circle. If he tracks the back of your hand with his nose, great! Click and treat. Start with one or two steps, then three or four and slowly build up until he can walk a whole circle with his nose on the back of your hand. If he switches off or looks confused, you've done too much too soon. You'll need to go back a step. If he looks confident and happy, gradually bring your hand into your leg and rest it against your thigh. If he walks along by your side in the heel position, he's got the message. He needs to realise that if he keeps his nose near your hand, he will get clicked and treated. Now try it all on the other side!

Follow The Hand

1 Begin with your dog facing you in a stand. Make sure you have his attention and you have your treats and clicker at the ready before you start.

1

Work In A Circle

Hold a treat between your fingers and extend your arm so your dog can see the back of your hand. Take a few steps forward. If your dog follows without jumping up, click and treat out of your hand.

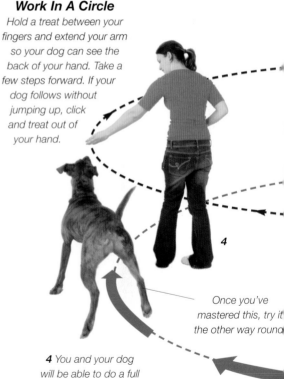

4

Once you've mastered this, try it the other way round

4 You and your dog will be able to do a full circle in no time at all.

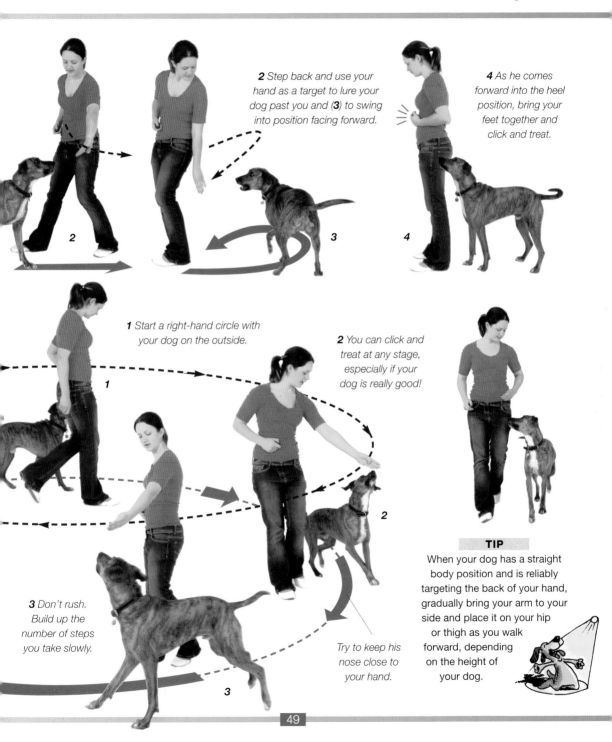

2 Step back and use your hand as a target to lure your dog past you and (**3**) to swing into position facing forward.

4 As he comes forward into the heel position, bring your feet together and click and treat.

1 Start a right-hand circle with your dog on the outside.

2 You can click and treat at any stage, especially if your dog is really good!

3 Don't rush. Build up the number of steps you take slowly.

Try to keep his nose close to your hand.

TIP

When your dog has a straight body position and is reliably targeting the back of your hand, gradually bring your arm to your side and place it on your hip or thigh as you walk forward, depending on the height of your dog.

Starting Simple

2 Spins

Teaching spins and twists to your dog will increase his spatial awareness and stop him getting dizzy on the dance floor!

Stand with the dog standing in front of you. Take a treat in your right hand and show it to him. Move the treat in a clockwise circle and if he starts to follow the treat, click and let him have it. Ask him to follow your hand in the circle a little bit more each time. If your timing is good, throw the treat a little ahead of him in the circle after each click. Eventually, he will be able to do a whole spin! Remember that your dog will be unable to spin on the spot if you start the exercise in the Sit – he will just corkscrew into the ground! And hold your treat at nose level – too high and he will jump up, too low and he'll lie down. Add a command for the clockwise action, when he is reliably following the treat in a complete circle on the spot. Gradually dispense with your lure, stand up straight and fade the hand movement. If at any time your dog looks bewildered, you can always add your training aids back into the equation to reassure him. In no time at all, he will be spinning like a top!

Don't stop now. Do this exercise with the treat in the left hand luring him in an anti-clockwise circle. He needs to be able to spin in both directions and the commands you choose should make this clear; for example, "Twist" means revolve to the right and "Spin" means revolve to left. I use these exercises in agility training to teach directional commands and ensure my dogs learn their lefts from their rights. You may find that he is better turning in one direction than another. Dogs like humans will have a preference and it is important that you spend time in training making sure your dog is as ambidextrous and proficient on both sides as possible.

A Clockwise Twist

1 Make sure your dog is in the stand to start this move. Let your dog sniff the treat in your hand and use it to begin to lure him round in a clockwise circle.

1

Fade The Hand Signal

Finally fade your hand as a cue so that your dog will spin on the verbal command alone.

TIP

Don't do too many repetitions at one time or your dog will get dizzy. And remember that big dogs may take a little longer to get around than small dogs with nifty feet.

2 His nose should follow your hand round.

3 Click when your dog is bending and moving in the direction of your hand movement, not standing still.

4 Some dogs are able to do a whole spin the first time; others may have to bend a few more degrees each try.

2

3

4

Reach further out to give big dogs room to pass under your arm.

Spin The Other Way

1 Use your left hand to teach your dog to spin in the opposite direction. *2* It helps to use a different command to distinguish left- and right-hand spins.

1

2

Starting Simple

III) Circles

I like to teach my dogs to interact with any object I offer them in an inquisitive but controlled manner. It stands them in good stead for doggy dancing where many moves are done with props. You will see dogs jumping canes, standing on stools or pushing trolleys. If you teach your dog to always approach garden and household items with an open curiosity, he will never be afraid to try and figure out what you want him to do with it. So what can you teach him to do with that pole you've just stuck in the ground? Circle it!

You have already taught him spins, so this should be easy. The method is similar but instead of revolving on his own axis, you will be asking him to circle around the pole. Start with him in the heel position on your left and hold a treat in your hand. Lure him around the pole. As soon as he starts to bend, click and treat. Ask him to go a little further each time. When you click, you can drop the treat a little in front of him so he has to bend around the pole a little more to get it. Can he go a full 360 degrees? Try directing him without the treat in your hand. Click and treat from your pocket. If he is circling like a little merry-go-round, think of adding a command like "Circle" or "Round". Gradually, fade the lure and your hand. If your dog circles the pole without your help, click and treat. Make sure that you are able to circle in both directions and consider having a different command for each one. In addition, you can extend the exercise to almost anything that crosses your path. How about circling a tree in the garden, a fire hydrant, your mother-in law or yourself!

Round And Round

1 Start with your dog at your side and a treat in your hand. 2 Begin to lure him around the pole and use the treat to encourage him to bend round further (3). 4 Then throw your treat in an arc in front of your dog, so he continues circling as he goes after his treat.

1

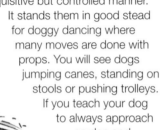

The Other Way

Don't allow yourself a favourite direction. Once you have tried circling one way round the pole, try the opposite and give it a different command to distinguish it.

Throw the treat in the direction of travel.

2

3

4

Fancy Stuff

If your dog will circle around your body (**1 and 2**), you will never need a prop and can practise anywhere and anytime.
In this variation, you revolve one way while your dog goes the other!

This handler has been able to dispense with the treat.

Note how the dog is concentrating intently on his handler's movements.

1

2

TIP

With practice, you can do away with a lure. Hold your arms still while your dog works on the tilt of a shoulder or a verbal command. Don't do too many circles as some dogs get over-excited and start barking.

Starting Simple

Backing Up Through Poles

1 Before you start teaching this trick, make sure that your dog is happy to walk through the poles. They should be far enough apart to accommodate his shoulder width comfortably and tall enough so that he can see them either side.

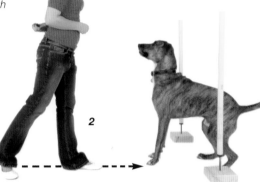

2 Stand facing your dog with his bottom between the poles. Take a step towards him; he will take a step back from you.

4 Backing Up

I never tire of stressing the importance of doing every exercise on both sides and in all directions. Time to reverse! The earlier your dog learns to "back up", the easier he will find it to back through your legs or walk in the opposite direction to you. "Backing up" or walking backwards is a good way to increase his rear end awareness. For some reason, dogs don't always know where their bottom is! The exercise also has practical implications for everyday living. For example, when you are strolling down the pavement with your dog and meet a young Mum with pram coming in the opposite direction, who's going to jump off the kerb and walk in the road? Tell your dog to "back up" and then walk behind you. There will be room for all of you!

We all take a few steps backwards from time to time, but we rarely cover any great distance at speed. As a motor skill, walking backwards is rarely used so it needs to be developed slowly. Imagine, strolling to work, shopping at the

supermarket or running up the stairs – all in reverse! It wouldn't feel natural and you'd be a bit apprehensive because you wouldn't be able to see where you were going. So watch your dog. Hold a treat or toy in the air in front of him. Does he scoot back a few paces in anticipation of you throwing it? If you take a few steps towards him, will he jump back a little more! Take advantage of this natural behaviour and build on it. Refine and shape it with a bit of barrier training.

1 **Build** Build a channel out of chairs, the settee and a wall, or poles evenly spaced in the ground. You might be able to find a ready-made hallway that will fit your needs. The channel should be wide enough so that your dog can walk through comfortably without touching the sides or twisting around and it should be about three or four of his body lengths long. It will keep his "walk backs" in a straight rather than crooked line.

2 **Accustom** Introduce him to the channel. Walk him through it a few times so that he gets used to the feeling of the barriers on either side. If he slips out of any gaps, you might have to do some remedial building, but if he is comfortable and at

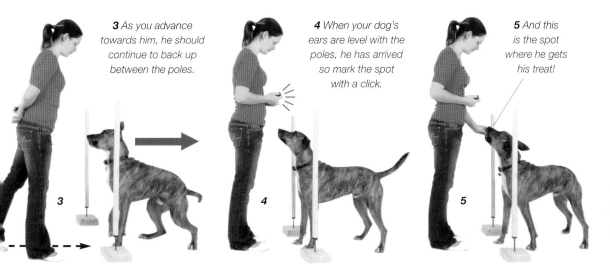

3 As you advance towards him, he should continue to back up between the poles.

3

4 When your dog's ears are level with the poles, he has arrived so mark the spot with a click.

4

5 And this is the spot where he gets his treat!

5

ease, walk him through the channel one more time and turn and face him so that you are standing in the channel's mouth. Unless he is very thin or very pushy, he won't be able to squeeze past you. And the only way out is behind him.

3 Take a step As you move towards your dog he will take a step backwards. Quickly click and treat him by tossing the titbit at him so it falls at his feet. Be quick or he will step towards you. You need to do your utmost to click for backward movement and treat when Juan is away, not near you.

4 Again Call him back to you so he is directly in front of you and you can repeat the exercise. Take another small step towards him. With luck, he will start to walk backwards a little more each time without you stepping forward on each attempt. Add a command like "Back".

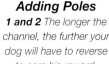

1

5 Don't be greedy! Gradually build up the distance a few paces at a time, especially at first when he is not fully conditioned to operating in reverse. If he can walk back all the way to the end of the channel, it's time to have a go without the barriers! But remember, he is relying on you not to reverse him into a chair or a wall. Don't break that trust!

Adding Poles
***1 and 2** The longer the channel, the further your dog will have to reverse to earn his reward.*

Click and treat at the last pair of poles.

2

Starting Simple

5 Through

Teaching your dog to run through your legs is the springboard for future leg weaving exercises. It will also increase your dog's confidence in you. A dog that will happily run through your legs is not afraid that you will collapse and sit on him. He's safe! He believes that your legs will stay straddled and not suddenly scissor shut and cut him in half! It's another trust thing. Dogs have a great respect for their handlers, especially their legs. Who can blame them? At some time, we have all accidentally stepped on our dog or fallen over them. Convince your dog that there is no need to be apprehensive about your feet and he'll be happy to weave between them.

1 **Straddle stance** Stand in front of your dog with your legs in a straddle. Don't have your legs too close together – there needs to be enough space for him to run through. And don't have them too far apart or you'll topple over.

2 **Restrain and throw** Bend over and place your hand on his collar so that you will be able to restrain and direct him. Let him see you throw a biscuit through your legs. You can use a toy if you are sure he will bring it back! Wind him up with a "Where's your treat?" and aim and release him to the treat. He should be excited and keen, but committed to the shortest route through your straddled legs. Don't let him cheat and deviate around them. Do this a few times. It's a great

Rev him up. Look what I've got! Do you want it?

1

Through Your Legs

1 Start by facing your dog and holding his collar. Stand with your legs wide enough apart so he can easily pass between them. Your dog should be focused on the treat or toy in your hand and raring to go.

2

2 and 3 Let your dog see you throw his treat or toy in a straight line through your legs. And then release him.

game and will familiarise the dog with the gap between your legs. If he wants to keep playing, progress to the next stage.

3 **Stand up** Will he run through your legs if he doesn't see a treat on the other side? Stand in front of him with your legs straddled, but remain upright and hold the treats behind your back. This time do not restrain him with your hand. If he sticks his nose through the gap, click and throw the treat behind you so that he has to pass through your legs to get it. Don't click and treat if he cheats! He will quickly get the idea that although he can't see a treat, one will be coming and land on the other side of you. When he does, add a command like "Through" or as one of my agility friends says, "Tunnel"!

4 **Variations** If your dog has mastered the art of "Through", you can keep him guessing with a few variations. Sometimes you can throw the treat behind you so he keeps running or sometimes you can hold on to it to lure him back into the heel position on the left or right side. Varying the exercise in this way will keep him on his toes and make sure that he is paying attention to you and not losing his focus.

TIP
Don't forget to try it on the other side too. You want your dog to be comfortable turning in both directions.

1

2

Back To Heel

1 Instead of throwing the treat behind you, keep it in your hand and (2) lure your dog back into the heel position.

4 Don't throw too far at first. Going around your legs is cheating!

5 But when your dog has the idea, you can throw your treat further so that his whole body passes through your legs. Off he goes!

4

5

Starting Simple

1 Hold a treat in your hand and make a fist.

2 Resist sniffs and licks. Wait for your dog to lay his paw on top of it. When he does, click and praise him.

Give A Paw *The first thing many people say when they meet your dog is "Does he give a paw?" Teach your dog this simple trick and you will not only impress your friends, but be laying the foundations for more complicated paw work.*

6 Paws

Every dog has four paws and you can increase your dog's dexterity with each of them by means of tricks. "Giving a paw" or "Shake hands" is every pet owner's favourite and this simple move can be the start of more complicated stuff like teaching your dog to limp on one foot or wave goodbye. You could even teach him to offer his hind leg next time someone asks him to shake hands! Let's not race ahead! Teach him to give you a front paw first!

How about this as different way to Give Me Five?

Get his favourite treat and hold it in your left fist in front of him at eye level. He will know it's there but how can he get you to open your hand and let him

3 *Now open your hand so he can see the treat and eat it.*

4 *Instead of your fist, offer your palm. He's shaking hands.*

3

4

eat it? What a puzzle! He'll try sniffing and licking your hand, but hold tight. He will be able to smell the juicy piece of sausage in your hand, but won't be able to get at it. How frustrating! In desperation, he might start to dig at your fist with a paw. As soon as his paw touches your hand, click and quickly open your fist so he can have his reward. If you are too slow, he might think that you want him to excavate your fist rather than touch your hand with his paw. Repeat. He will soon figure out that the clicks and treats will come only when he raises his paw and puts it on

your fist. If he's got the picture, offer him your hand palm up without holding the treat. He might give it a sniff and then the penny will drop. He'll hit it with the paw! Click and treat your clever dog! When he demonstrates that this is kid's stuff, give the action a command like "Paw" or "Hand".

You can have a lot of fun with this one and amaze your friends. Your dog can give a paw to your children's buddies and your boss at work. And don't forget to teach him to use his left paw as easily as his right one. Just start again, but use your right hand.

Both Paws Together
When your dog lifts two paws off the ground, he will need somewhere solid to rest them like your knees.

Present your forearm as a platform for your dog's paws and the pose will look less like a marriage proposal!

Starting Simple

7 Pose

If your dog is a bit of a poser, this is the exercise for you. The all-time favourite doggy pose is the "Beg". What dog doesn't look cute sitting on his haunches to peer over the edge of the dinner table? Holding a pose for just three seconds takes balance and strength, so it is important to build up duration gradually. If yours is the type of dog that can't sit still for long and has ants in his pants, he'll have to learn patience too!

With the dog sitting in front of you, ask him to give you a paw. Hold a treat above his head and as he reaches up for the treat, he will be using your

above *Not all dogs have the confidence, conformation or strength to balance on their bottoms. Offer your forearm as a support so they can get their front feet off the ground.*

hand for support to steady himself. His other foot will come off the ground as he stretches for the treat. Bingo! He is in the "Beg". Click and let him have his treat while he is still upright. Do this a few times and when he is easily getting in position, give the pose a command. If you think "Beg" is too demeaning a command, you can always use "Say please"! I use "Meerkat" because that's what my terrier cross looks like when she sits up on her haunches.

Keep your hand outstretched for as long as your dog needs support for the pose. With practice he

1 Face your dog and place him in the Sit. Have a treat at the ready.

1

Sit Up And Beg

Many dogs can do this appealing trick without aid or prompting. They have learned that balancing on their haunches looks cute and earns a biscuit. Other dogs need a little extra time and help, but they soon look just as sweet and deserving of a treat.

To stay in contact with the treat, his front feet will rise.

2 Take the treat forward and above your dog's head.

2

should be able to hold the "Beg" position for a little bit longer and a little bit more independently. Try it. Hold the treat above his head and give your command. Will he lift himself into the pose without your help? You won't find out if you don't try. And remember, he does not get clicked for jumping up and grabbing the treat out of your hand. His bottom must stay glued to the ground. That way he will have a solid base if you teach him to hold this pose and put his paws over his eyes.

Star qualities Some dogs will be better at twisting than posing. Others will excel at heelwork but need more work with their paws. Each dog is an individual with different strengths and weaknesses. So you might need to practise one kind of move more than another. But if you have fun teaching any of these basic exercises, you will have fun learning more doggy dancing. You can extend and develop these tricks into something stunning and suited to your dog's unique personality and star quality. I hope that I have whetted your appetite, so just get started!

Right Your dog can beg from the Sit or the Stand. Make sure you differentiate between the two. For dramatic effect, this handler says "Be a bear" for when her dog is sitting in the beg...

...and be a BIG bear when he is standing!

TIP

Give this pose a name – "Beg" or "Sit pretty" – so your dog knows what to expect. Will he perform without a treat attached to his nose? Will he hold the pose for more than ten seconds? Try and see.

3 When both feet are off the ground, praise and treat.

4 If you have been kneeling, rise to a stand. Your dog's bottom must remain on the ground.

3

4

SKILL BUILDING

It is easier than you think to teach your pet a trick. And the kick you'll get out of working as a team is truly addictive. Once your dog has mastered rolling over, you'll start looking for new training challenges and soon have a long list of moves and stunts at your disposal that will amaze your friends and family.

Using Vocal Communication

We take it for granted that we can teach our dogs a whole range of words, but it's worth thinking about our choice of words for commands. A clever dog may have as large a vocabulary as a small child, but he doesn't understand language in the same way that we do, so your must keep commands clear and simple. A dog's linguistic expertise is really quite limited.

Vocabulary It has been estimated that dogs can learn up to around 200 words. If you try and write a list of the words that your dog knows, I think you will be surprised at how long it is. And he has probably absorbed a few without you realising it. Did you consciously choose to teach him your husband's name or has he picked it up by listening to you call out to him?

Meaningful lessons You should aim to teach your dog words that will be meaningful to you both. Given that you may have a limit of around 200 words in the canine lexicon to play with, do you really need him to learn the words like "tabasco" or "balloon". It's quality, not quantity of vocabulary that counts.

Words don't always speak louder than actions And it is not just words that are meaningful. If you say nothing and point to the floor does your dog obediently lie down? If you put on your coat, does he rush for his lead because he thinks he is going for a walk? Body language is the communication of choice for dogs.

Right If you lure your puppy into the Down position, you will be teaching him a strong hand signal.

Choosing cues Whether you choose a verbal cue or body signal, your dog should react. It always makes me sad to see an old dog struggling to comply with the "Down" command. Those joints can't do the job like they used to, but the spirit is willing. The command you choose will stay with your dog for its entire life, so choose carefully. If your cue for your dog to twist is wiggling your hand in a circle like you are taking the lid off a jar, you will always have to use it. Dance with your hands behind your back and the likelihood is that he won't twist!

Signs and sounds Did you say "No" or "Go"? The context in which a word is used will often remove some ambiguity, but not always. Choose cues carefully. Did the dog hear "Bend" or "Bow"?

Slip of the tongue Choose verbal commands that are easy to say and slip off the tongue. Something short is best – one or two syllables. And something that is easy to remember. You don't want to make your dog wait while you rack your brain for his cue to hide his eyes with a paw.

Multi-dog families If you have more than one dog, try to keep all your commands the same for all of them or you will make extra work for yourself. Don't use "Down" for one dog and "Flat" for another and then wonder why both remain sitting.

Keeping A Focus

Some dogs can manage the moves and keep a good position, but tend to keep their heads down and their eyes on the floor instead of looking up at their dance partner. This spoils the whole effect – you want your dog to be gazing at you with adoration (even if it's your pocketful of treats that is bringing that soulful look into his eyes). Scent-oriented breeds such as hounds are particularly prone to this problem. Having been bred to think with their noses, they won't automatically find it more interesting to look at you than to sniff the floor. Tackle the problem with the "Look at me" game.

Left Hold a treat between your lips in order to focus your dog's attention firmly on your face.

you with getting a click. He won't need the lure of cheese to know where to turn his gaze. Gazing at you is more productive than studying the ground.

2 When your dog has the idea, make him hunt for your face. If he is sitting in front of you, turn your head away to the left. Did he step around to find your face? Good! Click and treat as his eyes meet yours. Try it again but this time turn to the right.

3 Make it an action exercise. When your dog is targeting your face, make him work even harder to find it. Just before he gets to you, dash off in the opposite direction. If he runs to catch you up and looks up at you, click and give him a super-size treat. He is having to work even harder to establish contact so make sure the reward matches the extra effort he's putting in.

Look at me For clicker-trained dogs that enjoy their grub, this game is a must and it will teach the dog to remain mesmerized by you!

1 Get out your clicker and have a handful of yummy treats at the ready. There are a number of ways you can tempt your dog to look up at your face. You can hold a treat up to your cheek or squash one behind the bridge of your glasses. He will look up and every time he does, click and treat. Some handlers put a treat between their lips and spit it out after the click. Repeat a few times and say "Watch" so that your dog will start to associate the act of looking at

4 Just how good is your dog at this game? Will he keep looking up at you if you drop a tissue, pound coin, ball or cube of cheese? If he looks at what you have dropped and not you – oops, must try harder! He has to be transfixed by your smile to get his click and treat. Try again. Remember the higher the value of object dropped, the harder it will be for him to keep staring at you.

Eventually your dog won't want to look anywhere else but at you even if you forgot to apply your make-up. Tell him to "Watch" during heelwork or when you leave him in a Stay if his eyes start to wander and his head drops. It should do the trick.

Catch Up Games

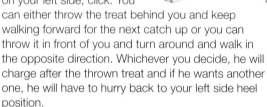

Keeping your dog's attention focused on you is crucial, both for speed of learning and for a polished performance– you don't want a dog who is easily distracted. Teaching him to concentrate on his studies is one of the most important lessons of all, and is best taught by fun – such as catch up games. Does your dog look bored or lag behind in heelwork? If so, then catch up games are for you. Your dog will literally have to run to catch you if he wants a click and treat.

Catch up! Get yourself ready with a bum bag full of your dog's favourite treats and your clicker. Throw a treat away from you and as soon as he goes after it, turn away and walk in the opposite direction with another treat in your left hand. He will gobble the treat you threw and turn to look to see where you have gone. Somewhere nice? As soon as he catches you up on your left side, click. You can either throw the treat behind you and keep walking forward for the next catch up or you can throw it in front of you and turn around and walk in the opposite direction. Whichever you decide, he will charge after the thrown treat and if he wants another one, he will have to hurry back to your left side heel position.

When he has the idea, ask for a few paces of stunning heelwork before you click and throw the treat. When he can quote all the rules of the game back at you, you can increase the number of paces in the heel position. And you can ask him to play catch up on the right hand side too, by having the

3 The sooner he finishes, the sooner he can run back to your side for another click and throw of a treat.

He'll have to be quick so use treats that are easy to chew and swallow.

TIP

Keep moving. Don't wait for your dog. Because a click and treat from you is guaranteed, he will soon stop wasting time and energy sniffing or scavenging on his way back.

1 Have treats and clicker at the ready. Throw the treat away behind you so that your dog has to leave your side to find it.

2 While your dog finds and eats the treat, continue walking away from him.

treat in your right hand. Are straight lines too easy? Try zig-zags and different paces. If you run, your dog will have to run too. A right hand circle will make him really work to catch you up on the left because he will have farther to go. A great exercise for a dog that lags. If he has little legs, you could walk with your dog on the inside of a left hand circle.

Catch him unawares You can throw in a catch up game anytime. If you think your dog is trudging along and his eyes are starting to close, bide your time.

When his eyes are almost shut, quickly step to the side or turn away from him and keep walking. Ooops! That should wake him up. When he catches up, click and treat. It is a good game because it will keep him alert and paying attention. Vary the direction and speed that you dart off but always make sure that he knows that it is worth returning to your side by rewarding him with a click and treat.

These are fun ways to teach a dog to keep his eye on you. Why should he expend energy looking for biscuit crumbs on the floor when he hears a click in the catch up game?

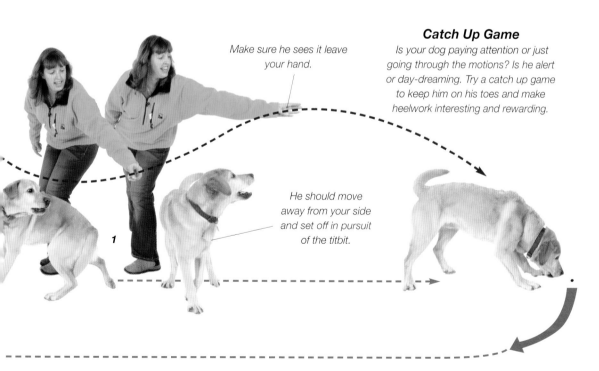

Catch Up Game

Is your dog paying attention or just going through the motions? Is he alert or day-dreaming. Try a catch up game to keep him on his toes and make heelwork interesting and rewarding.

Make sure he sees it leave your hand.

He should move away from your side and set off in pursuit of the titbit.

1

Getting Closer To Little Dogs

A common problem with small dogs is that, even if they have good attention, they may tend to drift away from their owners' sides during heelwork. The natural response is to reach down to reposition him closer to your leg, but often this will cause the dog to move away. There is a simple explanation for this.

Whatever their size, all dogs love to look up at their owner's smiling face. However, to get a good view without cricking his neck, a little dog has to move away from you. As soon as he does, you bend down and reach out for him. He probably thinks you are going to grab him so he moves further away to stay out of reach. The problem can be compounded if you have ever accidentally stepped on him. No wonder he is a bit foot shy and wants to keep some distance between him and your size nines. Don't despair! There are a number of things you can try to help bring a small dog closer to you.

Look straight ahead When you practise your heelwork, stand up straight and face forward. If you want to see what your dog is doing, cast your eyes down, but keep your head still. Chances are he will be there by your side and not digging into someone's treat bag that's been left on a chair. Set up a full-length mirror on one side of the room, stand on the other and heel your dog towards the mirror. You'll be able to see your little companion without bending down.

Stand up straight You will never be able to know that a small dog is there by your side by feeling the weight of his shoulder against your thigh. He just isn't big enough. Instead of bending down to see if he is there, extend your arm with a target stick. Click him when he touches the end with his nose and treat. Once he is happy to follow the end of the target

Right Give your small dog a target, like a piece of tape or sticking plaster on the outside of your leg, that he can reach for a nose-touch.

stick as you walk, you can progress to holding it close to your leg. Click and treat when he is walking where you want him and gradually collapse and shrink the target stick.

Sticky plasters Or you could put a small plaster on the outside seam of your trouser leg nearest to him. Teach him to nose-touch it when he is in the heel position. Start by putting the plaster over a treat and click and treat when he investigates. Click and treat. He will be offering you a nose touch in no time at all. You can do the same thing by sewing a button on the spot that you want his nose to contact. Many trousers have stitchwork designs on the legs. Perfect for the miniature dog to target.

Playing footsie I play footsie with my small dogs. I massage their tummies with my feet. I hide treats between my tootsies. Games like these go some way to ensuring that my dogs have a nice association with my feet. Try it. See if your small dog will lick your toes. It may help to get that vital bit closer.

Keeping A Distance
It's hard to know where your little dog is without looking down. You won't be able to feel him pressing on your leg.

Bending Down
You have to bend over to attract his attention with a treat. You could end up on painkillers and in need of an osteopath!

The lure must be within reach, if you want him to follow it.

He should be here...

TIP

To check your posture, rest a mirror against a wall as you train or have a friend video your heelwork. Are your shoulders back? Is your head up straight?

But he won't be able to see you without standing back.

A Better Way
1 Try using a target stick so that you don't have to bend down.

2 Once your dog is following it, bring it closer to your leg.

3 Gradually fade the target stick, by collapsing it into your hand by your side.

4 Stand up straight and have faith that your dog is there alongside you.

1   2

3

4

Working On The Right

For people making the transition to dance from obedience work, a common problem is that their dogs become confused when asked to heel on the right. In obedience competitions, all heelwork is done on the left – heeling on the right just doesn't happen!

However, heelwork to music dogs are taught to perform their movements on all sides of their handlers in order to demonstrate to the judges their flexibility, dexterity and versatility. This is easy with a puppy, but often hard work with an older dog that has spent years doing everything on the left hand side.

Above *A well balanced dog will be happy working on the left or on the right and forwards or backwards. Dogs drilled in conventional obedience exercises are left-side-orientated and may take longer to become ambidextrous.*

Old dogs, new tricks Both you and your dog may have established a preference for the left and whenever he is in doubt or confused, this is the side to which he will return as, in the past, this is where he has earned his rewards and your smiles. Moreover, one side of the dog is more developed and muscled than the other because all your work has been done on this side. Physically, it's easier on the left so this intensifies his preference even more. No wonder he is resistant and you are uncomfortable asking him to walk on the right. It's like wearing shoes on the wrong feet. Be patient. You'll get there in the end.

Back to basics How did you teach your dog to heel on the left? Go back to basics and start all over again but this time on the right. Did you teach him to follow a lure on your left side when he was a puppy. Try it on your right. Where that treat goes, so will he. Now put a treat in your right hand and tempt him into a position where his left shoulder is level with your right leg. When he is there, hold the treat above his head and next to your body. While he is looking up at the treat, click and run your hand down your thigh to give him his slice of frankfurter or cube of cheese. After a few repetitions, your dog will get your game and you can add a cue like "Side" or "By me". He now has a command for the heel position on your right. Progress to taking a few steps forward with the treat in your right hand. He should follow and you can click and treat again. Gradually increase the number of steps and as he increases in confidence, try walking in a circle. Then a figure of eight. You'll be a pro in no time at all. With practice you and your dog will be as comfortable working on the right as the left.

1 Teach your dog to target your hand on your right side with a click and a treat.

1

The dog is beautifully positioned on the right.

2 Take a few steps forward. Click and treat if he stays with you.

2

Heelwork On The Right
Use the same training methods with which you taught your dog to heel on the left. Start back at the beginning.

3 Gradually increase the number of steps and try to complete a full circle.

3

Ambidextrous dogs Remember that the more work that you do on the right side, the stronger and more developed your dog's right hand side will become. But do so gradually. And whenever you introduce a new move to him, practise it on both sides. He should be able to twist in any direction and walk forwards or backwards on either side of you. He should be able to shake hands with either paw. Don't let your dog be lop-sided.

The aim is for you to have a dog that is balanced mentally and physically. Enjoy your training!

Teach On The Right
Can your dog twist on the right side of you as well as he can on the left? Have a go!

Working Across The Front

If you are going to compete in heelwork to music, you will need to be able to demonstrate your dog's ability to work in different heelwork positions. And also your ability to walk forwards, backwards and sideways! Once you have taught your dog to heel on both your left and your right, you need to teach him to heel across the front of your body. You can teach the across position just like you did the others. With your clicker and bag of treats.

Static practice Face a wall and stand about three or four feet from it. You've made a neat little channel. Throw a treat to your right side and have another one ready in your left hand. Hold your left hand by your side away from your thigh, at your dog's eye level. When he comes through the channel and touches your offered hand, click and either feed in position or throw the treat to your left out of the channel. If you throw, he will exit to chase it but will have to turn around and re-enter from your left to nose-touch your right hand for a click and treat. Working against the wall, a row of chairs or the back of the settee will help keep the dog in a straight line across your body. And he gets his titbit in the stand, not the sit or down. Repeat four or five times.

Next step If your dog is confidently targeting your hand, try clicking as he comes into position, but before he nose-touches your hand. Hold your hand a little higher or a little further in front of him. Your hand still acts as a target, but he no longer has to nose-touch it. He is getting the click for his position relative to you – the across.

Add a command Choose a command for this position and start saying it as soon as your dog is reliably placing himself in the stand across your thighs. "Across" is the obvious one!

On the move Sidestep to your left. Your dog should maintain his position across your body. Your hand is in front of his nose leading him like a beacon. Click and throw the treat behind him. If he wants more, he will have to put himself back into position. Gradually increase the number of steps you take before you click and throw the treat. Practise in a straight line in both directions. If you can keep your dog's movement smooth, across heeling can look very elegant.

Show off You can jazz up the "Across" to make it look ethnic or modern. Try to sidestep by taking a step with one leg behind or in front of the other. Hold your hands above your head or put them on your waist. Once you have taught your dog the across position, the hardest part could be deciding on how you are going to move sideways.

Teaching Across
1 Make a channel between you and a chair. Show your dog you are ready to train by getting out his treats. 2 Throw a treat so he goes through the channel to get it.

TIP
You can move sideways with the same foot always leading or one crossing behind the other. It shouldn't make any difference to your dog as long as you don't leave him behind.

Front Across Position

1 Use your hand as a target to maintain your dog in position. His body should be parallel to the front of your legs.

2 Step to your right or left (3) while your dog moves with you, his eye on your hand containing the treat. As your dog becomes more proficient, you can increase the number of steps that you take.

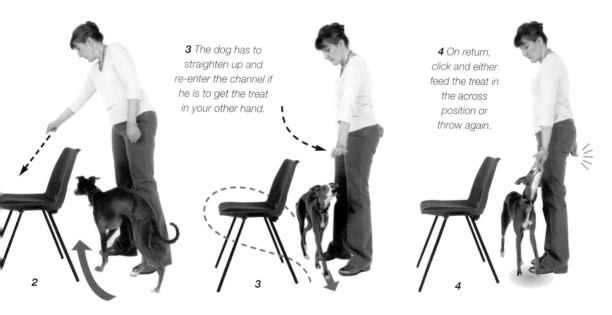

3 The dog has to straighten up and re-enter the channel if he is to get the treat in your other hand.

4 On return, click and either feed the treat in the across position or throw again.

Extra Height For Little Dogs

Pint-size dogs present a whole new set of training challenges. You look down at your dog from on high and see his back. With his little legs, it's hard to be sure whether he is trotting, cantering or galloping. At times, you may not even be able to tell if he is sitting, lying down or giving a bow. This can make it difficult to teach him new tricks, as you can't be quite sure what you're clicking – did he wave a paw, or just take a step forward? Who knows what is going on underneath!

The simple answer when training very small dogs is that you need to raise your dog up nearer to you. He needs height so you never have to bend down. They don't make elevator shoes for Chihuahuas, so think of alternatives.

Try a table If you lift up your dog and put him on a table, you'll be able to see what he is doing with his paws. Yes, that was a bow, not a Down! Grooming tables are ideal because they are a good size, stand at waist height and are covered in rubber matting so the dog won't slide off. Agility tables are another viable option or you can make one of your own. Take care to

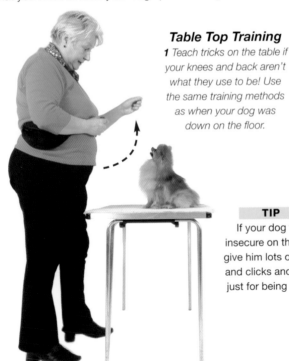

Table Top Training
1 Teach tricks on the table if your knees and back aren't what they use to be! Use the same training methods as when your dog was down on the floor.

2 For safety, don't encourage lots of bouncing or jumping up. It's a long way down.

TIP
If your dog feels insecure on the table, give him lots of praise and clicks and treats just for being there.

ensure that your dog will have enough room to perform his tricks without falling off an edge. Choose a surface that offers plenty of grip and make sure your table is solid. If it wobbles, your dog won't want to stay on it no matter how many treats you feed him. And it's a long way down if he takes fright and jumps off. Choose a table that is both welcoming and safe.

Use a plank Will your dog follow a target stick along a plank? Get an old builder's plank and check it for nails and splinters. Place it over two milk crates and voilà! A dog walk. Parade him across it. Pretend he is a model at a fashion show. You'll be able to see if he is prancing or strolling. Look for old gym benches or brick walls on which you can also practise. Not too high though and make sure there isn't a drop into a fast-flowing river on the other side! Mini dogs aren't good swimmers.

Stairway platform If you have steps in your house that turn a corner from one floor to the next, you have a ready-made training platform. Put your dog on the platform and stand a few steps below so you can get a good view of his feet. You will be able to spot any cheating. Ooops! There's the proof. He didn't complete a full turn when you asked for a spin – when you had been looking down from above it looked like he had.

I'm very lucky. I have steps up into my back garden that are the length of the rear of the house. I use them like a table or a bench depending on what moves I am training. So think laterally. You may have something at home that is perfect for giving your dog some extra height, but always consider the safety aspects when deciding. And when you have polished the performance, try it back on the floor.

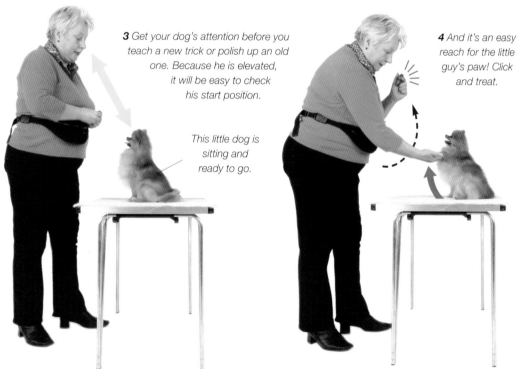

3 Get your dog's attention before you teach a new trick or polish up an old one. Because he is elevated, it will be easy to check his start position.

This little dog is sitting and ready to go.

4 And it's an easy reach for the little guy's paw! Click and treat.

Teaching To Walk Straight Back

Walking backwards in a perfectly straight line doesn't come easily to every dog. A dog who can walk in a straight line when going forwards may well start curving or zigzagging when asked to do the same thing backwards. You should bear in mind that walking backwards needs good spatial awareness, static reference points and trust in whoever is giving directions.

You are asking your dog to develop a very particular skill and there are many stumbling blocks along the way. Your dog loves you and wants to stay as close to you and your pocket full of treats as possible, not back away from you. And if he is keeping his eye on you, he won't see any obstacles behind him. Oops! There's the kerb. Here are some ideas to help him straighten up.

Barriers guide the way If your dog veers to his right when he walks backwards, try performing the exercise with a barrier or wall on his right hand side to give him a point of reference and help him to maintain a straight line. If he is more inclined to float off to the left, do it the other way with a wall on his left. Repeat this sufficient times and the notion of "straight" will embed itself into the dog's muscle memory. Test by seeing how he performs away from the barrier. I have seen some very determined dogs reverse at an angle back to the side of the wall and then continue reversing in a straight line. They have added the presence of the wall into their performance equation although that is not what their handlers intended at all!

Pick a destination You can train the walk back to a specific destination. This will not only keep your dog on a straight line with no deviations but it will mark a beginning and end to the exercise. He will not be backing into infinity. Much less stressful. If you have taught him to stand on a mat, use that as an end target. Start with him in front of you, and his mat directly behind him. Ask him to reverse and as soon as he has four paws on his mat, click. He will run towards you for his treat; thus setting himself up to do it all again. Repeat until he is executing the move confidently and then increase the distance that he has to cover. The mat stays where it is but you and he move a step further away. Progress slowly and always finish the exercise when your dog hits his mat satisfactorily. If you are after all four paws on the mat, don't accept less.

Guide poles Teach him to stand between two poles placed in the ground. The gap between them should be about 15cm (6in) wider than the dog on either side. Dogs have good peripheral vision and he will know when he is standing in the middle of the gap. Use the same method as with the mat. However, add two more poles every 1.2 to 1.5m (4 to 5ft). He will have to move through the first and subsequent two poles and get clicked as he reverses into place between the last set. The poles are way markers and the click occurs when your dog is between the final two.

Introduce a new command If "Walk back" is associated with reversing aimlessly in a zigzag, try something new and different like "Opposite" or "Contrary" or even "Sausages" as a command when you retrain this skill.

I hope that these training strategies are helpful and that your dog gets on the straight and narrow soon. Be patient and consistent and you will get results.

Back To A Mat

1 With the mat directly behind your dog, give your walk back command.

2 You have already taught the command, so your dog will start to reverse away from you.

3 When he hits the mat, he has arrived. Click and he can return to you for a treat!

4 If you want your dog to stand on the mat, click before he collapses into a Down and recall him for a treat.

Back Through Poles

1 With the poles behind your dog, give your command to walk back.

2 The gap between the poles must be wide enough to accommodate your dog.

TIP

Increase distance by adding more pairs of poles, but always click when your dog is standing between the end two.

3 When he is standing between them, mark his position with a click.

Speeding Up Your Weaves

A common problem that some handlers experience with weaves concerns manitaining momentum and speed. The dog may start weaving in time to the music but then he will slow down and by the third or fourth weave he may be lagging woefully behind the beat. If this describes your experience of weaving with your dog, try some of the following suggestions.

Done well, legs weaves look spectacular. Done badly, they look like something from the Ministry of Funny Walks. To achieve leg weaves that flow, think about how you have trained your dog. If you have taught your dog to touch your hand with each step, you may have inadvertently encouraged him to push his head up to meet your palm and pause for a treat between at every step. Instead of working a straight line ahead of you, he bobs from a heel position on the left to a heel position on the right. And if he doesn't get his anticipated piece of sausage, he slows down in protest. Try a few of the following ploys to speed him up.

Short and simple Keep it to the minimum. Don't do long lines of leg weaves across the garden. Your dog will get bored, lose his motivation and run out of gas. It is far better to have four steps of snappy legs weaves than dragging out eight painfully slow ones.

Limit expectations When you practise leg weaves, don't reward your dog after every step. Sometimes give him his treat after the first step and sometimes after the fourth one. That should keep him guessing.

Use a target This is an agility exercise I use for the weaving poles with my target-trained dogs. Try it with leg weaves. Place the target on the ground about 2.5m (8ft) in front of you – it can be anything like a square of carpet, a margarine tub lid, or a mouse pad. The dog has to do four leg weaves to the target to get a reward. If he runs to the target without weaving, he doesn't get a treat. This exercise should increase his drive and get him thinking about running a line through your legs rather than bouncing up and down. When he understands the rules of the game, you can gradually increase the number of legs weaves to six, eight, ten or twelve.

Keep your timing Remember that you set the pace, not the dog. If you feel that he is flagging, don't accommodate him by walking slower. If he isn't quick enough – oops, bad luck. He has missed his opportunity for a treat and game. He'll shoot through the gap between your legs next time.

Care with choreography Instead of dropping leg weaves from your routine, break them up into smaller chunks (four leg weaves rather than eight) separated by something that your dog likes doing that can act as a reward; for example a twist. His favourite move becomes an incentive to keep him weaving.

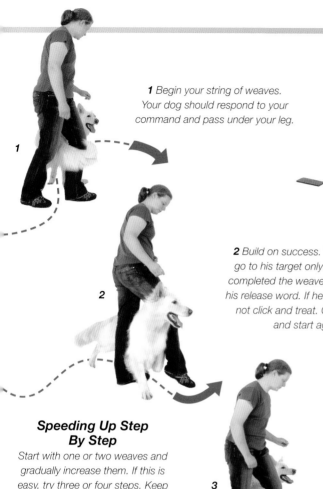

1 Begin your string of weaves. Your dog should respond to your command and pass under your leg.

Review Your Target Training

Before you add a mat to a string of weaves, quickly review your target training. Start by letting your dog see you place a treat on the mat.

2 Build on success. Your dog can go to his target only when he has completed the weaves and you give his release word. If he anticipates, do not click and treat. Call him back and start again.

TIP

Look for drive on to the target. If your dog needs more motivation, use a food bowl or a toy as a target to quicken his pace and interest.

Speeding Up Step By Step

Start with one or two weaves and gradually increase them. If this is easy, try three or four steps. Keep your dog keen to get to his mat and he will soon change up a gear.

3 The closer you get to the target, the more tempting it will be for your dog to break loose. If he is wavering, repeat your weave command.

When his nose touches the mat, click and treat him.

TIP

Practise your leg weaves so that your dog is comfortable exiting from both the right and the left hand side of your body and forward on to the target.

4 As your dog finishes the last leg weave, praise and release him to the mat. He's done his job!

Weaving Little Dogs

Small dogs can look wonderful weaving in and out of your legs, but sometimes you find that bending down to lure your mini-dog through your legs has affected your own posture. It's easy not to notice how far you lean over while you're dancing – if in doubt, try and obtain a video recording of your routine, which will show you whether there is room for improvement.

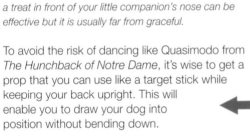

Above Hunching over your dog so that you can dangle a treat in front of your little companion's nose can be effective but it is usually far from graceful.

To avoid the risk of dancing like Quasimodo from *The Hunchback of Notre Dame*, it's wise to get a prop that you can use like a target stick while keeping your back upright. This will enable you to draw your dog into position without bending down.

Use an umbrella An umbrella is the perfect prop for your music and you can use it like a target stick. It will give your arm extra length. No more doubling over to lure your dog through your legs. Instead, teach him to nose-touch the end of your umbrella tip as well as the handle. If you have already taught your little dog to follow the end of a target stick, he should be able to quickly transfer this behaviour to each end of your brollie.

Step right, then left Start with your dog on your left side and hold the umbrella with two hands in the middle. Step forward with your right foot. Slide the umbrella to your right side and lower the end of it so that your dog can see it between your legs. If he goes through your legs to touch it, click and treat. Step forward with your left leg. Slip the umbrella through your hands to your left side and lower it so that he can see its opposite end. Click

Using A Target Stick

1 Increase the length of your arm with a target stick so you can stand up. Your dog can follow the point for a click and treat.

1

2 And he'll happily pass between your legs to track the point from one side to the other.

2

and treat if he goes through your legs to touch it. Now you've got the idea. Build up the number of steps and start to click and treat intermittently. Make it a game of catch the point of the brollie. Oh, there it is. Ooops! It's on the other side. Let him win every now and again or your dog will stop trying.

No more stooping When he has the idea, he will be weaving back and forth with gusto. As you pick up speed, fade the nose touch. He will start to respond to the mere downward dip of the umbrella. With luck, your shoulder movement will be enough of an

indication to tell him where he goes next. But if not, you have your umbrella to remind him of what to do with his target.

And think of all the other things you can do in a routine with a prop like an umbrella. Your next dance could have you dressed as Mary Poppins!

TIP
There are lots of thing in your house that you could use as target stick – umbrella, broom or cane. If you choose one of these as a prop, make sure it is relevant to your music.

Fading The Nose Touch
Progress from lowering the target stick right down to your dog with each step to keeping it level with your waist.

Your dog will have to keep his eye on it.

Raise your right arm as you step left.

1

2

3

1 Move your stick quite quickly to the other side. Don't wait for touch.

2 As well as your stick, he will have to watch the movement of your shoulder and arm.

3 If they drop, your dog will scoot through your legs to the other side.

Weaving Big Dogs

Weaving between your legs is quite easy for a small dog, but quite a challenge if you want to try it with a bigger breed. If you have a really substantial dog like a German Shepherd, and especially if you are not very big yourself, you need to consider whether this move is actually practical for you.

Weaving a large dog takes skill and it helps if you have long legs. The gap between them needs to be big enough for your dog to squeeze through from head to tail. He can easily dip his head to avoid hitting you in the crotch but he can't dip his shoulders. However, you can adjust the size of the gap in a number of ways.

Stride length Try it. Are you closer to the ground when you take giant steps or when you take itsy bitsy ones? Lengthening your stride is not necessarily the answer for weaving big dogs as it can make the gap long and narrow instead of short and wide. You will need to experiment.

Get a leg up If you can lift your leg high as you step forward, you will create more space underneath for your dog to manoeuvre through. However, it is hard to maintain forward movement if you are doing a series of leg weaves that involves touching your toe to your forehead with each step. And to be visually effective, your dog needs to be weaving directly underneath you. It is safer too. If he is too far in front, you could stumble over him.

And swing! Draw an imaginary line on the floor and weave along it. It is not a tightrope so don't be afraid to swing your legs out and plant them on either side of the line. Rather than chopping your legs like scissors, walk a little like John Wayne. The gap will be a little wider for a little longer if you take your dog through on the diagonal.

Practise the solo walk We've talked the talk! Now you have to practise the walk without the dog. There are fewer legs to get entangled and it's safer. If you think you've got what it takes, then add the dog to the equation.

Adjust your timing Don't forget that it will probably take longer for your dog to shoot through the gap because there is so much of him. Master the art of weaving before you try to increase speed. Go slowly so that you can make sure that you aren't taking your second step while he is still directly underneath you. Look down and if the coast is clear of his hind legs and bottom, it's safe to proceed!

If all else fails, you could always consider getting a smaller dog.

Stepping Up
Lift your leg high enough for your dog to fit underneath, but not so high that you topple over.

Weaving Backwards

Once you have mastered the weave forwards, you may become ambitious and want your dog to weave through your legs forwards as you walk backwards. This is a really spectacular move if you can manage it, but a real challenge.

It is so much easier to walk forwards. Placing one foot behind the other instead of in front? We just aren't built for it. Our eyes face forward and our knees are hinged. They only bend in one direction – and that's not backwards.

Walk the walk Try walking backwards. It will feel uncomfortable. Most people shorten their stride and walk more slowly when they are going in reverse and this reduces the gap between their legs. They can't see where they are going and are frightened of losing their balance. This makes it harder for your dog to squeeze through the gap than when you were walking forwards and he is likely to push you to try to make the space bigger.

Leg height Now try standing on one leg and lifting the other behind you while keeping it straight. Unless you are very supple, it won't go up very far. And bending the leg you are standing on won't help to get it up any higher. To get a higher leg swing behind you when you walk back, you will need to bend forward. That's the way we are built! Your waist is your fulcrum.

Cheat a bit If you want to avoid too much seesaw action when you walk backwards, cheat a little. Instead of lifting your leg straight back, keep it slightly bent and circle it to the side before you bring it down behind you – a bit like a frog. This should help you to momentarily create a bigger gap for your dog and he might stop trying to bulldoze through your legs.

A lot of people find it difficult to do anything in reverse gracefully. I am one of those! Doing anything

backwards takes a lot of time, patience and even more practice and, at the end of the day, it can still look extremely awkward. So, if you achieve your goal – good weaves while you walk backwards – and can do it with style and pizazz, it will certainly be a skill that you will want to show off and include in your dance routines.

One Leg Behind The Other

1 It's not easy to walk backwards and look elegant, but try! Check for obstacles in your path. Resist the urge to lean forward when you lift your leg behind you.

Pivot point for your legs and upper body.

1

2

2 Your dog will be able to see where he is going, but you won't. Don't worry – he'll find the gap if it's big enough!

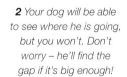

Teaching A Jump

Jumping over a cane is an eye-catching move that takes advantage of your dog's athletic abilities. But, if you have already taught your dog to use a target stick, you may run into problems teaching your dog the jump unless you make it easy for him to distinguish between the cane and the target stick. The two items look very similar, especially if you present the cane in a similar way, and you may end up with a dog who keeps trying to touch the cane with his nose instead of leaping over it.

Jumping stick Buy a jumping stick or alternatively make one oneself. A piece of dowel or plastic pipe about 1.2m (4ft) long

1

will do. Paint it something easily visible. You don't want it to blend into the background colour of your carpet or the lawn. Choose something robust that won't break or splinter. Leave the bamboo canes holding up the beans in the garden.

First steps Put the stick on the floor. With your dog on the lead on your left side, walk him over it. He'll have to step over the stick to continue walking forward with you. Do it again with your dog on your right. Repeat several times.

Jumping Over A Cane

1 Initially just walk your dog over the cane as it lies on the floor. 2 Then kneel and hold your cane a few inches in the air with its point on the ground. Your dog should be a few feet away in a Sit waiting for your next command.

3 Show your dog the treat. As he gets up to investigate, throw it so he hops over the cane as he moves towards it.

2

3

Add a hop Now place him in a Sit wait. Move a few paces away and kneel on the ground facing sideways to your dog. Hold the stick in the hand nearest to your dog and about 15cm (6in) off the ground. Place the tip on the floor so that he will have to hop rather than step over it. Have a treat in your other hand. Show him the treat and tempt him over the stick to get it. When he begins the hop, give your "Jump" command and throw the treat for him to chase. If you give him the treat from your hand, make sure that he has cleared the stick fully and that he doesn't have his front feet on one side and his back feet on the other. Practise a few times a day until he is moving comfortably towards and over the stick.

Now the jump Hold the stick parallel to the ground. Your dog should understand the "Jump" command. You can raise the stick a little higher, but not too high or too quickly. You don't want to encourage him to duck underneath it.

Front, side and back Try holding the stick out to the side or in front of you. Vary the position of the stick so that your dog has to look for it and gets accustomed to jumping in different places relative to you.

A cane, umbrella, or peacock feather When he understands the "Jump" command, he should jump over anything that is put in his path once he has been familiarised with it. But choose props carefully. You don't want him to tangle a foot and hurt himself.

Size matters Even with turbocharged boots, your dog will never be able to leap over tall buildings in a single bound. Jump height should be reasonable for the size of your dog. Don't set the bar too high. Jumping is also hard physical work. Your dog may be able to walk for miles but he needs to develop a different kind of fitness for jumping. Don't overdo it or he may injure himself.

Have fun jumping together!

4 Hold your cane a little higher and parallel to the ground. Make sure your dog has room to take off and land safely.

Jumping is hard work. Take plenty of breaks.

4

5

5 Progress from kneeling to standing. You may have to bend down if you have a little dog that can't jump very high.

Jumping Through Your Arms

Teaching your dog to jump through your arms adds another useful dimension to your routine. But many dogs who are confident jumping through a hoop or a tyre for agility work are reluctant to adapt this technique to leap through your arms.

This is because dogs have trouble thinking that parts of our body are pieces of agility equipment. They are more accustomed to experiencing us using our hands to dish out treats or pat them on the head! Your dog is comfortable jumping at or through inanimate objects, but you are a different matter. He thinks it is disrespectful to treat you as an object or prop. Moreover, if you keep waving your arms in front of him, he may well interpret this action as an invitation to join in the Mexican Hat Dance rather than perform a specific trick.

1

2

Through Your Arms

1 Familiarise your dog with the hoop. Rest it on the floor so that he can easily walk through.
2 And lure him through the hoop to the other side with a treat or toy.

Keep him moving forward so that he can land comfortably.

3 Raise the hoop off the ground a little so that your dog starts to jump, rather than walk, through it.

3

4 Wrap your arms around the hoop. You can rest your elbow on your knee to help keep it steady.

4

Hula hoop Dig your old hula hoop out of the garage. Sit your dog in front of you and hold the hoop by your side with its bottom resting on the floor. Train jumping through the hula hoop the same as you did the tyre in agility. Lure him through with a treat or toy and make sure that his whole body, front and back legs pass through to the other side. When he is walking through without hesitation start using a command. You can use the same command that you use in agility too – "Through", "Hoop" or "Tyre".

Add a wrap Kneel on the ground and wrap your arms around the hula hoop. One on the top at twelve o'clock and one on the bottom at six o'clock. Hold the hoop low to the ground and as far away from your body as you can. Allow your dog a bit of a run up and give your tyre command. Easy wasn't it? See if it was a fluke and try again. Resist the temptation to look through the hoop at him. If you put your head in the way, you could end up with a bloody nose!

Now a little more Wrap your arms around the hoop a little more. You'll have to move the hoop closer to your body but try to maintain a circle shape. Is your dog still jumping for joy through your arms? Yeah! Give him lots of praise and treats. Repeat a few more times and have a rest.

Almost there Put your hula hoop away and try your dog with just your arms. Make the circle large. You don't have to clasp your hands together but can leave a foot or two in between them. When he is sailing through with ease, you can tighten the circle and bring it closer to your torso.

Bravo Your dog knows what to do! Try it on your left as well as your right. You can increase height and move from kneeling to standing, but be reasonable. You will never get a Chihuahua to jump through your arms if you hold them five feet off the floor – this breed just doesn't have enough leg length or spring.

But it is a very flashy move for larger dogs that seem to fly off the floor and float through the human hoop.

5 Try without the hoop. Your hands should be in the same position and your dog should aim for the middle of the "O".

5

6 Progress to standing and holding your arms a little higher. But not too high!

6

Catching A Dog

If your dog is small enough, teach him to jump up into your arms for the perfect finale to a dance routine. Some little dogs take to this move quite naturally; others, frustratingly, can jump up and down quite happily but don't seem to get the idea of jumping into your arms. For these dogs, you need to teach the move in stages.

Size When you teach this trick, size matters. Only Superman would be able to hold a Newfoundland in his arms without crumbling. You should be able to easily manage a small dog's size and weight, but what about the wiggle?

Wiggling Hold a dog off the floor and more than likely he'll wiggle. Fear of being dropped or resentment at being suspending in the air are all reasons for struggling. To eradicate wiggles, get your dog accustomed to being lifted and held. Reward him with praise and a treat when he is relaxed and still. A split second will do at first and gradually increase the length of time that you hold him. It will stand you in good stead if you ever need to carry your dog on the escalator. When he is happy to be held in your arms, then you can teach him to jump into them.

Take a seat Put his treats on the kitchen table and pull up a chair. I like sitting by the kitchen table because my dogs are always curious to know what's

A titbit will help him stop wiggling.

Your lap is a perfect landing platform.

1

2

3

Jumping Into Your Arms

1 Squat down on haunches and tempt your dog onto your lap for cuddle. 2 He needs to enjoy being held and have confidence that you won't drop him.

3 He will have to jump a little higher if you are sitting in a chair.

on top and that alone is enough motivation for them to jump onto my lap. But you can sit by a window ledge or anywhere else handy to rest a treat pot. Invite your dog onto your lap with an "Up" command or pat your chest. Click and treat him when he arrives. Place him back on the floor and repeat.

Take off Which part of your body is going to be the springboard? Are you going to hold your knees together and bend them slightly so that he will spring straight up or are you going to extend a leg sideways so he climbs a diagonal? Experiment.

Take a cushion When your dog is happily jumping onto your lap, raise your game. Put a cushion on the chair so you are still balanced but he has to jump a little higher. Then another till you are almost standing.

Use a wall as support If you have the type of dog that is a canine missile and capable of jumping up with so much force that he knocks you over, stand against a wall with your knees slightly bent for support. Such good exercise for your thighs and bum too!

Free standing Move away from the chair or wall. When he jumps ... now you catch.

Word of warning The downside of this trick is that it is a great way of plastering muddy paw prints onto your clothing. Also don't wear shorts or you'll end up with track marks on your thighs from his nails. And lastly, be prepared for a few embarrassing moments if one of your dog's front legs disappears down the front of your open-necked T-shirt.

TIP
Help your dog jump up by bending one knee before you straighten up.

Support your dog's bottom with one hand when you catch him.

4

5   6

4 Sit on a pile of cushions to raise yourself a little higher off the ground.

5 Have at go at standing up. Your dog will spring off your thighs. 6 And push up into your arms to be caught. Wrap them around him.

Jumping On Your Back

It's always effective when you can pick up on an action that your dog carries out spontaneously and build that movement into part of your dance routine. Perhaps your dog likes to jump on your back when you're down on your hands and knees scrubbing the kitchen floor. Just imagine what a great trick this would be if you could teach him to twist or lie down while he is up there. Why stop there?

Can he sit up and beg? What about lying down on your back or putting his paw on your head? The dramatic and comic possibilities are endless.

Create a cue Your dog may be keen to mount onto your back but you have to teach him to do it on cue and not just because he needs a step up to see what's on the window sill. Use a verbal command like "Table" or "On top".

A friend can help Ask a friend to help you by luring

A friend can help by luring him up with a treat.

1

2

On Your Front
1 Lie on the floor so that your dog can easily get on your back by walking up your legs. 2 Prove to him that you won't break or wobble too much under his weight.

Hands and Knees
1 Progress to resting your elbows on the ground and your bottom on your knees. 2 And when your dog can cope with some extra height, try kneeling on all fours.

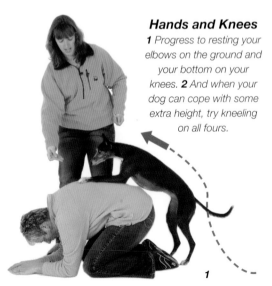

1

TIP
Your helper can not only direct your dog, but report on his performance. Make sure she knows what you are looking for.

2

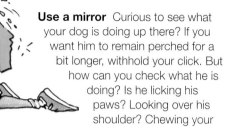

your dog up onto your back with a treat while you lie on the floor. You won't be too high off the ground and he can get accustomed to your lumps and bumps! Progress to your hands and knees. Think about the dog's approach. Do you want him to jump from behind you or from your side? Make sure that you present a firm and stable table top with your back. Nice and flat, not arched. Say your command as soon as he jumps. When he has landed, you click and your friend can give him a treat. Repeat a few times and have a break.

And you're off! Ready to start again? Get down on your hands and knees with clicker in one hand and treats in the other. Your friend is going to lure your dog up with a pretend treat. Give your command and when you feel his weight on your back, click and throw him a titbit across the floor. Has he quickly eaten it and jumped back on you for more? If so, he has worked out how to make you go click. If not, your friend can give him some more help until he has worked out what to do to get the treat.

Use a mirror Curious to see what your dog is doing up there? If you want him to remain perched for a bit longer, withhold your click. But how can you check what he is doing? Is he licking his paws? Looking over his shoulder? Chewing your collar? Take a mirror off the wall, rest it on the floor and practise opposite it. All will be revealed.

Additions Now that you have taught your dog to jump on your back, what next? Anything that he knows how to do on the floor and that doesn't take up much space, can be done on your back. He must have a thorough understanding of any move you transfer. Can he twist, sit up and beg or tap your head with a paw. If you crawl forward will he stay on your back in a Down? Will he tunnel under your tummy? Work through his repertoire and see what you like best.

TIP

If you always treat your dog from the same side, he will develop a preference. Reward from both the right and left to maintain a balance.

Here I am. Treat me!

Home Alone

1 No helpers? You'll have to click and deliver rewards yourself.
2 Go by feel or put a mirror against the wall opposite to see what's happening.

Giving A Piggyback Ride

If your dog is agile and lightweight, he can learn to jump on to your shoulders for a piggyback ride, a move which can form a striking and appealing part of your dance routine. However, you don't want to take the risk of dropping your dog from a height, which could injure him and will certainly damage his confidence.

It is best to teach this trick in stages making sure that your dog can execute each element easily and safely before progressing to the next.

On your knees Put your dog is a Sit-stay and walk a foot or two away and turn your back on him. Kneel down and sit on your heels. Hold a treat in your hand over your shoulder and lean forward so that he has an incline to climb. Release him and tell him to get the treat. He should be able to reach the cheese or biscuit by stretching over your back with his hind feet still on the ground. Click and treat.

And now higher If that was easy, hold the treat above your head. This time, if your dog wants the treat, he will have to jump onto your back and leave the floor. Be prepared to bring your free arm across your back so that you can cradle his hind legs for support. He should be resting his front legs on your shoulder. This is the piggyback position so click and treat. Your dog should feel safe and secure. Don't click if one paw is scrambling for purchase and the other is down your trousers.

Piggyback Rides

Begin training close to the ground. Height and movement comes later.
1 Kneel on the floor with your dog in a Sit behind you.

3 Bold dogs will jump on with all four paws but tentative pooches may land only two and need extra encouragement to get their back feet off the floor.

4 When your dog is comfortably perched on your shoulder, he has arrived.

2 Lean forward and release your dog to a treat held over your shoulder.

3

4

And higher still As your dog gains confidence, you can start to slowly straighten up to a stand. Continue to kneel on one leg but lift your bottom off your heels and bend one leg forward for stability. Gradually, work yourself into a stand. The dog knows the signal. When you lift your hand above your head and bend forward, he is in no doubt that you want him to jump onto your back.

Piggyback Your dog does not have suction pads on his feet, so get a good grip on him. Some dogs balance easily on your arm and shoulder. They drape themselves around your neck to look like the fur trim collar on a jacket! Once he is comfortable and settled, try to walk a few paces carrying him. As you gain in confidence, add a few more paces and then a few more. Increase the number of steps slowly but

don't overdo it. You don't want to get a bad back and, worse, if he is up there too long he could get bored and start to fidget.

A rousing finale This is a great move to finish a routine. You can give the judges and audience a wave as you carry your dog out of the ring on your back. And it avoids the problem of how to get him back on the ground. It's not easy to make a dismount that looks like the dog has floated back to earth rather than being dumped unceremoniously on the floor.

Have fun with this trick!

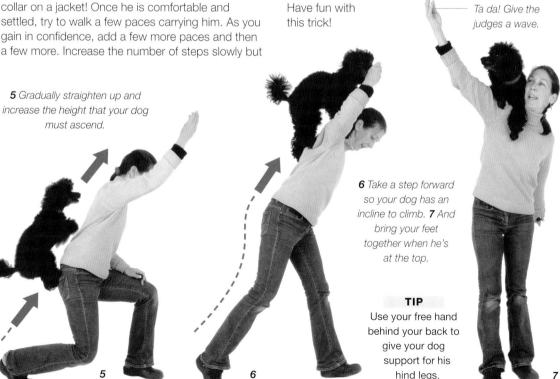

5 Gradually straighten up and increase the height that your dog must ascend.

Ta da! Give the judges a wave.

6 Take a step forward so your dog has an incline to climb. 7 And bring your feet together when he's at the top.

TIP
Use your free hand behind your back to give your dog support for his hind legs.

5

6

7

Paws In Front Of Eyes

Teach your dog to cover his eyes with a paw – it is a trick with enormous appeal that will fit into a variety of dance routines. With this simple gesture your dog can convey a range of emotions – bashfulness, embarrassment, cheekiness, despair or simply tiredness. This is one trick that may be difficult to build up in stages. If you click and treat when he lifts his foot off the ground, he may get stuck on this first step and stop at waving.

Shaping a trick like this can take a long while. Getting a dog to lift his paw isn't too difficult, but getting him to place it on his nose could take ages. You might find it happens more quickly if you encourage him to do so voluntarily. Then you can quickly click and treat right away.

Put something on his face If there's something on your dog's face, he will naturally use his paw to rub it off. Start with him in the Sit and put a bit of sellotape on his eyebrow or the end of his nose. Or loop your lead over his snout. Or place a scrunchie hairband loosely around his muzzle. These things are mildly irritating and he will want to be rid of them. As soon as he wipes his face to push them off, mark the action with your clicker and give him a big reward.

Try a tickle Some dogs will preen with their paw if something messes up their fur. Try blowing gently on your dog's cheek. Or misting him gently with some water from a plant spray. Anything that will give him a tickle and make him rub his face. As soon as he lifts a paw, click and treat.

The stoics Some dogs are real stoics. They can balance a lead on the end of their nose for hours looking sorry for themselves. They put up with any amount of misting or blowing without a wiggle or twitch. They delude themselves that you are teaching them an endurance trick. But play around and experiment, there will be something that will make them move. And praise, praise, praise any indication that they are thinking about shifting the loop of lead off their nose.

Choice of command The command you choose gives the game away. I like the command "Peek-a-boo" because it immediately makes my dog look playful and naughty. "Wash your face" is another one I like. "Hide", "Cover" or "Shy" are also popular cues for this trick.

Going for gold When your dog has got the trick off pat, see if he can do it in other positions besides the Sit. The trick will get a whole new set of connotations. If he can cover his eyes while lying down, it will look like he wants to go to sleep and will someone please turn off the lights? And how about the Stand? Will he hold his paw over his eyes and keep it there till you release him? What about using his other paw? Or both when he's lying down?

Whatever way you choose to use this trick, I am sure that your dog will look extremely cute when he performs it.

Left This is such a cute pose and can convey cheekiness, embarrassment or an itchy nose! Choose a command that fits the emotion.

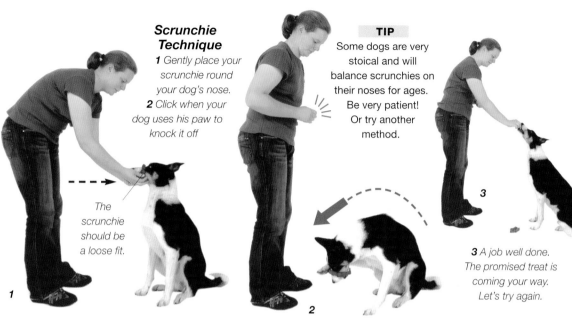

Scrunchie Technique

1 Gently place your scrunchie round your dog's nose.
2 Click when your dog uses his paw to knock it off

The scrunchie should be a loose fit.

TIP
Some dogs are very stoical and will balance scrunchies on their noses for ages. Be very patient! Or try another method.

3 A job well done. The promised treat is coming your way. Let's try again.

1

2

3

Lead Technique

1 With your dog in a Sit, loop the end of a light lead gently over the tip of his nose.

2 That shouldn't be there! Your dog will use his paw to remove the lead from his nose.

Now I know what to do for another treat.

3 Click when your dog's paw touches his cheek or nose and then he can have a treat.

Teaching A Bow

Dogs naturally perform a graceful play-bow when they want to invite another dog to play. If you teach your dog to do this on command, you will have a beautiful and useful addition to your repertoire of dance moves. The commonest problem when teaching this move is that the dog automatically sinks into the Down position rather than lowering his front end only and leaving his back end up in the air.

Confusing cues If you have tried to lure your dog into a bow with a treat, he could be getting confused. Look at it from his perspective. When he was a puppy, you held a treat between your fingers, attached it to his nose and lowered it to the floor between his front paws. And you didn't release the treat until all of his body, including his bottom, was grounded – a Down. If you are using this method to teach him the bow, the hand signal you are using is identical – how is he to know that you want something rather different? And although you may be clicking in the right place (when he is in the bow position), are you giving him the treat after he has collapsed into the Down? If so, he is never going to wiggle his bottom in the air at you!

Finger on the tummy If you kneel by your dog's side, and lure him into the Down you can physically maintain the bow position by gently placing your hand or a few fingers under his tummy so that he is encouraged to keep his bottom in the air. Not always easy with a big dog.

You will be able to feel him shift his weight to keep his balance. Click when he is in position and make him reach forward into the Stand for his treat.

Target stick Take your hands out of the equation and teach the bow with a target stick. Warm your dog up with a few nose touches on the stick and then set to work. With him standing in front of you, swing the target stick from behind you, past your ankles and place it on the ground between his paws. He'll bend and his front end will go down as he nose-touches the stick. Quickly click and return the stick to a resting position. Again, he should return to the Stand for his treat.

1

Luring Into A Bow

1 Kneel by your dog in the Stand and lower a treat to the ground. 2 His nose will follow it between his front paws, lowering his chest to the floor.

Support his tummy gently, give a little tickle.

1

Where the nose goes, the rest of the body follows. 2

Target Stick Bow

1 Practise a few nose touches with your target stick.
2 Swing it from behind and place its end on the ground between your dog's paws.

2

3 When your dog folds down into a bow and touches the end of the target stick with his nose, click.

3

Cheese, chicken or sausage will taste yum!

4 When your dog pops up for his reward, he will be in position to repeat the exercise.

Press-ups

Whichever method you choose, bring your dog back into the Stand for his treat after you click. He will be less likely to fold downwards if his frankfurter slice is offered in the upright position. It will also balance his muscles – he'll look like he is doing press-ups.

4

TIP

Some dogs collapse through the bow into a Down when following a treat or target stick. Prevent this happening by bringing your dog back into the Stand for his reward.

The Finished Product

Try a bow with your dog facing you or standing at your side.

Bowing to your partner is a nice start to a routine.

TIP

Does your dog respond to a verbal command for this trick? Choose "Curtsy" for a girl or "Bow" for a boy.

Mastering The Crawl

If you want your dog to crawl forward on his tummy, the first step is to teach a reliable "Down". Does your dog respond to the command the first time? Will he lie down anywhere and any time you tell him? If the answer is "Yes", you are ready to make a start. Don't make the mistake of trying to teach the crawl by force – urging him forward by his collar won't work. If you pull him by his collar, he will pull in the opposite direction. You need to give him a good reason to crawl and stay on his tummy. Try the techniques that I outline below and you should have success.

Follow the titbit Tell your dog to lie down and hold a treat in front of him on the ground. You can crouch beside him or, if you have long legs, bend over him. Does he move forward an inch or two without standing up? Fantastic. Try again and as he moves forward click and release the treat while he is in the Down. If he stands up, keep holding the treat on the ground. He will remember his puppy training and lie down so try again. Now he can have his titbit. Don't attempt a 50-metre crawl on your first attempt! Build up distance slowly. If you choose to follow this method, start adding your "Crawl" command as soon as your dog is reliably following the treat across the floor. The disadvantage of this method is that you build in a dependence on a hand signal. Unless you, too, are going to crawl along the floor, you will have to gradually unfurl yourself into a stand with your arm at your side. If your dog gets confused, you can always bend and point to the floor with a finger.

Follow the target stick This method allows you to remain standing upright. In addition to a good "Down", you must have a good nose-touch on the target stick. The progression is the same but instead of holding a treat on the floor in front of the dog, rest the end of your target stick an inch or so from his nose. If he creeps forward, click and give him a treat. Add a verbal command and when your dog is looking good and performing reliably, fade your target stick.

Commands When your dog understands what he has to do to make you click, add a command like "Crawl", "Creep" or "Slither".

Up and down If he is popping up and down, you can use your free hand as a guide by placing it gently on his withers. Or you can ask him to crawl under a chair which naturally prevents his body from lifting.

Going the distance Slithering along the floor for great distances is not something a dog would do naturally. He can get to places much faster on all four feet. Practise in short bursts. He will need to develop different muscles to propel himself forward on his tummy, so don't overdo it at the start.

Luring To Creep

1 Kneel by your dog. Put him in a Down and get him interested in a titbit.

2 Slowly move it away and click if he stretches forward to follow.

Fading The Lure

1 You will have to fade your lure, if you want to stand up straight. Try to do this gradually.

2 Don't have your hand so low to the ground. Take one or two steps backwards. Praise your dog for staying flat and creeping forward.

Target Stick Crawl

1 Dogs that can nose-touch a target stick or cane in the Stand are good candidates for this technique.

Try some touches while he is in the Down.

TIP

If you move the stick too quickly, your dog will pop up. Go slowly and rest your free hand gently on his bottom if he needs some subtle persuasion.

2 Can he follow the end of the cane as you drag it across the floor?

Under A Chair

1 Use a chair as a barrier to keep your dog low to the ground.

2 If he wants the treat, he'll have to stay flat.

Teaching A Roll Over

The roll over is a great trick and a real crowd pleaser especially if your dog performs it with energy and enthusiasm. Some dogs catch on quickly, but others take a little bit longer. In order to succeed with this trick you must first learn to be patient.

Starting To Roll

1 Kneel on the floor opposite your downed dog. Show him his treat. 2 Move the treat behind his head to lure him onto his side.

Prerequisites for success Before you start, you must have a good "Down". Make sure your dog responds to your first command to lie down, not your second or third. Can he lie down while you are sitting in a chair, standing up or at a distance? The Down is your starting position so practise it in different locations – for example, your kitchen, the garden or local park.

Going belly up Many dogs feel exposed and vulnerable when they are belly up. If your dog is hesitant to show you his tummy, give him an intermediary reward at this stage. A few extra clicks and treats or a gentle tummy tickle could be all that is needed to make him more confident. Work on this before asking him to roll over completely.

Teaching the roll over

1 Start with your dog in the Down and kneel in front of him with a treat in your hand. Allow him to sniff the treat but don't let him eat it.
2 Move the treat to the side and round the back of his head. As he turns to follow the treat, his shoulder will drop and he will lie on his side. Continue moving the treat in a circle around his head so that he is lying on his back. This is a hard position for your dog to maintain balance. As you continue moving the treat, he won't want to lose sight of it. To keep it in view, he will flip over onto his other side and come back to rest on his tummy in the Down.

3 As soon as your dog starts to flip, say "Roll over", click and immediately give him his treat while he is still in the Down position. Tell him he's clever!
4 He will learn to associate the verbal command, "Roll over", with flipping. The circling movement that you have made with your hand can be gradually minimised and turned into your hand signal.

Pop up problems If he keeps popping up just as your bring the treat behind his head, put your free hand gently on his shoulder. As he follows the titbit, use this hand to guide him. Don't exert force and resist the temptation to roll him manually. You can help but your dog has to learn to perform the trick on his own.

Select appropriate surfaces Don't ask a dog to roll on a surface that might hurt his back or be uncomfortable. Practise on soft surfaces like the lawn or carpet, not concrete or wooden floors. And remember to avoid puddles!

Don't stop! Once you have taught one roll over, why stop there. How about multiple roll overs? Do one roll over and praise and treat. Ask him for a second one. You'll need to reward after each roll over but while he is eager to keep going, give your dog a supersize reward after two or three. Don't do too many or he'll get dizzy! And try a roll back. Use the same training steps, but circle your hand in the other direction.

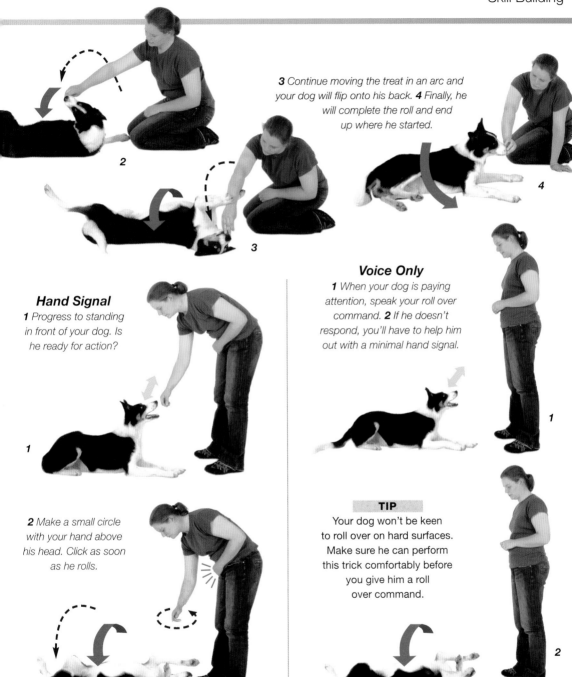

3 Continue moving the treat in an arc and your dog will flip onto his back. 4 Finally, he will complete the roll and end up where he started.

Hand Signal
1 Progress to standing in front of your dog. Is he ready for action?

2 Make a small circle with your hand above his head. Click as soon as he rolls.

Voice Only
1 When your dog is paying attention, speak your roll over command. 2 If he doesn't respond, you'll have to help him out with a minimal hand signal.

TIP
Your dog won't be keen to roll over on hard surfaces. Make sure he can perform this trick comfortably before you give him a roll over command.

Pretending To Sleep

A dog posing with his chin resting on his paws as if he is sleepy forms an extremely cute picture. How do you teach this one? You might think you can start with your dog in the Down and then let him follow a treat to the ground with his nose, but the likelihood is that, as soon as he eats it, his head will pop back up. This approach also leaves you stuck down on your hands and knees to hold his treat on the floor. Using a target or target stick is much simpler!

Target stick When your dog is in the Down, collapse the target stick and place it front of him on the ground between his paws. If he nose-touches it, click and treat him with his head back in an upright position but the rest of his body still in the Down. Be sure that the stick isn't too far away from his nose. You don't want him to start crawling forward on his belly or to stand up to reach it. Remember it is the head that should move, not the rest of him. Do lots of repetitions. If he finds the exercise easy, you can add a command like "Head", "Sleepies" or "Pillow". Will he go "Sleepies" without the prompt of the target stick? Great! If not, try again with the stick or wait a bit longer for him to think it through.

Other targets If you don't have a target stick, what about the lid from a tube of snack biscuits, a piece of carpet or a mouse pad? Teach your dog to nose-touch the target with a clicker and slowly lower it to the ground. Continue to click and treat when he gives it a nose-touch. Practise in different places – the kitchen, garden or park. If your dog understands what is required, ask him to lie down and put the tube lid between his front paws. Impossible to touch with the tip of his nose in this position. Easier to touch with the chin. Click and treat. Keep practising. Will he go "Sleepies" without the lid? Why not try and see.

Sweet dreams By slowly withholding his click and reward, you can extend the time that your dog will keep his chin or nose on his target. It is worth thinking about a release word that will let him know that the exercise is over or using a command to mean the opposite action. You might choose "Sleepies" for head on paws and "Wakey, wakey" for head off paws.

Somewhere to hang your head Dogs will rest their heads on many things besides their paws. Your dog could go "Sleepies" on a cane, your outstretched arm or leg or on a skateboard. Can you get him to place his paws on a stool by the foot of the bed and lower his head onto them? You'd swear he was saying his prayers. There are so many ways to look cute!

Make sure you've got his attention.

Sleep With A Target Stick

1 With your dog in the Down, move the end of the target stick to the floor.
2 Your dog's nose will follow it.

1

2

Sleep With A Pot Lid

1 When your dog is lying down, place a pot lid between his paws. 2 Command him to touch it with his nose and he should lower his head to the floor.

A treat on the lid is an incentive.

1

Withhold the click for a second to increase duration.

TIP

When teaching "Go sleepies", you can use anything that will fit comfortably under your dog's chin as a target. A pot lid, mouse pad or small square of carpet – even a little pillow.

2

3 He will soon find it easier to rest his chin rather than his nose. Be ready to click and treat.

3

Sleep On A Chair

1 This chair has a "treat window". Ask your dog rest his paws on the seat. 2 And he will lower his head to see the treat come through the window.

What a nice place for a rest!

1

2

Teaching A Puppy To Stay

It's never too early to lay a basic foundation for later exercises. Young puppies aren't ready for demanding routines, but you can start teaching your puppy a few basic commands right from the start. One of the most useful things you can do is make an early start on the Sit-stay.

Puppies are such wiggly worms, it's hard for them to stay still even for a minute. There's a big, wide world out there to explore! So don't expect too much too soon. But you can teach your puppy from an early age to relax in the Sit and wait for his release word.

Puppy stays Kneel on the ground and lure your pup into a Sit beside you with your left hand. Give him his treat. Place his lead under your knees and take your right hand across the front of your body and rest it on his collar. With your left hand, gently stroke his bottom. Your hands are there to guide him back into the Sit in case he tries to stand up or move away. Wait for the tension to escape from his little body. When he is still, calm and relaxed, praise him and say "Sit-stay". A few seconds will do. Give him a treat and say his release word. "OK", "Off you go" or "Finish". This release word signals that the exercise is over and the puppy can move around again.

Praise calmly Don't hold your breath during this exercise or your puppy will wonder why you've gone puce. Praise in a calm tone of voice while he is chilled and keeping his bottom on the floor. This is the action and psychological state that you want to reinforce in your puppy. Don't praise if he twitches! And resist the urge to give three loud cheers after you release him from the exercise. You don't want your puppy winding himself up, waiting to spring into the air as soon as you say "OK".

Sit Beside Your Pup

1 Kneel on the ground and lure your pup into a Sit by your side.
2 Place one hand on his collar; the other on his bottom. Stroke him gently till he relaxes; then say "Sit-stay".

This hand is on bottom duty. Don't stand!

Kneeling on the lead frees both your hands.

1

2

You talking to me? Avoid saying his name during this exercise. Otherwise he will look at you and try to get up to find out what you want, especially if you have been playing name games with him.

Boost your chances of success You will have a greater chance of success if you introduce the Sit-stay exercise after your puppy has had a romp around the garden and enjoyed a good meal. Sitting still is very hard for puppies. It is best to try it when his appetite is sated and he is tired.

Longer and longer It's hard for a puppy to achieve a state of Nirvana when every earthly thing around him is so new and stimulating. Sit-stays are very boring! Don't do too many and hold them only for a few seconds at a time. Increase the duration slowly.

Your aim is to teach your puppy a calm and relaxed mental state while he is in the Sit. If he can achieve this as a puppy, he will be able to relax during his Sit-stays as an adult and will be more likely to remain where you place him.

TIP
Don't say your dog's name after you have given the Stay command. Your dog might think that you want him to get up and come towards you.

Ensure that the lead remains quite slack.

Standing Beside Your Pup
1 Try standing with your pup on the lead and sitting quietly by your side.

2 If he is calm, tell him to stay and take a small step to one side. If remains in the Sit, praise him.

3 Return to his side. Praise again. Click and treat while he is still sitting before releasing.

Teaching An Adult Dog To Stay

A reliable Sit-stay is vital to a canine performer and her dance partner. It's no good you doing a wonderful twirl around your dog if he keeps getting up to join you as you make your moves. You need to teach a solid Sit-stay in the first place.

Staying put The Sit-stay is a basic obedience exercise with practical implications for everyday life. For example, you can park your dog by the picnic table while you go and buy an ice cream. And it is an exercise you can include in your freestyle routine once it has been mastered and proofed.

Sit means Sit
I like my dog to understand that "Sit" means "Sit" until the next command, whether that be a release word or a cue for a specific action like "Fetch". Once in the Sit, he must keep sitting! To teach a good Sit-stay get out your clicker and treats.

1 Place your dog in the Sit by your side. Praise him for being a good boy, click and treat before he moves. If he moves after the click, put him back in the Sit and treat him there.
2 Command him to "Sit" and take a step to the side. Tell him he's a "Good boy", click, and return to him and give him a treat. If he gets up, put him back in the Sit, take a step away and back again and then give him the treat. The treat is coming, but he has to remain in the Sit and wait for it to be delivered to him. Getting up will only delay its arrival.
3 As your dog's competence grows, take two steps, then three, then four. Always tell him he is clever for sitting before you click and go back to him to give him the treat. Gradually build distance between yourself and your dog.

1

4 This time, praise, click and praise again before you go back to treat him. If he is still sitting for his second helping of praise, he really is a good boy!
5 Start varying your position relative to the dog. Stand off to the right and left as well as facing and behind him. This last is the hardest because the dog will almost certainly turn his head to watch you and might shuffle on his bottom.

Dealing with distractions When you think your dog has a really good Sit, add some distractions and find out how good it is. Will he still stay in the Sit if you pat your head, bend to tie your laces or put your hand in your pocket? If you jump up and down on the spot, does he leave the Sit to jump with you?

Testing time With your dog on the lead, tell him to "Sit". Very gently pull on the lead. Is he still sitting – what a good boy! Click when the lead is taut, and treat. You are clicking your dog for resisting the tension on the lead and trying to remain in the Sit.

Once you have taught your dog a solid Sit-stay, he should be able to resist the temptation to twirl with you around the dance floor.

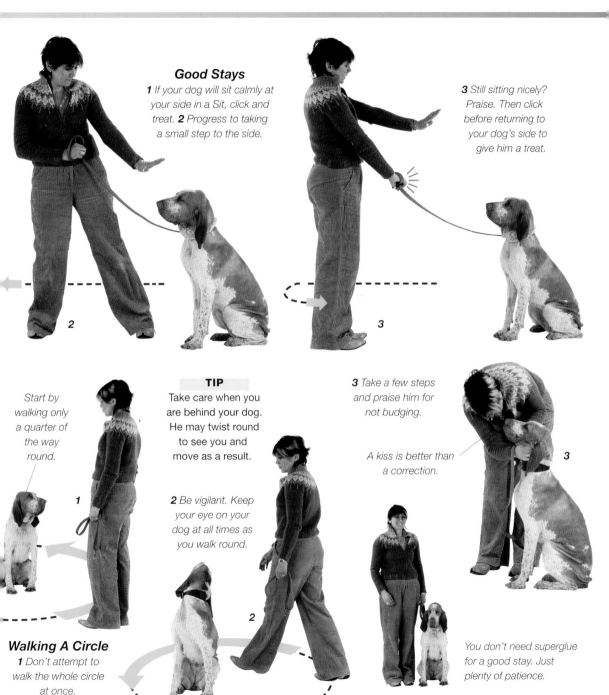

Good Stays

1 If your dog will sit calmly at your side in a Sit, click and treat. 2 Progress to taking a small step to the side.

3 Still sitting nicely? Praise. Then click before returning to your dog's side to give him a treat.

2

3

Start by walking only a quarter of the way round.

1

TIP
Take care when you are behind your dog. He may twist round to see you and move as a result.

2 Be vigilant. Keep your eye on your dog at all times as you walk round.

2

3 Take a few steps and praise him for not budging.

A kiss is better than a correction.

3

Walking A Circle
1 Don't attempt to walk the whole circle at once.

You don't need superglue for a good stay. Just plenty of patience.

Teaching The Wave

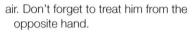

A lot of dogs learn to "shake hands" or "give a paw". It isn't just a cute trick, but a useful exercise to teach your dog so that he can greet new people with a handshake instead of jumping up on them. But why not build on this basis to teach your dog to wave? Not only will he be able to wave goodbye to friends, but he will have acquired another useful move for his dance routine. A dog who knows how to shake hands is halfway there already, so it's a shame not to take him this one step further.

Extension The "wave" is an extension of the "shake paws" trick. You will be building one trick upon another. For a shake you offer your open palm to your dog and he puts his paw into it. It is a strong invitation. There is no doubt in his mind what you want him to do. For a wave, he will have to raise a paw in the air, just like he does for a "shake", but there will be nowhere to put it.

Making a start
1 Tell your dog to Sit and Stay. Click and treat him for staying. He is such a good boy! And you don't want him to move towards you when you train a wave.
2 Review what he already knows. Ask him to "Shake" a few times and reward him for being so clever.
3 Offer him your outstretched palm as if you are going to ask him to shake again. As he lifts his paw, click and quickly withdraw your hand. You are clicking for his paw batting the

air. Don't forget to treat him from the opposite hand.
4 With a few repetitions, your dog will start to wave his paw more and more with less and less prompting from you.
5 Gradually change your hand signal from an outstretched palm to a wave and start using your new command "Wave" or "Bye, bye". You have differentiated the two tricks.
6 Can he wave with his other foot? Start the progression again on the other side.

Don't allow creeping If your dog can't resist the urge to move forward when he sees your outstretched hand, sit him on a step or low table. If he creeps towards you, he'll fall off his perch. So much easier to stay put.

Beyond cute Your dog will look extremely cute waving "goodbye" to your in-laws, but is this the only time you expect to perform this trick? If you are going to incorporate a "wave" into your dog dancing routines, you will need to keep practising. Teach your dog to wave when he is facing you and also on your left and right side. And can he wave while he is standing? Stand by his side and give him your verbal cue so that he lifts his left paw as you raise your left foot. Do it in time to the music and you will look like you are marching side by side!

Left Big dogs with long, slender legs, like Groenendaels, can show off their paw work more easily than little dogs with short legs.

1 Start with your dog in the Sit facing you. Tell him to "Stay".

2 Refresh his memory. Do a few "Give a paw" tricks into your hand.

Waving A Paw

A dog that waves a paw could be saying "Hello" or "Goodbye". It is a lovely way to make new friends.

3 Hold your hand higher and palm out towards your dog.

4 Your dog will lift his paw to try and reach it. Move your hand away. His miss is a wave so click and praise him.

We're marching together in time on the spot.

Right If your dog works from a verbal cue, make it look like your dog raises a paw as you lift your foot.

TIP

Teach your dog to wave both his right and left paws. If he can wave from different positions, you can really jazz up this trick.

Below This little dog can balance on his skateboard while waving at his friends.

Standing On Two Legs

A dog that can walk on his hind legs is defying gravity and this move can look very dramatic in a dance routine. If done well, it is extremely graceful with the dog copying his handler's footfalls with each beat of the music. Teaching this move requires some skill as dogs generally have a natural preference for being on all four paws, rather than on two.

If you have taught your dog to sit up and beg for a treat, you're nearly there.

1

Physical conformation First of all you must decide – is your dog a candidate? Not all breeds and sizes of dog are suited to standing on their back legs. Dachshunds have long backs and standing on their hind legs can put too much strain on their spines. Newfoundlands are too big and heavy to get off the ground. However, miniature and small breeds are naturals and spend half their life standing on two legs just to see what is above their heads on the kitchen table.

The first prerequisite Teach your dog to sit up and beg. This exercise builds muscle power in the dog's back so that he can hold himself upright and balance. Tell him to sit and hold a treat above his nose. When he lifts his paws a few inches off the ground, click and treat. Do it again and this time encourage him to lift his legs a little bit higher by offering him your arm as a paw rest. Click and treat. You don't need to physically hold him up in the air but you need to encourage him to rise.

A little higher Hold a treat above his nose so that he has to stretch up higher and stand on his back legs to reach it. Again, you can offer him your other arm as a paw rest. Click and let him have his titbit while he is still in the upright position, not when his front feet are back on the floor. As your dog becomes more accomplished at achieving and holding the up-right position, he will no longer need your arm. Decide on a command like "High" or "Up" and say it as you

raise the treat in the air. The lifting of your arm will become your hand signal. A second or two is enough.

Back and forth Your dog can learn to walk forward and backwards in the high position. Watch his feet. Most dogs will take a step backwards while trying to hold their position. Click and treat. Slowly build up to two steps, and then three or four. Remember that he will not be able to see where he is going and will be relying on you not to walk him into a wall! Add the "Back" command for moving backwards. Teaching a dog to walk forward is the same but in reverse. Click and treat for one step towards you and slowly increase the number or steps.

Three parts There are essentially three parts to this trick. Your dog has to learn to lift his front paws off the ground, to stretch up on his hind legs, and to take steps forwards or backwards. Don't rush through them. Walking on hind legs is physically demanding and can take a long time to train. Think how your muscles would ache if you had to crawl everywhere on your hands and knees. Be patient and keep training sessions short. The result will be worth the wait.

Standing Up

1 Hold a treat above your dog's nose. To reach it, he'll stretch up. Let him rest his paws on your arm.

2 Lure him higher so he has to stand out of his Sit. He can use your arm for support. 3 Reward him with the titbit while he is up.

4 Soon he won't need an arm rest to support him. When he sees you lift your hands, he'll lift his front feet off the floor.

TIP

A dog that can dance on his hind legs has the wow factor, but build fitness first and keep training sessions short.

In Front

You could be standing together in the wind on the prow of the Titanic.

Behind

Moving together like a choo-choo train. Is that Casey Jones coming on down the track?

In A Spin

Pirouetting on the spot adds extra difficulty. It's a very flashy move for dogs that love spinning.

And Facing

The nearest you will get with a big dog to dancing in a ballroom hold!

Going Round In Circles

Teach your dog to run a circle round you as you dance to add speed and drama to your routine. Some breeds find this easier to do than others. Collies and other herding types are naturals and circle so quickly they have difficulty stopping. Other breeds may not catch on as quickly, and often lack the speed that makes this move so impressive.

However, even if you have a slower dog, you can speed up his performance by luring him round with a treat in both hands.

Two feeding stations
Start with your dog on your left side and arm yourself with titbits. Make sure the value of the titbits in your left hand match those in your right. Show him the treat in your right hand and lure him across the front of you body. When his nose is by your right thigh, feed him from your right hand. While he is chewing, reach behind your back with your left hand and draw him to your left side. When his nose is by your left thigh, give him his treat. He has completed a full circle, but you have broken it into two halves with a feeding station on each side of your body. If your dog likes his grub he will be eager to hurry from one to the other. Try it a few more times. You'll find that every time you practise, your dog will need to be lured less.

Favourite toy If your dog has a much loved toy, you can use that to encourage a good circling movement. Hold the toy in one hand and pass it to the other in

1   **2**

Doing The Rounds In Halves
1 Stand with your dog at your side. 2 Start the circle by luring him across your front with a treat.

front of you. Then pass it to the other hand behind you. You will still have two reward stations on either side of you, so remember to allow the dog a game of tug at each one. The faster you pass the toy, the faster he will chase it around you. Wind him around you with the toy and then throw it for a retrieve.

Vary the rewards Whether you use treats or a toy, you will want to start varying when and where your dog gets his reward. Sometimes on the left and sometimes on the right. Sometimes after half a circle and sometimes after two circles. Keep him guessing and he'll keep circling.

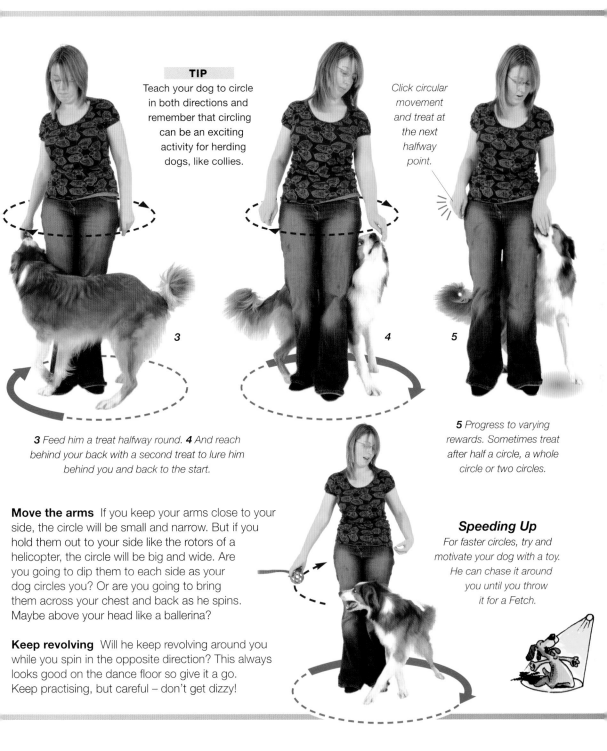

TIP
Teach your dog to circle in both directions and remember that circling can be an exciting activity for herding dogs, like collies.

Click circular movement and treat at the next halfway point.

3

4

5

3 Feed him a treat halfway round. 4 And reach behind your back with a second treat to lure him behind you and back to the start.

5 Progress to varying rewards. Sometimes treat after half a circle, a whole circle or two circles.

Move the arms If you keep your arms close to your side, the circle will be small and narrow. But if you hold them out to your side like the rotors of a helicopter, the circle will be big and wide. Are you going to dip them to each side as your dog circles you? Or are you going to bring them across your chest and back as he spins. Maybe above your head like a ballerina?

Keep revolving Will he keep revolving around you while you spin in the opposite direction? This always looks good on the dance floor so give it a go. Keep practising, but careful – don't get dizzy!

Speeding Up
For faster circles, try and motivate your dog with a toy. He can chase it around you until you throw it for a Fetch.

Learning To Rewind

If having your dog circle you looks impressive, what about having your dog circle you backwards? It sounds really difficult, but if your dog already knows the heel position and how to walk backwards, you have the prerequisites you need. With a little patience you can have your dog winding himself round your ankles in reverse just as confidently as going forwards.

Stand in the corner Stand in a corner of the room with your back to the walls and your dog in the heel position. Make sure the channel behind you is wide enough to accommodate him, but not too wide. Having it the same as his shoulder width is a good guide.

Reversing In A Corner
1 Stand with your back in a corner, your dog on your left.
2 Reverse your dog behind you through the channel. When he reaches the other side, treat.

First go halfway Give your dog your walk back command and have a treat ready in your right hand. He will reverse around you. The walls act as a barrier and will guide him in a curve around you. Watch his bottom pass your right leg. He will keep reversing and bring his little nose level with the treat in your right hand. Let him eat it! Do a few more repetitions and soon his movements will be smooth and flowing. Choose a new command to use like "Reverse" or "Rewind". With a little more practice, he won't need the wall as a barrier to guide him and you can perform the move free-standing.

Second half When he can reverse behind you without any aids, you are ready for the second half of this trick. Stand in the corner of the room and this time face the walls. Put your dog on your left side and give him his "Rewind" command. When he gets halfway around and reappears on your right side,

tell him to walk back. The wall will guide him back into the heel position as he continues to reverse. When he gets there, treat him from your left hand. As soon as he starts moving backwards without your prompt, you can drop your walk back command. He will know he has to keep on going to till he reaches your side.

Altogether now! If you have both halves off pat, put them together. Your dog will rewind around you in a full circle that you can always break down again if needed.

Other training methods There are a variety of training methods to choose from if this one doesn't work for you. If you have an empty closet or broom

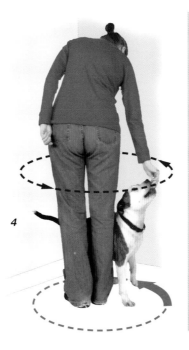

Hold it still and give your dog room.

Round A Brollie

If your dog can rewind successfully around you, try it with a prop like an umbrella.

Without Walls

Now you can come out of the corner. See if your dog will rewind round you without their guidance.

3 When your dog has mastered going behind, turn and face the wall. 4 The channel will be across your front and your dog will complete the circle.

cupboard, get inside with your dog and shut the door. Instead of two walls, you'll have four. You can try the whole trick all at once, although it would still be a good idea to treat your dog when he is on each side of you. Or you can stand in the middle of a puppy pen. The sides of the pen act as barriers and you can usually adjust the circle to the size you require. Just make sure there is enough room for your dog to move backwards, but not so much that he can turn around and go back where he started. That's cheating!

1 All the way round? Try two circles!

2 And treat at different points round the circle.

PART TWO

PERFORMANCE CRAFT

Once you have built a repertoire of tricks and
choreographed them to music, it's time to think about
public performance. Facing an audience needn't be
painful. Pleasing the judges is not impossible. And
everyone gets nervous. No matter what happens, you
will get a round of applause from me for doing your best.

Dressing Up

Q *My dance partner is a Jack Russell named Hurricane. We have devised a dance routine to Barnum & Bailey's favourites and I've made Hurricane a little jacket with a big frilly collar and buttons. I've also made a pointed hat with a pompom. I was going to paint his nails but thought this might be too much. What do you think?*

A I think Hurricane looks extremely cute in all his new gear and he must be a very patient little dog to let you pick his wardrobe. When dressing your dog there are a number of points to consider.

Respect Whether you are going to be competing at a Kennel Club-licensed show or performing a routine for the local nursing home, you mustn't deny your dog his dignity. There is a fine line between what is cute and amusing and what is demeaning. Don't get too carried away. It's called doggy dancing because the dog is recognisable as a dog and is the star of the show. Make sure he's not too well disguised or they might think your partner is a small child or a diminutive adult.

Kennel Club shows The rules say that dogs may only wear "dressed collars". Diamonds, bow-ties or beads are acceptable as long as they hang around Hurricane's neck. Anything else and you will lose marks. The judges need to be able to see how your dog moves and what he is doing with his paws. They don't want to see Hurricane tripping on the sleeves of a costume no matter how well made or fitted it is.

Demonstrations and displays You have a little more freedom performing at displays or exhibitions. But be sure that Hurricane is comfortable in his jacket. You don't want him to overheat or be so disturbed by one of the buttons that he sits and scratches in time to the music. Hurricane must be able to move freely in order to give you his best performance.

Canine closets Most dogs already have a number of items in their closets that have been specifically designed for canine wear. They fit well, are easy to move around in and the dogs are accustomed to wearing them. Does Hurricane have a body harness or winter coat that you could decorate and jazz up with a few sequins?

Practice run It is a good idea to get Hurricane accustomed to his costume before you go on stage. If you tie a large ribbon on his collar for the first time at a show, don't be surprised if he spends most of his time trying to get it off. If you try out your costume in advance, you have time to down-size to a smaller ribbon that looks just as charming if things don't go as planned.

Painting his toenails probably is carrying dressing up a little too far – a trim and polish will do the job. Why don't you book him in for a make-over with your groomer instead? And while he's there, treat yourself to a visit to the hairdresser. You'll both look and feel a million dollars when you go into the ring the next day.

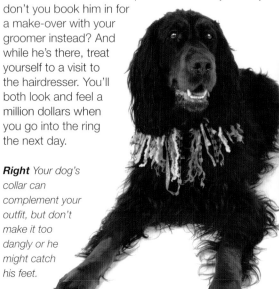

Right *Your dog's collar can complement your outfit, but don't make it too dangly or he might catch his feet.*

Choice Of Costume

Q *Our local dog training club organised a display of dog dancing at the village fete and it was so entertaining. All the dogs were so well trained and the costumes were amazing. I dance around the kitchen to the radio with my Springer Spaniel, Sorrel, and would like to learn some of the moves I saw; however, I'm a size 16 and there is no way that I am wearing a costume with sequins! What should I wear?*

A You don't need sequins to sparkle on the dance floor with Sorrel. But, if you are interested in performing in front of an audience or competing at a show, then you need to consider what you are going to wear. Handlers try to choose an outfit that will complement their music; for example, a ball gown for Fred Astaire's famous "Dancing Cheek to Cheek" number. How far you dress up is your decision. You could get a loin cloth and stamp your feet to the music from the *Jungle Book* or you can wear a T-shirt and jeans and bop to an Elvis tune. Costumes help you get in the mood, but think about the following.

Comfort Make sure that you are at ease in your clothes. It's no good digging out your old Sixties kaftan for a Santana number if it is so tight across the shoulders that you can't move your arms. And will you be too hot layered in furs for a rendition of "Take back your mink"? Will you be too cold skipping across the floor in bare feet to Sandy Shaw's dulcet tones? Stay in your comfort zone. If you feel silly wearing fishnets, don't choose music from the *Moulin Rouge* because Heaven help you if you break down on the motorway on the way home from the show and need to call for assistance.

Practicality Sorrel doesn't really care what you look like, but he would complain if your string of pearls keeps hitting him in the eye every time you lean over. Shorten them! Be practical. If your hat keeps falling off, an elastic chin strap will solve the problem.

Character Some handlers claim that they become a different person when they dress up. Their costume helps them get into character. Dressed as a nun, they become Maria or at least Julie Andrews in *The Sound of Music*. Slip on a pair of glasses and they become Harry Potter. Who knows? You, too, might find that the old you disappears when you put on someone else's clothes.

Generic And the generic look of black trousers and waistcoat and or jacket is very acceptable. Not all music lends itself to a period or character costume. Black on black is the outfit of choice for many handlers and they always looks smart and professional. And you've the option of jazzing yourself up with an colourful shirt or dare I suggest it … sew on a few sparkles!

Whatever you wear, you want the audience and the judges to be looking at your dog, not you. Don't be too outrageous and beware of plunging necklines and short skirts. You can look good without resorting to glitter!

Left The general pose gives no clues, but you know that this pair will be dancing to "Jailhouse Rock" even before the music starts.

Star Tricks

Q *My dog does lots of tricks. For an American Cocker Spaniel, I think she is the greatest and that's why I named her "Star". She can stand on her hind legs, sit, roll over, lie down with her head between her paws, sit up and beg and she can weave between my legs. Does she need anything else except music to be a doggy dancer?*

A You've made a good start. At the very least, every footballer must be able to kick a ball. Every cook must be able to break an egg. Similarly, every dog dancer has a few tricks up their sleeve, but doggy dancing is more than a collection of canine antics strung together while the music plays in the background.

In the context of doggy dancing, a trick is a learned behaviour that will amuse, amaze or astound depending on your ability as a trainer and choreographer. A carefully designed move will demonstrate a dog's dexterity or create a specific illusion. And done well, it looks as if the handler has cast a spell on his dog – the effect is magical. You make a trick special by training and choreography and ensuring that it is relevant to the music.

Training Ask yourself how well you have trained Star to roll over. Will she do it to the left, the right, in front or behind you? Will she do it if you stand on a chair or stand ten feet away from her? Will Star roll over the first time you command her or do you need to repeat your command? Will she roll over after eight paces of heelwork? And if Star has to choose between rolling over and chasing that crisp bag in the wind, which will it be? You need 100 per cent reliability and this comes with training and raising your performance criteria to a new level.

Choreography Great! Star can roll over anywhere and anytime. It is the perfect move to include in a routine to "Roll Over Beethoven". But Star rolls too quickly and has finished her move before Chuck Berry can spit out the lyric "Beethoven". Should you think about having her do two rolls or would the second roll carry her into the start of the next musical phrase? These are the sorts of decisions you have to make when you choreograph a routine. It's not always easy to be spot on the beat.

Interpretation of the music

A trick should be relevant to the music you have chosen. If you love the music of Wagner, do you really think that rolling over is in keeping with the *Twilight of the Gods*? You would do better to teach her to play dead! Star's moves must be appropriate to the emotion of the music to be meaningful. It's no good teaching her to retrieve your bowler hat if one of the god's thunderbolts would be more appropriate to the music and better fit the mood you want to create.

You've had fun teaching Star tricks. You'll have even more fun creating a routine.

Right *If your dog can balance on her hind legs, fit the trick to a musical phrase like "Reach For The Stars". She'll look great performing like this in your new routine.*

Choosing Music

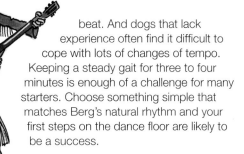

Q *I have been going through all my old records and CDs, trying to find a piece of music. I have had lots of fun reliving the 1960s, 70s and 80s but am still undecided. How do I pick one piece? I want to dance to them all and Berg, my German Short Haired Pointer, is losing patience!*

A Choosing your music can indeed be time-consuming. Suddenly you start paying attention to the music played at the supermarket. You listen carefully to the tunes on the radio while you are driving along in your car. And what was the name of that programme's theme song on the television? Worse, you start buying some of the CDs at the petrol station to check out in case there is a composition that hits the spot. Here's how I make my choice.

Do you like it? You will have to listen to it over and over and over again. Make sure your choice of music is something you like because you will end up humming it in your sleep and, if you practise long and hard enough, you will know every note in it as intimately as your own face.

The right tempo? Watch Berg. Is he elegant and long-striding? Is he hard-pressed to break out of a walk into a trot? Perhaps a fast, racy tune is not for you? You don't want to pick something that makes Berg play catch up with every musical phrase. On the other hand, if Berg does everything at a hundred miles an hour, you are safe opting for something quicker with a faster

Right Watch your dog carefully to spot his natural gait and rhythm and pick music with a similar heartbeat.

beat. And dogs that lack experience often find it difficult to cope with lots of changes of tempo. Keeping a steady gait for three to four minutes is enough of a challenge for many starters. Choose something simple that matches Berg's natural rhythm and your first steps on the dance floor are likely to be a success.

Can you live up to it? You want to be able to meet the judges' expectations when they hear the introductory bars of your music. Will they be sitting back in anticipation of a programme full of difficult and flashy moves? If you are a beginner, save the big theme tunes like *Chariots of Fire* for when you have the experience to get the judges on the edge of their seats. Pick music that inspires you but will allow you to deliver what it promises.

Can you make it your own? Or has someone else already done it? Avoid selecting a tune that a handler has already choreographed and used successfully in competition. There are bound to be comparisons and they may not be favourable. Similarly, don't choose music that has been danced to death by many other competitors. "Oh, no! Another *Singing in the Rain*!" There's enough music out there for everyone. Go for something no one has used before and be an original.

Your choice of music is an important starting point for your routine. Don't keep Berg waiting any longer. Make a choice so you can start spending time with him working on your choreography.

Let The Music Play

Q I've caught the heelwork to music bug and I've a routine for my Norwegian Valhund, Fuzz. My problem is that I'm limited by where and when I can practise. I have always done my dog training in the morning before going to work and I'm worried that playing Meat Loaf on my CD player will be an unappreciated wake-up call for the neighbours! Any suggestions?

A Quite right. Not everyone is a Meat Loaf fan. Do some shopping and invest in an iPod or an mp3 player and earphones. It will be money well spent and you'll be able to train Fuzz anytime and anywhere without causing a disturbance.

Deaf ears Fuzz needs to listen and respond to your commands, not the music. He may yowl when he hears the chimes of the ice cream van, but that is the extent of his musicality. Pop, jazz, classical – it's all the same to him. Fuzz will never tap his paw in time to a tune but with your direction, he can look like he was born with rhythm and can interpret a song. You can achieve this transformation with practice and you won't be guilty of noise pollution if you train with an iPod.

Anytime With earphones, you will be the only one that can hear your music. The children can do their homework undisturbed. Your husband can read his paper in peace. You can practise your routine early in the morning or late at night and no one will complain about the noise – unless you shout out loud or Fuzz starts barking.

Anywhere Where you can practise will be independent of lengths of extension leads. The only

Left Not everyone in the neighbourhood will necessarily share your taste in music, but if you play it on an iPod, only you will hear it.

plugging you will be doing is in your ears. If you want to go through your routine at the playing fields, a camp site or a car park at the local supermarket, there is nothing to stop you – except perhaps an inquisitive security guard who will wonder what you are doing!

Pre-recorded If your music is pre-recorded onto an iPod or mp3 player, you won't have to carry a selection of CDs or cassette tapes everywhere with you. It's bad enough trying to remember to pack Fuzz's favourite treats and props without worrying about your soundtracks.

Warm-ups If you arrive at your show early, you can warm up in the ring with Fuzz before the competition starts. You will not be allowed to take in sweets, but you can take an iPod or mp3 player. It's a great opportunity to map out your routine on the floor space. But watch out for fellow competitors who will be doing the same. They, too, will be listening to their music and not looking where they are going. Collisions are quite common.

Out loud If you practise with earphones, do make room in your training schedule to run through your routine with the music playing out loud. You don't want Fuzz to freak the first time he hears Meat Loaf boom out from a set a speakers.

So, no excuses now. You've got the dog, now get the iPod. Get training. And your neighbours can dream on in peace till they hear their alarm clock.

Picking Props

Q *I would like to try some doggy dancing with my greyhound, Lilly. I already go to obedience lessons with Lilly and the heelwork to music class follows mine. It really sounds like fun and I watch them troop in with their dogs and carrying their props every week. I see some very strange things being brought in from the car park – sometimes it takes two people to carry them! Will I need to take up weightlifting as well as buy a bigger car if I want to join in?*

A No need to sell your old car. Props are great fun and you do see some very imaginative choices at class and at shows. But there is more to a good prop than sheer size and weight!

Relevant A good prop will complement your music and help you get into character. If you are dancing to a track from a Bond film, you could carry a Martini glass or a replica handgun. You wouldn't choose a Masai shield or bow and arrow, would you? Props need to be relevant to your routine.

Above Make your prop relevant to your music. The lyrics say "The wheels on the bus go round and round". And that is what you can also do with your dog.

Part and parcel A good prop will be an integral part of the dance. As a choreographer, you will design your routine to show Lilly interacting with your prop in different ways. She might circle it, stand on it, retrieve it or follow it. She might crawl under it, tap it with a paw or rest her head on it. Your prop won't be idle, but part of the action!

Ready made You may already have a potential prop at home. It is surprising what you can dig out from under the kitchen sink. Or you may decide to buy one especially for your routine. Don't be embarrassed at the supermarket check out. The lady at the till probably thinks all the artificial flowers you are stockpiling are for a forthcoming wedding reception, not a performance of *An English Country Garden* with your dog, Lilly. Toy stores and charity shops are prop cornucopias – plastic swords, hula hoops, skipping ropes, toasters, milking stools, hand brooms … shop till you drop.

DIY You can build a castle, fashion a teepee or make a throne fit for a king – whatever you think will fit in with your music. Are your DIY skills up to the task? You don't want your carefully constructed spaceship to disintegrate as you carry it onto the floor. If the leaves are falling off your home-made palm tree, where will Lilly and the judges be looking? The aim is for something that creates the right mood and focus, not distraction.

At the end of the day, the star of the show will be Lilly, not your props. Remember that big does not always mean better. A clever handler can create the illusion of a specific place or time with minimal props or even none at all. And they have less to pack into their car on the way home!

Are You Ready?

Q *I've been training Elvis, my Whippet, for a year and I think the time has come to enter him in a competition. We've a routine ready to debut, but my trainer says to wait a while. How do you know when your dog is ready to go into the ring?*

A I will never forget the first time that I performed for the judges. I was so proud of how I handled myself and my dog. Your first time in the ring will be a very special and lasting memory so make sure that it is a good one. Don't be too hasty to fill in your entry form.

Is your dog prepared? Assess your dog's performance in class honestly. Elvis must be able to perform a few tricks to perfection and string them together so that they flow. Can he cope with the new variables that a competition introduces into the doggy dancing equation – a strange venue, a crowd of new people and a nervous handler? Prepare your dog by:

- Putting your hand up for displays and exhibitions. Grasp the opportunity to practise your routine in front of an audience ... and be able to treat your dog in the ring. No judges to mark you, so relax and enjoy the experience.
- Take advantage of progress tests run by the Paws 'n' Music Association. You'll cover all the basics and it's good way to test your dog in an environment that is very similar to a real competition. There will be a little bit of pressure, but you won't be overwhelmed.

- If you see a training day or workshop advertised, ring the organiser and put your name down. Working your dog in front of a class of strangers and an instructor you respect is just as nerve-racking as dancing for the judges.

Are you prepared? Even the seasoned doggy dancer gets nervous at a show. You and Elvis are a team and your dog will pick up on any negative thoughts you have racing through your mind as you wait for the music to start. Make sure you can cope with the extra pressure.

- Offer to help at a show. Volunteers are always needed and it's a great way to learn what goes on behind the scenes. You'll learn the ropes and meet fellow competitors. More importantly, you'll find out what to expect when it's your turn to walk out onto the floor.
- Learn to think positively. If you stand by the side of the ring wishing you had done more work on your "Rewinds", Elvis will make your doubts his own.
- Do you know your routine inside out? Can you recite the order of your moves one after another without pause for breath? Elvis relies on you to take the lead on the floor. If you don't know what is coming next, neither will he.

You can do Elvis more harm than good by taking him into the ring too early. If you and Elvis are inadequately prepared, you will leave your first show feeling disappointed and frustrated. Elvis will wonder what he has done to let you down and doggy dancing won't be fun anymore.

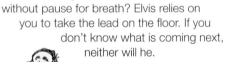

Conquering Nerves

Q *I don't know if you can help me. The night before a show I start getting nervous. I can't sleep and keep tossing and turning. In the morning I start feeling sick and can't eat anything in case I bring it back up. After I've done my class, win or lose, I'll feel great again. On the other hand my Tibetan Terrier, Suki, shows no nerves at all. Why can't I be more like her?*

Above *There are many herbal remedies that are said to help you relax. Give one a try and see if it works.*

A You are not alone. Anyone who has competed in a heelwork to music class, performed in the school play or taken part in some public sports event has suffered from nerves. The trick is to get the right balance. A little adrenalin rush will keep you on your toes but too much will keep you in the toilets for most of the day.

Relax This is hard to do consciously because how can you hope to relax when you are putting so much effort into chilling? Persevere. It is surprising what you can achieve with practice. A warm bubbly bath, soft music (not your heelwork music) and a glass of wine before bed can work wonders.

Displacement activities Clean the oven, cut the grass, have a game of football with the kids. Displacement activities can stop you getting pre-show jitters. You won't have time to think about the competition the next day and you'll be too tired the night before to care if you have packed your props.

Meticulous preparation Make a list of everything you have to do before the show. Have you run through your routine one last time? Tick. Have you sewn the pocket back on your costume? Tick. Did you pack a road map so you don't get lost on the way to the venue? Tick. The more you tick, the less you have to worry about and so can get a good night's sleep.

Listen Your body is preparing for your heelwork to music class as if you are going into battle. With an empty stomach, you can run, jump and fly to the best of your ability. So eat a good meal the night before the show and skip breakfast the next day or just nibble on something that releases quick energy.

Herbal remedies Some people swear by Bach Rescue Remedy or other Bach flower remedies that aim to calm nerves. Why don't you give one a try? It won't do you any harm and it might do you some good. Just don't overdose yourself!

Yoga can help Find inner peace. Keep yourself calm with meditation. Make your mantra something positive and reassuring. Repeat your dog's name over and over and over.

Experienced competitors will have developed a pre-show routine to help them relax and keep their nerves under control. Finding one to suit you can be a bit hit and miss What does the trick for your best friend may not be right for you. I rely on biting my finger nails and eating chocolate. And I try to make sure that I've had plenty of rest the week before a show in case I can't sleep the night before.

Be A Star

Q *I've been asked to do a display of doggy dancing for my Gardening Club which is raising money for Guide Dogs this year. Although I am a regular competitor at heelwork to music shows, the thought of performing with my Golden Retriever, Lee, anywhere else gives me the jitters – even if it is for a good cause. Can you give me a good reason to conquer my nerves and agree to do it?*

A Oh, go on and dive in! You will not only be helping to raise funds for a deserving charity but you will be a worthy ambassador for doggy dancing.

Ambassadorship Lead the way. What can you do with a dog once you've got one? Doggy dancing is one of the many growing canine sports that helps keeps our pets stimulated and fit. If you and Lee look like you are having a great time together, other dog owners will be tempted to join a training class too and have some fun.

Mistakes are overlooked If you make any mistakes in competition, those crafty judges will deduct marks. Not so for displays. If Lee misses a cue, no one will notice. If he does something really naughty or plays the clown, he'll get a laugh. Because everyone watching will identify with you in the belief that that is exactly what their own dog would do under pressure. The audience will love you whatever happens.

Friends and neighbours They will be there to support not criticise you and they will be impressed! Many people with a dog don't have a properly trained

recall and their dog's best trick is probably eating a biscuit in under 60 seconds. You and Lee will seem like magic. It may only be a spin or a bow to you but to the people watching it's awesome.

Valuable practice Displays are a great way to get ready for competition. You can take treats and toys into the ring with you. If you think Lee needs an extra incentive, go ahead and give him a bit of cheese or frankfurter. No one will mind and no one will mark you down. You will both be getting ring experience and you will still be able to reward him for getting moves right.

Take what comes Displays and exhibition dancing are a bit of a lucky dip. The floor space is always bigger or smaller than you've been told. Be prepared for anything. If you expect a small group of spectators, don't be surprised if you are faced with an audience with standing room only because it's sunny and everyone has taken their grandmother for a day out. The sound system is either too loud or too quiet. Don't expect the facilities to be on a par with those at competitions. They may be worse or they may be better, so be flexible.

Pull out all the stops at displays and demonstrations.

Above *Take the plunge and have a go! You'll never find out how big a star you and your dog can be until you hear the audience clapping your performance.*

Don't let anything hold you back. You don't have to be great on the day or even good. You just have to make sure your training is positive. Have fun with your dog and you'll be a star.

A Name For Fame

Q *I am going to enter my first heelwork to music show with my rescue crossbreed, Frolic, and I am very confused. My friend told me I have to rename her. What is she on about?*

A I think "Frolic" is a great name! It's short, easy to say and conjures up joy and playfulness. The most important thing you will ever teach your dog is her name and your dog should be listening for it even when asleep. Her name will precede every command you give her throughout her life. When your dog hears it, she should snap to attention for some fun.

Best names I try to avoid people's names for my pets after hearing someone shouting for a "Brian" in the park and retrieving not her dog but someone else's husband. Names mislead you if not picked with care. My friend regretted naming her puppy "Vodka" after hearing the kids yell for their pet in the garden to the bewilderment of the neighbours. And how confusing it would be to name your agility dog "Clover" and use the jump command "Over". "Frolic" is a great pet name and ticks all the right boxes for me. There is no need to change it for heelwork to music.

Kennel Club shows

To compete at a Kennel Club Show, your dog has to be a member of the Club. She must be registered either on the Kennel Club Breed Register (for pedigree dogs) or the Activity Register (for everything else) which makes your dog subject to the Kennel Club rules and regulations governing events like agility or heelwork to music. If you are purchasing a pedigree dog, the Kennel Club registration certificate is usually given to you when you collect your puppy and the pedigree name has already been chosen by the breeder. For rescue or mixed breed dogs, you choose the fancy name and it is not unusual for a dog to be well into adulthood before being added to the Activity Register.

Fancy names Let your imagination soar. What about "Fantasy Flying High over Frensham", "Twenty-First Century Disco Girl" or "Fancy Frolicking Fun with Phantoms"? There may well be other "Frolics" on the Activity Register so it is important to give her a distinctive name that will make her unique even if it does sound a bit long-winded. You don't have to teach Frolic her registered name and she doesn't have to respond to it. It's just for documentation. A good thing too because by the time you spit it out, your music would have ended!

If you want to compete at heelwork to music competitions licensed by the Kennel Club, you don't have to rename your dog. But you will have to register her on their Activity Register and give her a fancy name that will immediately identify her on paper. Good luck and enjoy your first competition.

Left *This little dog looks too small for a big, long, fancy name.*

Help!

Q *I have put my name down to help at the next show. My dog is too young to compete but I thought it would give me a good idea of what to expect when I do. What sort of thing will I be asked to do and will I have time to watch the competition or will I have to work all day?*

A I'm so glad to hear that you are going to volunteer your help. Without people like you, heelwork to music competitions would grind to a halt. There are a number of jobs that need to be done at a show, some are more specialised than others. Here are some examples:

Show manager The show manager is appointed well in advance and is responsible for any number of different things ranging from competitors' running orders to ordering the rosettes. The show manager delegates jobs to the volunteers, but if there are not enough helpers, she will do them herself.

Movers and shakers These volunteers are the most active at the beginning and end of a show. They sweep the floor free of dog hair and crumbs. They erect the barriers or fencing that surrounds the dance floor. They put pens and paper on the judges table. They are real multi-taskers.

Booking inners All competitors must book in on the morning of the show and hand in either CDs or cassette tapes of their music to the organisers. This helps the show run smoothly and ensures that the classes follow one after the other without hiccup. Imagine how awful it would be if you got onto the floor and your music was missing. Or if you missed your turn because no one knew that the competitor drawn to run before you hadn't arrived.

Music man The man in charge of the sound system will be busy all day. It is a specialist job and needs technical know-how. The music man has to be at the show early to set up his speakers and sound system and he is there all day to operate the button that starts each competitor's music.

The judges The judges have to know the rules and regulations for every class. They write the marks for each performance on a judging slip that will be passed to the scorekeepers. And, like yourself, they are volunteers giving up their time to keep the show running.

Scorekeepers Each competitor's performance will be marked by three judges and then given to the scorekeepers. Many shows these days have customised computer programs that calculate rankings and places. It's another specialised and important job. If the marks are not put into the program correctly, the wrong dog could win the class.

Runners These are the volunteers that collect the judges' marks and take them to the scorekeepers. The essential quality that a runner needs is patience. Some judges take longer than others to complete their slips.

Callers The caller makes sure that every competitor is present and ready to go into the ring in the order drawn. It's a great way to put faces to names and make new friends although there isn't much time to chat. The majority of competitors will be warming up their dogs and trying to remember which move follows which. If the competitor doesn't make herself known to the caller, she could miss her turn. She won't get another opportunity so the caller may have to do a bit of hunting. She could be standing just outside the door biting her fingernails.

Stewards If you are a steward, you will be asked to help competitors in or out of the ring. At the entrance, they may need help with props or holding their dog. At the exit, everything happens in reverse. If you are manning the exit, make sure that you allow the competitor time to congratulate her dog and don't forget to return the lead.

Commentator If you love a microphone in your hand, this is the job for you. You get to introduce each dog and handler as they enter the ring. You can offer information on the dog's breed, name and so on. Not everyone in the audience is an expert and many would appreciate learning a little more about the sport. If the judges are still pondering the last dog's marks, you can entertain the crowds with a few jokes. But don't get carried away. This is not an audition for the X-Factor.

Reporter Some shows will assign a volunteer to be show reporter. Do you think you have any literary aptitude? You can watch each routine and write a few lines about it for the newsletter. But be careful. No one wants to read that they look ridiculous in a wig or that they are an appalling handler. It is not always easy to be truthful and yet positive. Try to avoid upsetting your new friends with any unguarded comments.

I hope you enjoy your day helping at the show. I'm sure the show manager will allow you time to watch the competitors. You'll learn a lot about doggy dancing as well as how a good competition is run. And don't be surprised if you are asked to help again next year.

Below Helping at shows and demonstrations is a good way to learn the ropes of doggy dancing.

Be Prepared

Q *My Rhodesian Ridgeback, Rupert, and I have entered our first show. We are very excited. I'm only a beginner so I'm not expecting a rosette, but I want to have a good day out. What should I remember to take with me?*

A It is always best to be prepared. Competitions can be held anywhere. A leisure centre, a village hall or in a marquee as part of a country fair. You never know what amenities will be available, so the more self-sufficient you are the better.

The dog First and foremost, don't leave Rupert at home! You might want to give his coat a quick brush before you present him to the judges so pack your grooming kit. If you have a dog that likes to roll in unpleasant smells, include a few wet wipes or towels to clean him off. There is nothing worse than having to spend the day with a dog that smells of skunk. And remember a supply of poo bags.

Training bag This should contain your clicker, a fresh supply of treats, targets and Rupert's favourite toys. Throw in your training diary and a pencil. You'll want to assess and record Rupert's performance identifying weak spots and strengths so that you can plan next week's targets. Your first competition will provide your base line.

Documents These include your running order, the show schedule, directions to the venue, parking passes and Kennel Club Record Book.

Music Don't forget that! Best to have two copies. I pack a CD as well as a cassette recording to be on the safe side. CDs can be scratched and cassettes can unravel. Without a back-up, you'll have to hum the tune.

Costume Make sure it is ready. Sew on your sequins, tie your bows or polish your armour. Make sure it is clean and ironed and don't forget accessories like shoes and jewellery.

Props These are easily forgotten, especially if they are everyday household objects. If you use a foot stool in your routine and have been resting your feet on it while watching TV the night before, make sure you put it in your car before you go to bed.

Catering pack There may be a posh and expensive tea room at the venue or only an ice cream van. Rather than go hungry, pack a few sandwiches and a flask. And shove in some biscuits to munch on the way home if you are stuck in traffic. Don't forget Rupert's meal if you anticipate a long day away from home.

Toilet requisites Often the only available public conveniences are of variable standards. There are never enough of them and they always run out of paper and soap. Pack plenty of tissues and stock up on hand wipes.

Your purse or wallet There may be stalls selling all sorts of goodies – food, books, clothes or toys. You'll want to treat yourself or Rupert with a purchase whatever happens in the ring.

Expect bad weather The weather in Great Britain is always unpredictable. Pack an umbrella, wellingtons, hat and gloves as well as your shorts and sandals. And Rupert? Have you towels, a reflective coat, and a cage fan in your luggage?

Start with the bare necessities for your first heelwork to music show. You'll be surprised how the list of essentials grows the more shows that you enter.

Ready, Steady, Go

Q *I'm all set to go. It is my first heelwork to music competition with Mimi, my Maltese Terrier. When I get there, what do I need to do and when? I am besides myself with nervous anticipation.*

A So glad to hear that this is a red letter day on your calendar. Try to calm down a bit and get a good night's sleep so you can arrive bright and early at the show.

Opening times Check the schedule to see what time the show opens. Before the first class starts, you will be able to practise with Mimi in the ring. Although you won't be able to take food with you, it's an opportunity to get Mimi accustomed to the flooring and any ring decorations that she might find distracting. Take care to avoid collisions with the other competitors who are marking out their routines or rehearsing a few last minute manoeuvres with their dogs.

Booking in Take your music with you when you book in for your class. You will have been sent the deadline for booking in, usually about eleven o'clock in the morning, with your pre-drawn running order. And find out how many dogs are booked in before you. You'll be going into the ring a little earlier if a few of the competitors drawn in front of you haven't shown up.

Get your bearings Once you have introduced Mimi to the ring and have booked in, it's time to get your orientation. Take a few moments to work out where the judges are sitting, where the toilets are, how far away the exercise area is, what coins operate the coffee machine and so on.

Find a seat Find a seat, watch a few competitors and relax. Enjoy the performances. It will be your turn soon enough.

Your turn You are responsible for making sure you are available for your class in the correct running order. When your turn approaches, get ready. Make sure that you and Mimi have taken a trip to the toilets, get your props and warm up. Report to the ring but not too early as hanging around too long could fuel your nerves.

In the ring Hand the steward your lead and go into the ring to your start position and face the judges. When you are ready, give the sound man the nod and your music will begin. Don't forget to breathe and smile.

Scoring Leave the ring to the sound of applause (hopefully)! Catch you breath while the three judges finish marking your routine. The scores will be averaged, and announced and displayed in the venue.

Prize-giving It may be your first competition, but never underestimate yourself. Prize-givings usually take place after each class and, if you have done well, your name will be called out. You and Mimi can rush into the ring, shake hands with one of the judges, collect your prize and take your place in the line up. And keep smiling. You'll want to look good in the photographs.

Before you leave Don't forget to collect your music and, if you want a DVD or print-out of the scores, make sure you place your order before you go home.

Enjoy your big day.

How To Be A Winner

Q *I have just started competing with my young dog, Tamzin, and we were awful! I'm an experienced handler and I know I did everything wrong. At the first hiccup, I fell apart and did things that I would never do in the comfort of the training hall. I came out of the ring desperately disappointed in myself and how I had handled Tamzin. Can you help me avoid this happening again?*

A You get full marks for recognising that your dog's poor performance was a result of your poor handling. Many people are too quick to blame their pet. The dog is stubborn, naughty or dumb. They forget how proud they are of the routine in training. Fortunately, there will always be another show. You may have got it all wrong this time, but you can try again and get it right.

Post-mortem After the show, sit down and think about your performance. What were the strengths and weaknesses? What could you do differently to improve? Reflect, ponder and be very honest with yourself. But be aware that you can't change everything all at once.

Set some goals Choose no more than three goals – the simpler and more achievable, the better. For example, you may decide that you must heel Tamzin into the ring at the next show rather than let her run in willy nilly. She'll start under control and continue in that vein. Or your goal might be to smile at the judges before you start your routine so you don't look stressed – smiling will help you relax and breathe normally. Perhaps you might decide to ignore any barking rather than shouting at her. Maybe you give yourself the simple challenge of doing whatever it takes to keep Tamzin's tail wagging for the length of your music. You might not get

to perform any of the moves you planned but if Tamzin looks happy, so will you. I always write my goals down on a card so that I can read it before I go into the ring. It helps me focus and reminds me of what I have to do when I step onto the floor.

Review and develop Your goals will change as you and your dog develop as a team and you find out what does and doesn't work for you. For example, once you've cracked getting Tamzin to heel in competition like she does in training, you might decide that you should concentrate on improving your posture in the ring. There will always be things to get better no matter how successful a competitor you become.

Congratulate yourself And don't forget to give yourself a pat on the back. If you have achieved a goal, give yourself a treat – anything from a bar of chocolate to dinner at your favourite restaurant. Then settle down to start the whole process over again. Training your dog is easy. Training yourself to compete is much harder but the same rules apply. Keep at it and you'll find yourself always exiting the ring as a winner in your own eyes.

Right Your dog will always do his best for you so don't blame him if it all goes wrong. Instead, look critically at your handling during the routine.

Judges' Marks

Q *I was sure that my rough collie, Laddie, and I were going to win the Starters' Freestyle class last week, but our names weren't even called out for a place. I checked the score sheet and was surprised to see such low marks. What can I do?*

A It does sometimes happen that what we think is a fabulous routine is not what the judges are looking for when they award marks. In this case, you must content yourself with the knowledge that Laddie did the best he could for you and try to remember how thrilled you were with his work.

The judges Three individuals with a good knowledge of the sport and the rules and regulations will be invited to judge each class. They will have qualified a dog out of a Starter's class and have some experience of competing at the level they are judging. In addition, it is likely that they will be entered at the show with their own dog but in a different class. Don't expect any favours if one of the judges is your trainer or a friend.

The marks The judges will mark three elements in your programme, each with a maximum of ten marks.
- Programme content will take into account factors such as the difficulty of the moves as well as their appropriateness to the conformation of the dog.
- The accuracy and execution of movement section assesses how quickly a dog responds to cues as well as the suitability of props.
- Musical interpretation looks at rhythm, phrasing and expression. The choreography should be balanced and flowing. Costumes should be complementary to the routine.

One day someone will get a perfect score of ten in each section, but it hasn't happened yet.

The judges' mark is final Once a mark is recorded, it is final. You should not argue with the judge, protest or scream and pull out your hair! Such behaviour will not make a good impression and you may find yourself reported to the Kennel Club for impugning the decision of the judges. Don't be confrontational or aggressive. Remember that there are three of them and only one of you.

Advice and guidance Although you won't be able to get your marks changed, you can query them. The majority of judges are approachable and friendly. They want to see the sport of canine freestyle grow and they want all the competitors to reach their true potential. Politely ask one of the judges if she has a few minutes to spare to chat with you. Point out that you are after constructive criticism so that you can improve your routine. Many judges keep notes; others keep it all in their head but they should all be able to justify and explain their marks.

See! Hear! Remember also that judges can only mark what they see and hear. If you obscured Laddie when he did his flashiest and most innovative move, the judges will have missed it. It is no good complaining that Laddie should gain points for three perfect back somersaults, if the judges couldn't see them.

It is always wise to check the score sheet to find out what areas to target for future training. And I hope it won't be long before you are giving the judges what they want and gaining top marks.

Thinking On Your Feet

Q *I can't understand it. I made loads of mistakes with Fritz, my Hungarian Vizsla. Yet we were awarded high marks and I got a rosette! At one stage, I had to fudge a whole set of moves because Fritz was not where I thought he was going to be and that put everything in a different order. How can I have done so well?*

A Never argue with the judges! If they thought what they saw was good, accept the high marks and my congratulations for being able to compete so well when things went wrong in your dance routine. You have joined the ranks of the great performers who can cope with the unexpected.

Perfection It is always just out of reach, especially with a canine dance partner who may be thinking about his fleas rather than what comes after eight leg weaves. Even top handlers will confess that there are times when everything does not go to plan and they have to do a bit of busking with their dog to get back on track. So don't be disappointed in yourself. You did well to carry on and complete your routine for the judges. Many competitors fall apart and freeze at the first sign of trouble.

Thinking on your feet And even better, you were able to think on your feet. You kept your dance programme moving forward by rearranging your steps and shuffling your moves. It is not easy to think clearly when your dog puts you on the spot. Had you planned for Fritz to be on the right and instead he popped up on your left? Did he catch you out by twirling really quickly instead of at his usual steady pace? Perhaps he anticipated giving you a paw and you weren't ready. Now what do you do? How you cope when things go wrong is the real test of a true performer.

Covering your tracks Remember that the judges won't have seen your routine before and they don't know what move follows what. If you suddenly have to be creative in the middle of the routine, the judges

won't know that it is because Fritz walked back for eight beats instead of four. They only mark what they see performed in front of them, not what they should have seen.

Skill box And aren't you glad that your training goes beyond what you include in your routine? If you are continually adding tricks and linking moves to Fritz's skill box, you won't ever have to stand in the middle of the floor wondering what to do next. You will be able to improvise and pull something out of your hat that should wow spectators.

Keep going! Have you ever been to a ballet and seen a ballerina signal to the orchestra to re-start the music because she missed a step? No. She stays on stage and covers her error so well that you are unaware of the omission. To the audience, it appears that everything is going to plan. Just like the ballerina, you and Mimi kept going and deserve applause, even a rosette.

Choice Of Venue

Q *I practise my routines in a carpetted room at our local leisure centre. Imagine my surprise when I entered my first show and the ring was in a marquee on grass. My Tibetan Terrier, Jojo, thought he was out for a walk in the park. He sniffed here and there but at least he didn't start digging holes! Are any more surprises on the cards?*

A When you go to a doggy dancing show, you could be performing your routine on just about anything from grass, rubber matting, felt, carpet to bare floorboards. You will have to be able to strut your stuff indoors or out. If you continue competing, you will get to know all the venues and their facilities. Be prepared.

Suitable shoes Starting with your costume. Match your footwear to the surface. Stiletto heels will sink into the grass, puncture rubber matting and make a tap-tap noise on wooden floors. If you remembered to pack shoes with rubber soles, now is the time to try them out. And they are probably a safer option if you are unlucky enough to step on Jojo accidentally.

Jumps and leaps Rubberised flooring or carpet with underlay are popular choices for dancing surfaces because they provide traction as well as cushioning for any high impact moves. But they are not always available. If you are going to perform a series of aerial manoeuvres on the village green, look out for natural hazards, such as molehills and rabbit holes. Also, just a thin layer of morning dew can turn a grassy playing field into an ice rink. Be careful not to fall over. Why not limit the number of jumps or accept a lower height from Jojo? Indoor venues are not necessarily any better because wooden floors can also be slippery and they provide little give on landing.

Wet and muddy Even if you are under cover, you can still get wet and muddy. In the shelter of a marquee, excess water drips off the ceiling and dribbles down the sides of the tent so you will have to steer clear of possible puddles. If you kneel on the ground you will no longer be pristine and Jojo may well transfer a few pawprints onto your costume. Make some last minute changes to your routine so you can stay as clean and dry as possible.

Distractions If Jojo likes to put his nose to the ground, he will be rewarded with a whole host of smells when you work outdoors. With the best will in the world, you cannot sanitise an expanse of grass. During the night an earthworm will have thrown a cast. If your competition is part of a larger extravaganza with food stalls, there will be the smell of burgers and onions wafting your way and it will be even harder than usual to keep Jojo's attention. Be prepared to take steps to control Jojo's sniffing behaviour.

As Jojo matures and you gain more experience and confidence when competing, you will be able to anticipate any problems in advance and take steps to deal with them. Another rainy day in Margate? With a few last minute changes, you can still steal the show.

No Clicking In The Ring

Q *Everyone complains that they can't take food or toys into the ring with them at shows. I can't work my dog unless I'm holding a clicker. Without it, Pax, my Yorkie cross, and I look complete beginners in the ring. With it, we look like we are going to be Crufts Champions! What am I going to do?*

A It always amazes me how holding something in your hand can make such a difference to a person's attitude. If you have a clicker in your hand and a treat between your fingers, what dog could deny that you are going to give a great reward for a great performance? So that is what your dog gives you. You are confident that you are going to get a good result, your body language is convincing and your thought waves positive. You trust Pax to deliver. When your hand is empty Pax knows it. There are no goodies any more. He might as well sniff the ground. Motivation is dropping, dropping, gone.

That positive feeling How are you going to get it back again? Look and act like you do have something in your hand. Stand tall. Believe in yourself. Smile. You've done the training. Pax is well schooled. Be confident. If you lose motivation, so will Pax. This is a team event.

New habits In training, cultivate new habits. Don't always hold the clicker in your hand. Hang it on your belt or hide it in a jacket pocket. Pax will still be able to hear the click and you will get accustomed to performing empty-handed. Or brief a friend and ask her to click for you. You will initially feel undressed without your clicker, but the feeling will pass.

Clicker word So many of us are in awe of the power of the clicker that we forget the power of our voices. Choose a word to mark good behaviour and follow it up with a treat. "Yes!", "Bingo" and "Wow" are all words you can say during training and in the ring. Pax will be happy to hear you praise him for a job well done.

Reward planning Clicker trainers have it ingrained into them to click and treat often and consistently. This often welds the device to their hand and they feel unable to train their dogs without it. They become reluctant to ask their dogs to work a little bit harder for a little bit longer before they are given each click. To progress, you have to raise your criteria and use your clicker more judiciously. It is not a question of simply slinging your clicker in a drawer. Motivate yourself to plan a reward strategy for Pax and he won't lose motivation or drive but will try even harder to please you.

Let go! Don't keep holding onto the clicker because you are afraid to let go. If you have followed a carefully constructed training programme and Pax can do cartwheels and somersaults in training, he can do them in the ring. Have faith in yourself and your dog. You will be a Champion.

Left You don't always need a clicker. Your dog will cross his paws as you cross your legs for just a smile. Put your clicker away and have faith in your training. Try it.

Finding Inspiration

Q *I need inspiration! I'm tired of the same old tricks and moves and I want to create a routine that will stretch my imagination and challenge my dog-training skills. Biscuit is a Labrador cross and is up for anything. We already have several successful routines behind us. Where should I look for new ideas?*

A Everywhere. It's not a question of where to look but of keeping your eyes open for new moves, music and props.

Competitions and displays Don't just go to the show, work your dog and then go home. Stay and watch what other competitors are doing on the dance floor. Is it your local fête? Don't miss the heelwork to music display. It just may contain a move or combination that you have never seen before.

Doggy doings OK. You are not interested in obedience, agility or flyball, but watch a competition anyway. You might be inspired by someone's handling or warm-up exercises.

Sporting disciplines So many other sports contain a dance element and you can watch them all on TV in the comfort of your own home. Gymnastics has floor exercises to music. Ice skaters are expert choreographers. Copy them but leave the blades at home.

The arts Do you love musicals? Don't simply get caught up in the story lines. Instead watch the foot work in *West Side Story, Guys and Dolls* or *Oklahoma*. You'll find ideas for costumes, props and steps. You may even want to move the furniture out of the way and get up and join the chorus line.

Keep fit videos It doesn't matter how slim you are, the aerobic gurus are experts at putting moves to music. Buy some videos and work through the exercise routines. You'll be as fit as a fiddle and get lots of new ideas into the bargain.

Celebrity challenge There have been a number of programmes recently that challenge celebrities to learn to dance, skate or juggle. Switch on the box and you can learn along with them.

Talent shows Entrants often have a knack for the unusual. It doesn't matter if their act is striptease or hula hooping, you can put it to music.

The school disco Volunteer to be an adult monitor at the next one. Watch the kids bopping to their favourite beat. Hey! That looked really good! Can you do it? If yes, include it in your new routine.

You Tube Spend some time on the internet browsing the You Tube website. Your will be surprised by the many different interpretations of *Swan Lake*. Performers range from frogs to pole dancers. You'll be entertained and find food for thought.

Mental management Don't forget to read the sport pages of the newspaper. They are full of stories of dedication and commitment. If Tiger Woods can take time off to re-shape his golf swing, you can retrain a twist. Emulate a few of them and you'll be surprised at the result.

You will be surprised where inspiration is hiding. Keep looking around you and be prepared to experiment. Who would have thought that a hockey stick would lead you to your next dance routine?

You Hum It And I'll Dance It

Q *I swear that my collie, Candice, has a musical memory. She has learned every beat of our music and knows exactly what comes next in our freestyle routine even when I forget to give her a cue. In fact, Candice is sometimes a bit guilty of anticipation. Is she special or are all dogs like this?*

A Of course Candice is very special! She is your dog and you love her very much, but I doubt if you would be able to rely on her remembering your whole routine. Candice can hear and recognise different sounds to a degree but she wouldn't be able to get up on a stage and give you a solo performance even if you promised her a whole roast chicken. You listen to the music to tell you when and what cues to give Candice so that she appears as if she is interpreting the tune, not the other way around. She needs to pay attention to you even though her hearing is excellent.

Sound sensitivity Dogs have good hearing and some dogs are more sensitive to sound than others. Is Candice afraid of fireworks or thunderstorms? Does she cover her ears if she hears gun shots? Does she yodel when the ice cream van rings its chimes? Or does she ignore all of these and carry on sleeping?

Recognition Any sound, be it words or the ring of a bell, can be endowed with meaning by dog trainers. Hunting and sheep dogs are taught to react to a whistle. And sometimes a noise is made relevant by us unintentionally. Does Candice get excited when she hears the door bell because she thinks that nice people are coming to play with her and give her treats as they have in the past? Dogs learn by association and repetition so it's no surprise that she gets excited.

Association I have no doubt that Candice has learned to recognise a few distinctive phrases of your music. When the drums roll, she jumps through a hoop. Or when the tempo switches to double time, she runs around the ring in big circles. You can rely on a few musical cues to prompt Candice, but be aware that she may decide she knows what's coming next better than you. Anticipation can be a problem. That's why handlers spend so much time teaching their dogs to listen for verbal commands or to watch for hand signals.

The whole experience It is always a good idea to practise with your music playing if you have the opportunity. It not only gets you moving naturally, but it gives your dog the chance to build up an enjoyable and pleasant association with the music. Candice may not know in what order to perform her tricks but she will hear it and think, "Oh, goodie. We're going to do some stuff together and there is going to be lots of fun and lots of treats." She'll be eager and alert to your every command and able to give a performance that makes it look as if she has written the piece of music herself.

Left Is it bedtime? Listening to a lullaby makes this little dog so sleepy, he can't hold up his head any longer.

Editing Your Music

Q *Help! My chosen piece of music is too long for my class. I'm allowed a maximum of three and a half minutes (a five per cent overrun is permitted) and my recording of "I Could Have Danced All Night" goes on for four and half minutes. It's my absolute favourite. Do I have to try and find something shorter?*

A If it is your favourite piece of music, I'd stick with it instead of changing. You will have to listen to it over and over again, so it's better to have something you like. There are a number of options open to you.

Another cover Have a look in your local music store. You may find another cover of "I Could Have Danced All Night" which is shorter and just right for you. It could be an instrumental rather than a vocal production. Perhaps it will be a more jazzy or soulful rendition compared to your copy at home. The tempo and phrasing may be a little bit different, but the tune will be essentially the same. But it will still be recognisable as your favourite.

Cutting the introduction Make a copy of "I Could Have Danced All Night" on to another CD or cassette tape and cut it so that it is the length you want. Do you think the introduction is a bit fussy and long-winded? Don't put your finger on the record button until it is finished. But you will have to dive straight into your routine when you come to dance it.

Cutting the ending Or maybe the ending goes on and on and on. If the finale is built up in bite-size sections, just lift your finger off the record button at the end of one of these sections before the repeat starts. Very easy!

Fade Or make a recording of your selected piece of music and fade out the ending. Choose the place you want to fade to and turn the volume down as you approach it. Be careful not to do this too quickly or too slowly. And don't inadvertently twitch the volume knob or your recording will sound like it has hiccups. Try to keep it nice and smooth. It's a question of personal preference, but eight beats is about right for me, long enough to get into and hold a finishing pose.

Audio editing software There are a number of music editing programmes that you can download onto your computer. You can cut, copy and paste parts of your tune or add special effects like echo or noise reduction. Some are very sophisticated programs while others are more basic. They all claim to be easy to use and do a professional job. If you like playing on your computer, this could be your best option.

Word to the wise However you choose to shorten your music, the challenge is to find the best place to cut things short. Your music must retain a beginning, middle and end in order for it to sound like one whole piece. Good luck with the scissors and tape!

__Left__ If you need to shorten your music to fit your planned routine, listen to it carefully so you can identify the best place to make cuts.

Choreographing A Routine

Q *I've chosen my piece of music and I can do lots of tricks with Klinker, my medium-sized crossbreed. But I haven't a clue how to do choreography. Do you have any tips to get me started?*

A Doggy dancing is hard work! You not only have to be a dog trainer, but a good choreographer if you want to show Klinker off at his best.

Choreography The choreography tells the dancers, you and your dog, how to move to a piece of music. Good choreography will let you show off your skills. It will fit the music and entertain your audience. Bad choreography will make you look a dummy and send your best friend asleep. So it is important to take some time to try and get it right.

Listen closely Listening skills are important and can be improved with practice. Play your music over and over again. You'll hear something new and different each time – the sound of a violin, a change of tempo or a crescendo that you missed before.

Count the beats Tap your foot to the music. Most pieces of music are composed of a series of four pulses or beats so count one, two, three, four. Some beats will be stronger than others and these will occur in a regular patterns – four, eight or sixteen. If your music is being sung, listen to where the singer takes a breath and you will be on the right track.

Listen for the refrain Your music may have a refrain or chorus that is repeated over and over again. If so, fit a series of moves or single trick to the refrain that you can perform every time you hear it. For example, when The Beatles sing "I wanna hold your hand", you could train Klinker to put his paw in yours.

Tempo Keep an ear open for tempo, the overall pace of the music. The tempo will often set the tone of your routine. If your music is fast and furious, it is more likely to be chirpy and cheerful. If it is slow, it is more likely to be solemn and mournful. Make sure your moves are in keeping with the tone.

Starting and finishing pose Start your routine with something that will make the judges sit up and pay attention and finish with something they will remember. Don't just stand slumped in the middle of the hall and wait for the music to begin. What about putting your dog in a beg or sitting on a prop? And when the music ends, where is your dog? On your back? Lying in a down with a paw covering his face? Try to come up with something memorable.

Flash moves Some dogs have signature moves that are flashy. Is there something that Klinker does that is eyecatching and unusual? Make sure it is included in your dance programme.

Use the space Don't centre your whole routine in one corner of the room. Keep moving and cover the floor. Make use of all that empty space.

Orientation If you are dancing for the judges, make sure that you face them and that they can see you and your dog's best features. No judge wants to look at a competitor's bottom for three minutes.

There is no right or wrong way to choreograph a routine. These are just some of the points to keep uppermost in your mind. Some people just listen to their choice of music over and over again, get up and try some moves and then put it all together. Other people need to write it all down on paper and produce reams of diagrams and floor plans. Whatever works for you.

"Hmm. Once I get up, how do I get down again?"

Beginning And End
This is a great finishing pose. The judges won't forget you balancing your dog on your back in a hurry.

Point it to the ground for a bow.

Left *Umbrellas can be so versatile. Use it closed or open for imaginative poses and stunts.*

Above *A cane is an accessory that can be used to lure your dog into different positions and through different choreographed movements.*

And they make good jumping sticks.

Travelling Through Space

Q *I've just finished choreographing my routine and it is a real space saver. Josie, my Cairn Terrier cross, and I do all our stuff right in the middle of the floor. I won't get lost wandering hither and thither and end up in the wrong spot. This has happened to me in the past and I was so confused I tried to exit through the entrance. What do you think?*

A Everyone has tried to leave the ring by the same route that they came in at some point in their dancing careers. It's a common mistake and gives the ring stewards a chance to jump up and down on one leg to try and get your attention at the exit. It's not something that the judges will mark and it is no reason to do all your moves in the middle of the floor.

Start and finish You can start and finish your routine anywhere on the floor. Your starting and finishing points don't have to be in the same place – one can be in the centre and the other can be off in a corner – but they do have to be in the ring.

Floor space You are not being challenged to perform all your tricks on top of a beer barrel! Make use of the floor space or you will lose points. The dimensions and surface of the ring will be published in the show's schedule for example, "grass surface with a ring approximately 18 x 15 yd" as well as telling you on which side the judges will be sitting. A dance programme that flows and moves across the floor will keep the judges' interest.

Floor plan You don't need a complex floor plan to stay on the move. Sometimes something simpler is easier to remember and just as effective. Some handlers find it helpful to think of a number or a letter of the alphabet to use for a floor plan; for example, a figure of eight allows you to reach all the corners or a room as well as traversing the centre of the floor twice. Other handlers imagine their floor plan is a road map. The heavily used routes where they can get up speed are super highways and the less frantic, quieter tracks are country lanes. Whatever works for you to help you negotiate your way around the ring.

Catch your breath You can punctuate your routine with a few poses. If Josie can hold a bow or a beg, you will both have a chance to pause and catch your breath, but your dog must not be stationary for more than ten seconds.

If you choreograph your routine and have a simple floor plan in mind, you will not be wandering here and there aimlessly or getting lost. Knowing where you are going and what you are going to do when you get there, will allow you to perform your routine with confidence. Wherever you go, Josie will go and I am sure that she will be a highly competent co-pilot.

Above Poses are the perfect place to catch your breath. But don't remain stationary for too long and think carefully about how you are going to start moving again.

Dancing Deportment

Q *I've been reading the rules and I don't understand what is meant by "deportment". I think of deportment and I think of girls at finishing school walking around balancing books on their heads to improve their posture. What does that have to do with heelwork to music competitions?*

A Yes, that is the picture that springs to my mind too when I hear the word "deportment". I think of the good manners and taste that have been stamped onto the young people of any particular era or culture. Similarly you can stamp your dance routine with the type of deportment that will immediately tell the judges about its theme, dance type and place in history.

Changing times The rules of good behaviour are linked to polite society but these rules evolve and change with the times. For example, most young ladies no longer need to know how to manage a long gown or execute a curtsy. A handshake will do in these days of equality of the sexes. Nonetheless, we base many of our judgements about people on deportment. If you pick as your tune "The Rumble" from *West Side Story,* any curtsies or other cultivated gestures would look entirely wrong.

Dance appropriately The heelwork to music judges are looking for appropriate conventions of deportment in your dance routine. You need to choreograph movements that are complementary to your music and how you stand, walk and gesticulate should reflect the theme and type of dance. Try to meet the expectations that the music will arouse in the audience. For example, a few high capers will suit a traditional English Morris dancing folk tune. And marching along with a ramrod straight back is perfect for a military tune, especially if you throw in a salute to the judges. Deportment is an important tool to help you to interpret the music but it must be matched to your own capabilities. If you can't do high kicks, don't choose the can-can!

Inappropriate deportment Unless you are aiming for laughs, don't walked bow-legged like a cowboy shooting from the hip to the strands of a gentle waltz. That said, unusual juxtapositions can be very successful – a male dancer pointing his toes to *Swan Lake* will certainly catch the judge's attention. But it takes a lot gumption to pull it off. And what makes it funny is that the deportment is entirely appropriate to the music despite the dancer being a hairy man wearing tights.

Put your books back on the shelf. There is no need to try and balance them on your head for your heelwork to music routine – unless you are trying to conjure the atmosphere of a privileged girl's finishing school, of course.

***Left and above** Set the mood with expressive arms and postures appropriate to your music.*

Barking Out Loud

Q *I've had a bit of a barking problem with my black and white collie, Thomas. It is now largely under control but every now and again he'll emit a whine when he is excited. It's as if he thinks it's OK to make noise as long as his mouth is shut. Will I be marked down at shows for this?*

A Some dogs can make a noise even when their lips are zipped and they are sworn to silence. The less noise Thomas makes and the less the judges hear him, the less he will be marked down. The maximum numbers of marks that a judge can deduct for barking is four.

Proportional marking The rule of woof is that if the whole routine is spoilt, four marks are deducted. Half the routine ruined, two marks and so on. If Thomas only barks or whines when he is spinning but the rest of the routine is unblemished by extraneous canine noise, you would not receive the full penalty.

Continuous barking Loud barking that carries on non-stop throughout your routine will not only give the judges a headache but it will spoil their enjoyment of your performance and make judging difficult. How can they tell if you are in time if they can't hear the music. How can you hear the music? Can your dog hear your commands? Deductions for barking in this case would be a whopping four marks and a couple of aspirin.

Whimpers and whines How good is the judge's hearing? Loud music will cover up any whimpers that escape from Thomas, especially if he has his back to them and is on the other side of the ring. But you will certainly hear them and you will have to decide whether you ignore them or tell him to be quiet. How these whines are marked may well vary from one

judge to another depending on whether they have been heard and to what extent the noise ruined their enjoyment of your routine. Some breeds can whinge just like a musical instrument and it is impossible to tell if the noise is on the recording or coming from the dog.

Barks allowed There are occasions when it is acceptable for your dog to bark. Barking is excused if you have stepped on your dog's toe and he yelps in pain. And you can forgive a dog for grunting if he lands heavily on the floor after a jump. It is also all right to incorporate barking into your routine if it can be justified and is on cue; for example, during a rendition of "How much is that doggy in the window? Woof! Woof!".

Barking, woofing and whining should not be overlooked by the judges, but sometimes it is. Judges are not superhumans who can see and hear everything all of the time. However, if you know you have a barking problem your best course of action is to continue to address it rather than ignore it and risk losing marks.

Right *Listen to your dog's bark. Try to work out what he is trying to tell you.*

Handling Your Dog

Q *I am fuming! I have just come home from a show where I was docked for handling my German Shepherd, Dolly. All I did was pat her while she was heeling. My trainer keeps telling me to praise and reward her. Well, you can't use treats so I thought a pat on the head would be OK. Am I losing my temper over nothing?*

A Losing your temper is not very constructive. Instead try to understand why the judges deducted marks and the different types of handling that are discouraged.

Harsh handling Harsh handling is when unnecessary force or physical coercion is used on a dog. If you push your dog into the Down and she lands with a heavy thud and crack of bone, you've overdone it. If you pulled the fur on your dog's cheek to get her attention and she has squeaked in pain, you've hurt her. There are other ways to get your dog to do what you want and you will pay the penalty with the judges for acting in this way.

Intentional handling You've told your dog "Wave" three times during your routine and she looks perplexed, so you have gently tapped her paw with your finger to remind her what to wave. This is an example of intentional handling for training purposes. Your dog is not responding to your cues so you need to help her out. You will be marked down but it is better to be marked down than to allow your dog to wallow in confusion.

Accidental handling There will always be times when a dog brushes too close to its owner. Dogs can take you by surprise by jumping up or becoming amorous and leaning on your thigh. Well, no one planned for that. This type of physical contact will not be marked adversely.

Acceptable handling If handling is obviously an integral part of the routine, it will not be marked down; for example, a dog that jumps onto his

owner's back for a piggyback ride on the same beat at every performance. This is choreographed handling.

Rewarding in the ring There are many ways to reward your dog in the ring besides a pat on the head or a kiss and a cuddle. You can tell Dolly that's she is a star as often as you like without incurring any faults. If Dolly loves jumping in the air, let her do so as a treat after a particularly stylish stretch of heelwork. Or if Dolly has been struggling to grasp a new move and executes it perfectly in the ring, it might be worth stroking her head her anyway and losing the points. Or be a bit devious and change your choreography so that a pat on the head is part of the routine!

But shaking hands may be in the script and cued.

__Left__ Holding your dog in the heel position would not be acceptable at a competition.

So hold your dog's paw lightly.

SOLVING PROBLEMS

Training is never plain sailing. You can encounter problems at any stage during your doggy dancing career. No one is perfect and mistakes happen no matter how hard we try to avoid them. But by trying to understand your dog's behaviour and find solutions to problems, you will also find out a lot about yourself.

Mini Dogs Have Mini Mouths

Q *It takes ages for my toy poodle, Abra, to find, chew and swallow a treat. By the time Abra has located and finished her titbit, the rest of the class have moved on to the next exercise. We never catch up. Have you any suggestions that may help?*

A Everything about the toy breeds is miniscule. And that includes their mouths and tummies. Treating with titbits can be difficult. The smaller the treat, the harder it is for Abra to find, especially if you've thrown it a long way and it's hidden in long grass. The bigger it is, the easier it is to locate but the longer it takes to chew. And what is just a small cube of chicken for a Golden Retriever is an entire meal for Abra. He'll be too full to want any more.

The trick is to not only carry a variety of treats so you have a choice depending on what and where you are training but to polish your delivery of them.

Small is beautiful If you are going to be doing a lot of repetitions, ensure your treats are small enough for Abra to eat quickly without choking. Choose something he can eat neatly. You don't want to use food that will crumble and encourage him to hoover the carpet. The sooner he can swallow it, the sooner he'll be ready for the next treat, so go for something that has chewability rather than crunch – unless you are training Abra to do an impression of a nutcracker.

See it and believe it! If you are delivering a treat to Abra by throwing it, make sure he sees it leave your hand and land. You are a long way up and there are no prizes for throwing a slice of frankfurter the farthest. Lob it too far up in the air and he will lose patience waiting for it to float back to earth. He'll give up and ask, "Was that an unidentified flying biscuit or am I dreaming?"

Bowling practice Go to your local bowling alley and practise hitting those pins. It will help you to polish your treat-throwing techniques. Bend your knees, lunge and take the treat past Abra's nose and eyes. If he doesn't see that sausage slice at the start of your throw, he stands no chance of following it to its end. And release the treat in a low arc, not up into the clouds. Keep it on Abra's eye level. Don't throw too far. As well as a small mouth, Abra has short legs and you don't want to wear him out. If your treat rolls and bounces when it lands? Great! Abra will not only be able to see it but hear it.

Sticky You'll never be able to bowl a sliver of ham any distance. Some treats are determined to stick to your fingers. Practise flicking them off with thumb and forefinger and improve your aim. Oops! If that one hit the husband, maybe it would be safer keeping these treats for moments when you want to reward Abra directly from your hand?

You will soon be a titbit connoisseur and Abra will be leading his class.

3 The sooner your dog finds and swallows his treat, the sooner he'll be ready for more. If your dog fails to find a treat and looks like giving up, don't disappoint him. Throw another so it hits the ground near him.

3

Above Little dogs are big on personality but have little mouths and little tummies. Make sure your treats and titbits are little too.

Ready, Steady, Treat
Small treats last longer than big ones. Be prepared. Cut treats into bite-size morsels before you go training so you have a ready supply.

2 Your treat should be visible when it lands. Don't make your dog hunt for it.

Bowling A Treat
1 Lunge and sweep your treat past your dog's eye line so he will see it leave your hand.

Barking Mad

Q *I can't stop my dog from barking. It's worse at shows, especially when he weaves or walks backwards. Trio is a working sheep dog and gives everyone a headache as his woofs reverberate round the training hall. I know the judges are going to deduct points and dread him opening his mouth. Should I buy myself ear plugs?*

A No. If you wear ear plugs, you won't be able to hear the music. And worse, you won't be able to listen to what Trio is trying to tell you when he barks.

"This is so exciting!" And it is. You are jumping up and down and waving your arms in the air. You are scurrying here and there across the floor. How is Trio supposed to know that these antics are carefully orchestrated steps, not an attempt to wind him up? He will find a slower pace of music and softer choreography less stimulating. If Trio finds specific moves exciting, like weaving, send aways or walking backwards, leave them out until he can control himself.

"This is so confusing!" You've done a move millions of times. But suddenly Trio doesn't get it. He doesn't understand what you want him to do. Sometimes dogs have a mental blank, especially if their handlers are off-key, so they bark. Trio can wave a paw, but after heelwork? You looking like thunder and repeating the command over and over is only going to make him bark more. So, make sure you practise any new moves in different sequences and, if Trio looks muddled, blame yourself for not being as thorough in your training as you should have been. Start from the beginning again.

"You are so frustrating!" You will hear this bark when you have stopped in the middle of your routine because you don't know what comes next. And it is usually during an important competition that you will hear it. No wonder. You are much more comfortable performing at home or in training than at a show. With the judges watching, you'll be nervous, no matter how much you practise. Make sure you know what comes next, and give your commands confidently and positively. Trio won't have an excuse to open his mouth and complain.

"Come on, come on COME ON!" Hear this bark and you know Trio is putting on the pressure. If you don't lift your leg up faster and higher for the next leg weave, he'll explode. There is a hint of desperation in his voice and his body posture may even be a tad confrontational. If you don't hurry up and decide if you want him to circle to the right or to the left, he'll decide for you. Turn your back on Trio, leave the floor. He's on the verge of taking the lead and who wants a dance partner who is so vocal and rude? Be consistent and stop the fun as soon as he barks. I know that show entries can be expensive, but it's better to forfeit a few classes that forever losing points for excessive barking.

Not so much jumping, as barking for joy !

For many dogs, barking is as natural as breathing and can be as addictive as cigarettes. You can fit Trio with an anti-bark collar or carry a water pistol to spray him the second he opens his mouth to complain at you. They may help him to kick the barking habit; however, if Trio is barking because he is frustrated or confused on the dance floor, you must polish your handling skills and timing. Trio will be a quieter dog. He'll be able to hear what you are saying and will follow your lead, not his.

Snipping The Nip

Q *I have a very excitable working sheep dog called Bryn and recently he has started to grab my sleeves or trouser legs. There's no way I can do an arabesque with a dog hanging off my ankle! I'm afraid he is going to cross the line and nip me if I don't do something about it now. Can you help?*

A Nipping hurts. Have you thought of dancing to the theme tune from *Camelot* as an armoured Knight of the Round Table? Or choreographing your dance steps so that your arms and legs are always crossed to cover and protect the more sensitive parts of your body? You need to take steps now to snip nipping in the bud.

Herding instinct Nipping is in a collie's job description. Giving a dozy member of the flock a nip is all part of a day's work. When you slow down or hesitate, this is when Bryn will give you a nip to get you to move faster or change direction. Unlike sheep, we don't have a woolly fleece to protect our skin. We puncture.

Anticipation If you worry that Bryn is going to nip you, you are bound to be less focused on what you are doing and you'll slow down. You'll be thinking about tears in your clothing rather than mapping the floor. Bryn will know your mind is elsewhere and give you a nip.

Know your routine It's not uncommon for handlers to lose the plot and have to make up their routine as they go along. In the middle of a performance, they hesitate and substitute one move for another or slot in something completely new. Hmmm, what comes next? And this is the split second when Bryn will nip your sleeve to pull you back on track. You shouldn't need to take time out on the floor to think. Every move should be carefully planned in advance.

Commands and cues Bryn is not a mind reader. Fail to give him a command or cue clearly and he will think about giving you a reminder with his teeth that he is waiting for orders. Make sure commands are easy to read and understand. You don't have to shout but you do have to be clear. If confused, Bryn may nip in frustration.

Curb his excitement Keep it low key. Avoid over-stimulation. The more you throw your arms about, the more Bryn will be tempted to grab them. Keep your movements controlled and understated while Bryn learns to maintain composure. Stay away from circling moves that mimic herding – Bryn could mistake you for one of his lost lambs!

Still nipping If Bryn forgets himself in the heat of the moment, tell him to go "Down" and stand still until he has remembered his manners. Or turn your back on him and leave the room so he is alone on the dance floor. Either way, you don't boogie with partners that flash their big teeth and so the fun must stop.

With preparation and patience, Bryn should lose the urge to nip. Good luck!

Right *If your pet accidentally nips the hand that is feeding him, it will hurt.*

Mad Manic Collies

Q *Twister is a manic collie. He loves training but goes wild. I've tried exercising him before training to tire him out but his energy is limitless. I've tried doing lots of heelwork before class to calm him down, but that just wound him up even more. I need to reverse the polarity and help him relax. What can I try next?*

A You've got one of those mad collies that launch themselves into orbit. They love to work and must always be doing ... anything! You need to help Twister to keep his feet firmly on the ground and still in our solar system.

Herbal remedies Many handlers swear that herbal remedies such as skullcap or valerian help their dogs to calm down. But before you give any pills or potions to Twister, it's a good idea to have a chat with your vet about his hyperactivity. He is familiar with your dog and best placed to advise you on medication. And remember that although herbal remedies might help Twister to relax, he may still be unable to contain himself in highly charged environments like your training hall or show venues where everyone is jigging about and clicking their clickers.

Stay cool Dogs are quick to pick up on your adrenalin levels. If you are excited to get to class, Twister will be excited too. Don't turn into a nervous wreck in anticipation of Twister going hyper the moment you walk through the door. Instead of winding him up with lots of heelwork, sit down and keep quiet. Twister will follow your example.

Go slow You have all the time in the world. You don't have to lure Twister through a roll over at a hundred miles an hour. Keep your treat in your hand and keep the movement slow and steady. Don't run anywhere if you can walk. If you try and do everything as fast as possible, your adrenalin levels rise. Keep them low, by thinking slow. Twister will have time to metabolise your instructions without getting indigestion through excitement.

Planet Earth Keep Twister on the same planet as you. It's a team thing. If Twister gets something right, praise him. Do it calmly. Smile. Feel joy in your heart. Don't jump up and down and clap your hands above your head yelling "Good boy" in a squeaky voice. If you do, Twister is departing for the nearest launch pad. And if Twister gets something wrong or goes over the top, don't stamp your feet, throw expletives at him or grab his collar. That won't keep his feet on the ground. It will only excite him further. Instead use a marker phrase like "Oops" or "Oh dear" so that Twister knows he has goofed. Calmly start again and see if he can get it right.

Out of orbit If Twister is on the ceiling, it's too late. Twister has lift off. Once he is in orbit, rather than fight gravity, put him back into the car or into an indoor kennel in your training hall. You both need some time out to let your adrenalin levels return to normal.

Good luck and happy landings with your canine astronaut.

Above and right
Although you don't need a prescription to buy herbal remedies like valerian, you should discuss your pet's hyperactivity with your vet first.

Lacking Social Graces

Q *My two year old Beardie, Max, isn't very sociable. He wags his tail at other dogs and then tries to take a chunk out of them. There are so many dogs at shows – waiting to go into the ring, running around the exercise area or sitting with their owners. I'm so afraid that he is going to get into a fight. Should I give up and stop going out?*

A If only you could guarantee that all dogs would have good temperaments. For whatever reason, few are complete angels. They have pluses and minuses and it is this unevenness and unpredictability of character that makes every dog an individual surprise package.

Home alone Don't stop going out. You'll both go stir crazy. Together you can learn how to handle those awkward situations. The first person to visit for help is your vet.

Your vet There may be a medical reason for Max's behaviour and it's a good idea to rule that out first. If I have a tooth or belly ache, the rest of my family run for cover. I'm operating on a short fuse. It's the same for Max.

The dog trainer Your dog trainer will have experience of dealing with dogs like Max who lack social graces and behave like grumpy old men in public places. Discuss possible strategies for dealing with awkward or inflammatory situations. Not all trainers are qualified to give practical advice on problem dogs, but they are usually happy to support and implement recommendations from those that are.

The dog behaviourist Put Max on the behaviourist's couch. Does Max react to other dogs because he is nervous or afraid? Is he being protective, territorial or dominant? Are there psychological and environmental causes for his actions? He will assess Max and suggest a remedial programme you can follow.

Above *Take steps to help your dog cope in social situations, such as walking to the ring in the company of other dogs.*

Over to you In the long run, it is up to you to implement anything your vet, trainer or behaviourist recommends. Once you have an understanding of what is going on in Max's mind, you will need to be vigilant. Are there dogs playing chase behind you? How will Max react? Have you found a seat that gives Max enough personal space so that he can relax and be comfortable? Who will see the out-of-control retriever headed your way first – you or Max? Should you risk taking Max into a very crowded room and have both of you on tenterhooks waiting for something to happen or would it be easier to leave Max in the car or his crate until the room empties a bit?

You have time on your side. Max is a youngster and hopefully will get some doggy protocol under his belt as he gets older. The world and all that is in it will become less threatening and more familiar. With luck, his enemies will become his acquaintances and finally friends. But he may be like Greta Garbo – "I want to be alone". Stay on your toes. Max can be a happy dog with just you and the music for company.

Party Animal

Q *My year-old Rough Collie is a party animal. Kestrel loves other dogs and if he sees one, watch out! Get out the balloons and party poppers. Kes was (and still can be for a few minutes) absolutely brilliant at dancing. But lately he leaves me to look for four-legged friends to chase. If he spots a chum out of the corner of his eye, off he goes. What should I do?*

A Kestrel is still a baby and the big world out there is full of surprises and temptations ... and parties! Don't take it personally if Kes leaves you to boogie with a friend.

Where to party? You are half way there. You say you can achieve a few minutes of brilliant work from Kes. Well done. Continue to teach Kes that the best place to party is with you and in the ring. Make your training sessions irresistible good fun and call a halt to them when Kes still wants more – not when he is tired and has lost interest. That's the time he'll be looking around for a new playmate.

Distractions in training Wherever you go, you'll encounter distractions – squeaky toys, dropped titbits, new people and barking dogs with party hats. Distractions are everywhere. Some dogs find the lines painted on the gymnasium floor fascinating. Some are experts at finding biscuits squashed between floorboards. If Kes leaves you to investigate any of these, what are you going to do?

Rules of the game Make sure that the rules of the training games you play with Kes are clear and comprehensible. Perhaps he is confused with the "Down" and the "Bow". Maybe he is flummoxed by the prop you've introduced. If Kes doesn't fully understand the rules of leg weaving, he will go and look for some his canine buddies and a bit of rough and tumble. This he does understand.

What can you do?

- Don't let it happen in the first place. Make sure you have Kes's attention before you start training and stop before you lose it. Better lots of short sessions than a long one that gives Kes's eye an opportunity to wander.
- Have faith. If the other dogs in your class are on the lead or under control with their handlers, Kes's search for a playmate will be thwarted. He'll return to you as you are the only dance partner available willing to give him goodies in exchange for a few twists. Don't call him. Just wait. He'll be back if he wants some fun.
- And when he returns, you can give him a big smile. Quick ask him for a twist or to lift a paw. Yeah! You've played a short game by the rules and Kes has earned a biscuit. Those other dogs were real bores when compared to you.

Kes sounds a very lovable dog. You'll soon be not only his best friend but his favourite playmate. He won't want to boogie with anyone else and his career as a social butterfly will soon be a thing of the past.

***Left** I've had invitations from all my friends but the only one I want to party with is **you**!*

Class Bully

Q *I loved my heelwork to music until Beluga started coming to my class. Beluga is big crossbreed that picks on Pepper, my Papillon. Pepper has turned into a wilting flower and is always looking over her shoulder in case Beluga is going to pounce on her. I spend the whole class worrying about her instead of paying attention to my instructor. What should I do?*

A It certainly sounds as if the fun has gone out of your training and you will have to take steps to remedy the situation. First have a think about what is going on. It may not be as simple as it seems.

Reading the signs Is Beluga the class bully? Is Pepper the temptress? Does Beluga want to rip Pepper into little pieces or does she want some friendly rough and tumble? Does Beluga think Pepper has overstepped the mark when she is perched on your lap and yearn to put her in her place on the ground? Does Pepper think Beluga is a piece of dirt because he is lying down below her on the floor? Did they both zoom in on a piece of cheese left under a chair at the same time? Is their discord a result of poor social graces? It is difficult to tell from what you have told me. But it is certainly the case that it needs to be sorted out. Whether it is a clash of personalities, youthful exuberance or an unfortunate behaviour problem, you won't get anywhere looking at it from just one side.

Talk to your instructor Instructors are usually good listeners and want everyone in the class to have happy, well mannered dogs. If you explain how you and Pepper are dreading encounters with Beluga, I am sure that she will take steps to make you feel safer and more secure. Your instructor can give you her reading of the actions of Beluga and Pepper and try to help you relax and enjoy training with your dogs. Sometimes just understanding what is going on and why is enough to defuse matters. In addition, she may put a few plans into action that will make learning easier, for example she may ask you to take turns getting up on the floor or to sit on opposite sides of the room. Her most expedient and simplest solution may be to offer you or Beluga a different class.

Time is a great healer Things may improve over time without any intervention. Wouldn't you be surprised if Beluga and Pepper grew up to become best friends after being sworn enemies! And even when there is no rhyme or reason for dogs disliking each other, they can usually learn to ignore one another and be polite when necessary.

At the end of the day, they don't have to have puppies together; just get along well enough so that everyone can enjoy and have fun learning new things in class.

Right Please don't look at my dog and drool. He's not a snack!

Pressure Cookers

Q *Sizzle use to be a fantastic freestyle dog. He is a Staffordshire terrier cross whippet and we have been competing for about two years. Sizzle use to be so excited to go dancing that I had trouble walking him into the venue! But now, as soon as he enters the ring, his head hangs down and his tail tucks up under his tummy. He looks stressed and pressured and is reluctant to perform. This doesn't help my nerves and I'm very frustrated by Sizzle's behaviour. What can I do?*

A Our dogs take their cue from us whether we are at a show, training or at home. If I fall asleep and snore in front of the television, so do my dogs. If I stress, they stress. Always remember how sensitive your dog is to your state of mind. Your body language and tone of voice will tell Sizzle if you are relaxed or coiled like a spring. He can read you as easily as you read him and you're not helping each other.

Check up Firstly have your vet give Sizzle the once over. Whether the onset of Sizzle's reluctance to go in the ring was sudden or gradual, it is possible that there is an underlying medical problem at its root.

Learn to relax Be as cool as a cucumber. It's not easy but you can teach yourself how to relax. Recite a mantra, meditate your navel, stroke a rabbit's foot. Whatever will help you to control your nerves. Practise relaxing with the same commitment that you practise your heelwork. You'll find it will become easier each time if you do.

Show conditions It is unavoidable. Competition is about coping with pressure and controlling your nerves.

Start with a little challenge and gradually build your resistance. Take part in displays and exhibitions of dog dancing. It is also a good idea to sign up for training days and workshops. All of these things will get you and Sizzle accustomed to performing in front of strangers in new venues and prepare you for the high pressure events

Have fun Fun is what it is all about. Have you put more control and precision into your routine than Sizzle can handle? Is he worried that a mistake will earn him a frown? Has he stopped putting effort into his moves because there is no pleasing you? No wonder his tail is down. Ignore some of the mistakes. Have a game in the middle of your routine. Let him jump up on you and give you a kiss. Loosen up!

Attitude Attitude is more important than a perfectly executed pose. Start rewarding it. If you want a dog with a wagging tail, treat him when he wags it. If you want a dog with enthusiasm, let your control slip a bit. So what if Sizzle puts one foot on a stool instead of two. Do you want a dog that approaches your prop with trepidation or one that can't wait to interact with it?

As Sizzle's attitude becomes more positive, you will have less reason to feel nervous and you will both start looking forward to going into the ring together.

***Left** Dad is stressed. I've given up trying to make him smile. I want to go home!*

Stage Fright

Q *Do dogs get stage fright? My two year old Vizsla, Wanda, is a fantastic performer until she's on the centre of the dance floor. Then she looks blank and freezes. It is so embarrassing. Sometimes she does this when I am trying to teach her something new, too. Why is she doing it?*

A Even dogs get stage fright. And it is so unsettling. The music starts and nothing happens. Has Wanda gone deaf? Where has the keen and competent Vizsla gone? Why is she rooted to the spot? If it happens on a regular basis, your confidence in the ring will slowly be eroded making things ten times worse. Why do dogs get stage fright?

Multi-tasking Competitions are always a bit daunting for a young dog. You are expecting Wanda to look at you and spin as well as keep an eye on what is going on around her – what is that man doing with a video camera? She has not yet mastered the art of multi-tasking and there is too much going on for her to be selective so she just stands still to take it all in.

Perfectionist If Wanda is this type of dog, whatever she does, she wants to do it perfectly. Unfortunately the learning process is fraught with pitfalls. To move forward, Wanda has to take risks and have the courage to make mistakes. And rather than make a mistake, she would rather stay right where she is – thank you very much.

Confidence building The more confident Wanda is in her own abilities and your skill to direct her, the less likely she will be to shut down. Confidence grows over time, but it can be encouraged by simple training exercises that give you the excuse to lavishly praise and treat her. Repetition is another good tool for the dog that isn't sure of her own capabilities. If Wanda is hesitant to give you her paw, ask for it a second time, and then one more time for luck. By the third repetition, she will be sure that you think she is great.

Bonding together Spend quality time together and find out what makes your dog tick. Wanda will reciprocate by finding out how to do her best for you. Instead of thinking, "I give up! I can't do this!", Wanda will think, "I'll have another go because Mum will be there to help me get it right."

Too late Once your dog has shut down, the lights are out. There is nothing you can do to get them back on. It's too late to dangle a steak in front of Wanda's nose. Too late to wave a squeaky toy in her face. Remember that treats and toys are positive training tools. Don't let them inadvertently become associated with times of stress and confusion.

Many handlers become frustrated and impatient when their dog gets stage fright. You are to be congratulated for not jumping to the conclusion that Wanda is simply being stubborn or naughty. I applaud you for trying to understand why it happens before looking for remedies.

Right I can't do this. Everyone is watching. I might make a mistake. Please don't be mad!

Doing A Runner

Q *I enquired about heelwork to music classes at my neighbourhood dog training club. Sadly, they are full but the organiser invited me to come and watch. And oh my goodness! All the dogs were off-lead. If I let Wallace, my wolfhound, off-lead, he'd hightail it to the next county and wouldn't be seen again till the end of the evening. Can I ask to keep him on the lead?*

A You can ask. It never hurts to ask. But there are many reasons to unclip your leash.

Below Make it worthwhile. Reward your dog for returning to you with a treat or toy.

Free time All dogs need time off-lead simply to be able to enjoy being a dog. They love to smell where other dogs have been, roll in the long grass and play with their doggy pals. These are all acceptable behaviours during free time as long as your dog will return to you when called. An out of sight hound that doesn't respond to his name is courting trouble. If Wallace does a runner, whose dustbin is he raiding? Has he joined a gang of miscreant hounds? Has he caused a car accident when loping across the road? For his own safety, he needs to be taught a reliable recall.

Off-lead Any canine discipline will ultimately ask that the dog be worked off-lead. In doggy dancing, a lead can be more of a hindrance than an asset. The lead could get caught around Wallace's legs and trip him up. Worse, you could end up like a trussed chicken if he decided to try a few circling moves. And if you are working on a distance move, it just won't be long enough to stretch between you. The more complex the exercise, the more likely it is that your lead will get in the way. Ultimately, you want to be able to rely on your dog following commands off-lead. Start with the name game.

Name game The most important thing you ever teach Wallace is his name. He should be listening out for his name even when asleep. If he hears it, he should snap to attention in anticipation of some fun. And his name will preface every command you give him – or else how will he know to whom you are talking? Put some treats in your pocket and when Wallace is looking away from you, say his name in a happy voice. If he redirects his gaze at you, click and treat. Practise at home, in the garden and out on walks. Responding to his name gets a reward – not the names of your children or husband. Before you can teach your dog anything, you have to have his attention.

Many happy returns Got his attention? Good. Start your recall training. You may want to join an obedience class where an instructor can give you help and advice on teaching Wallace this important exercise. If you trust Wallace to come back when you call, he will be able to enjoy free time without endangering himself or others. And he will be able to progress to dog dancing and learn those fancy freestyle moves without tying you up in knots!

Sniffy Dog

Q *Diesel is a Jack Russell cross with very short legs and his nose is very close to the ground. He is a nightmare at training because all he does is sniff the floor looking for treats. He ignores every attempt I make to regain his attention. How can I compete against the pieces of cheese and frankfurter my classmates' dogs have dropped on the floor? I have the same problem outdoors where Diesel prefers rabbit droppings to me.*

A No matter how much you feed Diesel at home, he will still be tempted by rabbit droppings! Sniffing is an important part of being a dog. Often he is not being naughty but doing what comes naturally. He could be putting his nose to the ground for a number of reasons.

If training is boring ... Diesel is going to find something else to do, like sniffing. Too many repetitions and too few rewards can make training exercises tedious and dull. Liven things up with his favourite toy. Make dancing with you fun and Diesel will hold up his nose. Instead of sniffing he'll be watching your every move.

If you are boring ... You will lose Diesel's attention. Be an exciting companion rather than a stern disciplinarian. Stop frowning. If you trip over your prop, sit down on the floor have a laugh at yourself. Diesel will take his nose off the ground to see what is so funny and join in the merriment.

If your dog is stressed ... Many dogs relieve stress by sniffing. It is so relaxing and it is something they do really well. You can cause stress by asking too much of Diesel. Three roll overs in a row is enough.

He may not understand an exercise or your commands may be confusing. When he is out of his depth, he sniffs.

If you are stressed ... Your dog is sure to notice. Diesel will wonder what happened to the nice lady who sits and cuddles him on the settee in the evening. The woman at training acts like someone from another planet. Try and relax and be yourself. If you worry about Diesel sniffing the minute you set foot in your training hall, he will.

Below Dogs have sensitive noses and sniffing is a favourite way of learning about the world.

Dogs that think with their noses can be very frustrating. Why not try a few of the following suggestions:

• All venues have smells, but you can minimise them. Don't train after the puppy class. More tempting titbits end up on the floor than in their mouths!

• Teach Diesel a "Watch" command so that he will look up at you and not down at his feet.

• Add a "Leave" command to your toolbox so that Diesel backs off from any interesting treats he finds on the floor. The ones in your pocket are much tastier.

• Play catch-up games. Throw a treat away from you and walk in the opposite direction. Stretch out your arm with a treat between your fingers. When Diesel catches you up, click and throw the treat. Off you go again. So much easier and quicker to return to you for a click than expending energy looking for other dog's crumbs.

Be patient. Diesel will soon be looking at you instead of the floor.

Switching Off

Q *My boy, Finn, is a Miniature Pinscher. For the first few minutes alone on the floor in class, Finn and I are synchronised. My instructor is smiling. Things are looking good and then Finn strolls off to sniff the corner of the room. I call him and click him for coming back and we take up where we left off. Finn is only a year old. I'm not sure if he is being naughty or if I am expecting too much too soon. What should I do?*

A Dogs will switch off in the ring for all sorts of reasons. They are bored; they are stressed or they are confused. And some dogs are like a certain type of lawn mower. If you want the grass cut, you have to keep the safety button on the handle depressed. Take your hand off, and the power cuts out. As Finn is a young and inexperienced dog, this could be what is happening to him.

Keeping your finger on the button I bet Finn is paw perfect at home. In his own back yard, he gets lots of praise and lots of titbits. Power is on. Yeah! Here comes a piece of cheese! Yeah! She said I'm "Finn-tastic"! Finn is getting one reinforcer after another for doing the right thing. So he keeps doing them. But I bet you aren't so free with your rewards in class. Do you feed him less often or try and go without treats? Are you less relaxed, less vocal? No wonder Finn switches off – you've taken your finger off the button.

Power cuts No matter how hard you try to avoid them, they happen. Even the best trainers in the world will have power cuts. It is how you react to one that is important. Our gut reaction is to call our dogs and click and treat them for coming back. Or we run after them and try to entice them back with a chunk of liver. But look at it from Finn's perspective. He is inattentive and starts doing his own thing and you bring out the goodie bag. You are inadvertently rewarding him for ignoring you. Just as you have to reset your lawn mower by taking out the plug and putting it back in after it cuts out, you have to reset your dog.

Reset Finn will get bored studying that table leg and he will finish hoovering all the crumbs carelessly dropped on the floor. And then what? Provided there is little else to interact with in your training hall, he will return to you. So step out and click and treat him for walking with you in the heel position. Or ask for a spin and click and treat. Don't forget to tell him he is a "Good boy". You have reset his motor and your finger is back on the button. Finn is getting rewards for giving you attention and doing things with you.

Now you can finish what you started. The dreaded power cuts will become less and less as you and Finn have more and more fun training together.

Below Engage your dog and make sure that you keep his attention. Focus on finding the "On" button and press it.

Show Offs

Q *I'm so proud of Bronwyn, my terrier cross. I started clicker training her when she was a puppy and she loves dog dancing. I have only to bring out my clicker and she starts doing tricks. She spins, walks back, waves and barks. And I haven't even given a command. Am I lucky?*

A You are very lucky! You have a dog that loves performing tricks so much that what you do is of no consequence to her! Seeing a dog be so keen to please does warm the cockles of your heart, especially if you have had a couch potato pet in the past. But can you think how it might have consequences for future training or competition?

You haven't given Bronwyn a single command. You've haven't used a hand signal and you haven't said the word "Spin". You haven't done anything to indicate that this is the behaviour you want, yet there she goes and your smile is enough of a reward for an unprompted trick. Bronwyn is not listening or watching you for a cue. She is busy doing her own thing, working her way through her repertoire of tricks, one after the other. Why not teach her a "Wait for it" position, a position to wait for instructions from you?

Wait for it Where is the "Wait for it" position? The ideal position is a foot or so in front of you. If Bronwyn is facing you and in the Stand, she is on her feet and ready for action. She can see your hands and face and you can see her. Is she is studying the ground or gazing at you expectantly? Is she there waiting for a sign? Great. Click and treat.

It's a great place to be Don't be afraid to reward Bronwyn for being in this position by clicking and treating. This should be a great position for her. The fun starts here. It's not where you place your dog for being naughty, but the place that your dog waits expectantly to hear what's going to happen next.

Ears cocked Is she listening? When she is in the "Wait for it" position, click and treat for being in the correct spot and standing there. Do it again. And again. Now say something meaningless that your dog won't understand like "fruit salad" or "Mel Gibson". If Bronwyn is still in the "Wait for it" position and hasn't responded, quickly click and treat. She is listening and waiting for a cue that she has been taught.

And listening Now say "Spin" and click and treat Bronwyn for giving you what you asked. She should return to the "Wait for it" position. Such a good girl! So click and treat her for waiting rather than preempting you and trying something else that would get your attention.

There it is! The cue to stand on my hind legs.

Next time you bring out your clicker, Bronwyn will race to the "Wait for it" position. You better be ready for her!

I've been waiting patiently to be told what to do.

Left *When your dog has learned to "Wait for it", he has learned to watch, listen, attend and discriminate.*

Bounce, Bounce Bounce

Q *Panza is an Irish Terrier with attitude and on springs. When Panza walks by my side, it's not so much "Heel" as "Shoulder"! As for getting him to follow a target stick, he keeps jumping up in the air to try and grab it. If I wanted to teach him to be a kangaroo, it would be perfect, but I want him to learn to trot. How do I de-bounce him?*

A A dog with bounce will never have all four feet on the ground at the same time. If you can keep a spring in his step, Panza will look smart and stylish in his work. But if he continues to try and jump over your head, he will look demented and out of control.

The de-bounce It is very simple. Do not click and treat the bounce. With your target stick in your left hand, offer it to Panza to follow. Stretch out your arm and hold it above his nose and out of reach. Walk in a large clockwise circle with Panza on your left at a steady pace. Not too fast and not too slow. You will be looking for a trot, not a gallop.

Lower and lower It is very tiring jumping up at a target. Even dogs with lots of stamina, can't keep at it for too long. Have faith. Physiology and gravity is on your side. Panza will start with lots of ecstatic high jumping but his bounces will gradually become lower and lower as the target stick remains out of reach and moving forward. And no reward. Don't correct Panza or shout at him or tap him on the head with the target stick for jumping. Just keep walking forward as if you are going somewhere special and say nothing. Be patient.

A few steps Keep watching Panza. Look. He gave you a step or two without the bounce. Quick click and treat. He deserves a reward. Hold out your stick again and off you go.

Every time Panza walks a few paces without jumping in the air, mark it with a click and reward him with one of his favourite titbits. If he bounces, ignore it and keep going round in a circle.

By Jove he's got it! I think he has! It is more fun and less tiring to crunch a biscuit than bounce. And the quickest way to get a biscuit is to follow that target stick in a nice trot. The bounce gets zilch and soon disappears. It's so much easier to go forward on four legs.

When you have de-bounced Panza, you can start to extend the length of time you ask him to follow the target stick and trot. He may give a few initial bounces in excitement. Pay them no attention and they will disappear to be replaced by more rewarding behaviour that earns a smile from you. No one will mistake him for a kangaroo (unless you get him a pouch!).

Hold the stick in the hand closest to the dog.

Left *When your dog follows a target stick, ignore bounces and reward trotting.*

Try a circle to see greater stretches of his gait.

Toilet Troubles

Q *It is so embarrassing. I take Oreo, my young German Short Haired Pointer, into class and we do a bit of work. All is going well and then he suddenly takes off and goes into the corner and has a poo. It happens every time! And, yes, I do walk him before I take him into the training hall. Why is this happening to me?*

A If you work with dogs and food treats, accidents like these are bound to happen. Dogs poo and pee. But if they occur on a regular basis, you need to investigate why.

Medical reasons Does Oreo have an intestinal problem that needs the attention of a vet? Perhaps his diet is too rich or he has a food allergy. It's worth a quick visit to the surgery to rule out any medical causes for Oreo dropping his pants in public.

Not so great expectations Oreo had one accident and then another, and now you are expecting him to have a third. You get a little stressed and off-kilter. You are watching and waiting for him to toilet inappropriately. And all that stress goes straight to his bowels. No wonder he is emptying them in a corner.

Attention seeking Did you make a fuss when Oreo pooed in the corner the first time? Did you grab him by the collar, wave a paper towel in the air and run back and forth with disinfectant? How exciting! All eyes on Oreo! It is a great way for him to grab your attention and get you animated.

Preparing for the hunt Dogs like to make sure that they are running on empty before they engage in any exciting activities like hunting, chasing or doggy dancing with you. They perform better and are more comfortable without the extra weight of breakfast. What goes in, has to come out.

Toilet command Now is the time to use a toilet command to encourage Oreo to relieve himself before you take him into the training hall. Puppies are taught to associate a phrase or word with peeing or pooing and as adults they will toilet anywhere and any time they hear it. It's never too late to learn. Pick a time when Oreo is likely to relieve himself. As he sniffs the grass and squats or cocks his leg say "Spend a penny", "Wheezy, wheezy", or "Go toilet". Not too loudly or you'll make him jump.

Left Accidents happen. Make sure that you are equipped to deal with them when they do. If they occur frequently, it's worth investigating the cause.

Closed sign If Oreo is always running to the same corner in the hall, residual smells of urine or faeces will lead him to believe that this actually is the right spot to relieve himself. A table or chair positioned on that spot will make him think that the facilities are closed until further notice.

Prepare ahead If your class is in the evening, feed Oreo in the morning. He will have all day to run empty. Arrive at class early and give him the opportunity to go again. Don't rush him! He may need more than 60 seconds in the car park. If Oreo goes into the hall having done his business outside, you will be more relaxed and confident. If he does have an accident, chill. Calmly get the cleaning stuff. Don't flap. And don't be disappointed if, despite your preparation and self control, still Oreo goes into the corner and poos. It can take some time to build new habits.

Mistakes happen. I have seen dogs competing at Crufts suddenly squat and poo on the floor in front of hundreds of spectators. You are not alone.

Handling Handicaps

Q *Leo is an Affenpinscher who is extremely loveable but strictly on his terms. Because he is so cute, everyone wants to pick him up and pet him. He hates it! And he is not keen on being moved off the settee in the evenings when we get him ready for bed. Will his dislike of being handled hold him back in doggy dancing?*

A Dogs with the "Ahhh!" factor have to learn to tolerate some adoration, especially if they become dancing superstars.

Hands free Training methods that use luring, clickers and target sticks are popular with doggy dancers. They don't rely on physically manipulating a dog into a position. There's no pushing or pulling to get a paw here or an elbow there. But even with hands-free training methods, dogs will sometimes need to be handled. There will be occasions when you or your instructor might want to touch Leo; for example, if he is walking along a plank for a circus routine and stumbles, you might reach out to steady him. If you are teaching the "Bow" you might want to place your hand under Leo's tummy so he doesn't collapse into the "Down". Would Leo object and protest at this sort of handling?

Hands on Try this exercise and see if it helps Leo tolerate handling. Gently stroke Leo around his neck and under his chin. Click and treat as you are petting him. Do it again. And again. Is he enjoying himself? How about if you tickle or are just a bit rougher? A little gentle patting? Don't forget to click and treat. You will be marking your touch with the clicker and rewarding for physical contact. Touching is such a nice way to cement your bond with your pet. You can try the touch for a click exercise with family and friends, but do supervise very young children. Their patting can be a bit like thumping.

Touching you, touching me Teach Leo to touch you. Use the clicker to teach him to press a specific part of his body against your hand on command. His shoulder, hip or bottom. Will he rest his chin on your palm? Keep the exercises short and fun and start thinking of how you might use a body touch in your next dance routine. I remember the Bump. Do you?

Simply irresistible If Leo is irresistible, he has to learn to dish out autographs and accept his fans without grumbling. However, if all the attention is overwhelming and he is going to protest, politely tell whoever wants to pet and paw him that he distrusts strangers. Advise them to approach slowly. Give them a titbit to offer your reluctant diva! All said and done, they may be fans, but they have to respect your wishes. If you think Leo has had enough fuss for one day, tell them. Most people will understand. Enjoy your training and the adoration.

Left *Your dog can learn to enjoy being stroked, but he won't appreciate it if you click in his face!*

Fear Of Sticks

Q *I adopted Zeb, my Staffordshire Terrier, when he was ten months old. I don't know what sort of life he had before he came to live with me, but I think he must have been beaten pretty badly with a stick. Whenever I show him the target stick he backs away and barks. He won't go near it even though it has a ball on the end of it that is smeared with cheese. What should I do?*

A It is so hard to know what is going through a dog's mind, especially if you haven't had him from a puppy, but I think you are probably pretty close to the truth. If Zeb links sticks with beatings, he has good reason to avoid them. So, what can you do about it?

Ground level I bet that when you take Zeb for a walk in the woods, he pays no attention to the sticks on the ground. Is it only when you pick up a stick that Zeb backs off and barks? Start your target stick training at ground level. Rub some cooked chicken or sausage on your target stick and put it on the lawn at home while Zeb is indoors. Then bring him outside and wait. If he goes near the stick, click and treat. If he gets braver and sniffs it, click and treat. You will be clicking him just for showing some interest. It doesn't matter if he sniffs the handle, the middle or the end. He is near it and getting rewarded. Slowly progress to sitting near the stick while he sniffs it. Put your hand on it. Will he still touch it with his nose? Click and treat. Put the stick in your lap while he investigates it? Click and treat. Try kneeling. Click and treat. Take your time – days if need be – and gradually build up his confidence. Eventually you will be able to stand and hold the stick at your side and then outstretched without Zeb retreating away from you. Little and often is best and go back a stage if you think Zeb looks wary.

Long, long, longer A twig is not as threatening as a big stick, so start short. Collapse your target stick so that you can conceal the first 15cm (6in) in your hand. If Zeb sniffs the end, click and treat. When he is driving onto the end of the stick for a click and treat, extend your target stick half an inch. Click and treat. Over days and weeks, you can slowly make your target stick longer until it is at its full length. He will learn that you are not going to beat him with it, but that you are offering it to him so that he can touch the end for a slice of frankfurter.

Disguise Is Zeb frightened of the egg slice? How about an umbrella? How does he react to a penny whistle or a peacock feather? All of these can do the same job as a target stick and are not nearly as scary.

Following the stick Be sure to cultivate a love affair between Zeb and his target stick before you start moving it about and asking him to follow it. If you move the stick too quickly, Zeb may interpret this as the start of some physical threat, especially if you raise the stick above your head. Start slow and small.

Nothing You may choose not to persevere with a target stick. If Zeb has created a really strong negative association between sticks and physical pain, you will have to work very hard to change it. It is perfectly OK to give the target stick a miss. Although target sticks are very useful training tools, they are not the only ones. You may decide to spend your energies on exercises that give Zeb immediate pleasure and are more fun. You have the option of returning to target sticks at a later date if you want to try again.

Hopefully Zed will learn to disassociate the target stick with past blows and you will be able to use it as a training tool. Good luck!

Keeping Your Eye On The Ball

Q *My trainer is always shouting "Throw the ball!" Rafa, my black and white cross, is mad on tennis balls. Truth is, I know that if I throw the ball he normally won't bring it back. And even if he does, I can't get the ball out of his mouth. Rafa loves balls more than liver, sausage or cheese. But how can I include a ball in his training if he runs off with it all the time, and refuses to give it back?*

A The power of food in clicker training often means that a dog's toys are put in a drawer and forgotten. However, they are powerful training tools too and should not be forgotten. Well done to your trainer for recognising that balls, squeakies and tuggies can be valuable rewards – if your dog will relinquish them to you! If you want to include a ball in your training programme, try teaching your dog to give – to place a ball in your hand.

Smallest room in the house Start training this exercise in the smallest room in the house, the bathroom. Shut the door behind you and make sure you have your clicker and plenty of treats. Put the seat down on the toilet and make yourself comfortable. Bounce the tennis ball on the floor or against the wall. Rafa will pick it up and when he does, offer him your cupped hand. If he places the ball in your hand, click and treat. There is nowhere else for Rafa to go. Don't you dare get off your seat to pick it up for him if he drops it. Wait for him to come to you with his toy. It may take some time, but if you are lucky, Rafa will catch on quickly. Repeat the exercise until Rafa is putting the ball in your hand every time you bounce it. You are ready to progress to a bigger room.

Coffee breaks Sit down in your living room with a cuppa. Make sure the doors to the rest of the house are shut. Of course, you are armed with your clicker and treats. And you will be able to throw the ball a little further. But be careful. You don't want to knock over a lamp. Roll the ball along the carpet to a wall. If Rafa brings it back and places it in your cupped hand, click and treat. If not, wait. Stayed glued to your seat. You are not going to chase him. If he wants you to keep rolling the ball, he will have to return to you. Where else is there to go? Keep practising until you have a 100 per cent success rate.

Further And Further
When your dog is reliably dropping his ball into your hand, try rolling or throwing it. For another click and treat, he'll have to return it to you.

1 Let your dog watch you roll a ball across the floor.

The Hand Cup

1 Take a seat. Drop a ball in front of your ball-mad dog. He'll pick it up but there's nowhere for him to run.

Garden party Try the exercise in your garden. Relax in the sun lounger with your clicker and treats. Throw the ball a little way. Rafa will give chase and when he picks it up and looks at you, offer him your cupped hand. Did he drop it in? Fantastic. Remember to click and treat. If not, why should you get off your sun lounger? Wait and only offer your hand as a depository when Rafa is looking at you.

I think you've got the idea. Progress slowly to wide-open spaces with distractions. Chances are that Rafa may want to parade his ball around at class when there are other dogs around he wants to impress. And he may have a mad five minutes with his ball in the park on the first throw. Don't fret, he will settle down when he has got it out of his system. Start thinking of a good command – "Give", "Post it" or "Pocket".

2 Put your hand under his mouth. Click as he drops the ball into your hand for his treat.

2 And send him after it. When he has collected it and looks back at you, offer your cupped hand.

3 If he returns and drops it in your outstretched hand, click and treat as before.

Taking The Lead

Q *Dizzy is obsessed with his lead. He will swing on it for ages when we play tug. However, it doesn't end there. He will grab it out of my hands during heelwork and I have to be careful where I put it or he'll try and fetch it. Yesterday in class Dizzy chewed his lead in half. Can you help?*

A How would Dizzy's teeth fare with a metal chain link lead?

Leads Pick up the lead and it's the signal for a walk round the park to sniff the grass and meet up with friends. Not wonder dogs love their leads. Many handlers make their lead even more desirable by treating it as a toy. They play tug with it. They tie it in a knot and throw for the dog to chase. Or they use it as a target and send their dogs to it. Your lead is always with you even when you've left your toys and treats at home. To toy or not to toy – that is the question.

Your lead is a toy If you are going to use your lead as a toy, then Dizzy must learn the rules of play. The game only starts when you say "Get your lead!" And it ends when you, not Dizzy, have decided that you've had enough. Dizzy must relinquish his lead without a fight and on command.

When you pull and tug the lead, Dizzy will pull and tug right back until he hears the words "Leave" or "Drop", his cue to let go. These are the rules of any game of tug, whatever you use as a toy.

Your lead is not a toy If you believe your lead is an extension of your arm, a physical connection between you and your pet, don't allow Dizzy to chew on it. He may not draw blood, but it is just as disrespectful as mouthing your wrist. Go shopping and invest in a new lead and toy. Don't choose ones that are similar; for example, don't buy a plaited rope lead, if you want a plaited rope toy. And don't tie your toy to the lead's handle. Dizzy won't know where the lead ends and the toy starts. Once you've made your purchases, start a new regime. No games with the lead but Dizzy can chase and tug his new toy whenever you want to have some fun with him. Be consistent and vigilant. Praise Dizzy for interacting with his toy but if he snatches his lead, simply let go of it and walk away. Dogs that grab leads, don't grab your attention. Your message will be clear.

Warning If you do use your lead as a toy you could be asking for trouble. Imagine. As soon as you start your routine, Dizzy dashes out of the ring to bring his lead back to you. Elimination! Worse, your lead will always be dirty, wet and slimy from saliva. Do you really want to hold that? And you will go through a lot of leads, if Dizzy keeps chewing them. But the choice to toy or not to toy is yours.

Left If you play games of tug with your lead, make sure that your dog will let go of it on command.

Games of tug can be exciting and stimulating.

Prop Phobia

Q *Drat it! Ever since someone's elephant's foot umbrella stand fell over and hit my lurcher, she's refused to go into the training hall. Nova was doing really well until then. I've told her that it won't happen again, but she's not having any of it. How do I convince her that other people's props won't jump up and down on her toes?*

A Just when everything is going well, something like this happens to knock you back. One negative experience can jeopardise all your positive training. Props can be very scary, especially if they fall on you. Try and rise above it. If you have laid solid training foundations, you and Nova will soon be making progress in class again.

Vet check It is probably a good idea to have Nova checked by your vet to make sure all her toes are in one piece and they are not causing her any discomfort. Toes are delicate digits and she might be experiencing some residual pain that is keeping the memory of that elephant stand fresh in her lurcher brain.

Take a break The association between Nova's accident and training is writ large in her mind. Have a holiday. Or try another canine sport like agility or flyball. Nova will forget about the umbrella stand if she has something else to think about.

Don't force things The more you try to drag Nova into the hall, the more she will resist you. You could make matters worse. Encourage, but don't coerce. As a rule, it is worth praising and rewarding a healthy interest in objects that can be used as dance props. Your dog should be happy to interact with anything you offer her – no matter how bizarre. Introduce your props carefully so that they are viewed as something that signals fun. If your dog thinks it is an instrument

Left Check that your props can't fall over and frighten your dog or someone else's.

of torture or a focus for confrontation, you have made things more difficult for yourself than they need to be.

Are you bothered? Remember that Nova will always follow your lead. A chimney pot? A moose head? A step ladder? You're not impressed. You see them all the time. Common as muck. If you are bothered, worried or hesitant, Nova will be too. She will jump to the conclusion that the step ladder will indeed fall on her head.

Time passes Although Nova may always be suspicious of elephant's foot umbrella stands, she will eventually realise that they do not get up and pursue her across the floor. Time is a great healer. Nova is going to encounter many strange things as she travels through life and she will probably accept them unconditionally. And a little apprehension is not necessarily a bad thing, especially if Nova should meet any hedgehogs or toads in your garden!

Health and safety Have quiet word with your club's organisers. Suggest an area where all the props can sit until they are ready to be used. Why wait for a handler to slip on a skateboard and break a leg before tidying up the hall? Why wait for a handler's prop to be damaged before allocating safe storage space?

I hope Nova soon recovers her confidence and you are back training soon.

Role Models

Q *I really want to see my instructor work her dog. I've seen her perform but I would love to see her in class interacting with her pooch. I know I would learn a great deal just by watching (and so would my Sheltie, Teflon). But despite my pleading, she keeps refusing. Why?*

A I think she is paying you the courtesy of giving you her all and her everything when she is teaching you in class.

Primary goal The primary goal of any instructor is to impart knowledge and facilitate an understanding between owner and pet – not entertain or show off with their own dog. Your instructor is there to teach you and she is going to give you her full attention from 7 to 8 every Wednesday evening or whenever. Similarly, when your instructor takes her dog into the training ring, she gives him 100 per cent. Someone would get short changed if she tried to do both in your class on a Wednesday evening. However, there are exceptions.

Above *Watching how a handler unwinds with his dogs after a training session can be just as informative as close scrutiny of his ring performance.*

Demo dog If the class is having trouble understanding a move, your instructor may choose to demonstrate it as well as the progressions. Actions speak louder than words. But there are pitfalls. No matter how advanced, a demo dog can still mess things up. "Ah ... this is how not to do it ..." The result is a blushing instructor and the class is more muddled and confused than before.

Role model If your instructor is very accomplished, it is unlikely that her dog will make mistakes. She may take time to give your class a breathtaking performance of her dance routine in the hope that it will motivate you to bigger and better things. Great, it you are inspired but not so good if you think Teflon can achieve in a few weeks what has probably taken her months to create. Worse, you could become disillusioned of getting anywhere, give up and go home.

Every dog is an individual And what works for your instructor's dog may not work for Teflon. You don't know the history of your instructor's dog (he may be a rescue with a phobia about plastic cups). He may be bold while Teflon is mischievous. He may love titbits but Teflon loves rubber balls. You may learn a lot about how your instructor's dog works but not necessarily anything to help you with your own.

I love watching other people with their dogs and not just training. I like to study how they relax with their dogs – do they lie down in the grass together after a hard work-out and cloud-spot? I eavesdrop on them chatting to their dogs before they go into the ring at shows or slip the lead on for a walk. You'd be surprised at the baby talk! Also, seeing how other people handle their dogs when things go wrong is a great eye opener. And I've learned a lot. But when I take my dog to a class, I want the instructor to watch me. I want feedback on my commands and posture. I want 100 per cent from my trainer so I can learn even more.

Caught On Camera

Q *I am very lucky to have a husband who supports me in everything I do, even doggy dancing. He always comes to training to make the tea and get out the biscuits for fellow classmates. And he is always in the audience to watch my performances and give constructive criticism. He doesn't want his own dog, but wants to help me with ours, Bonnie the Boxer. How can I involve him more with my training?*

A Your husband obviously loves both you and Bonnie. And you know the saying, "Behind every successful woman, there is a man ... with a video camera!"

If Christmas is coming or his birthday is next month, buy your husband a video camera. It will become your most valuable training tool. He'll have fun learning how to get the best shots and you'll have a training record on film. The video camera never lies and you'll discover lots about yourself and Bonnie. Punch the playback button to see all your mistakes over and over again. Here are a few likely ones:

Posture Has your trainer been telling you that you are leaning over your dog? Do you keep denying it? Have you protested that you're standing up as straight as a broomstick? Then who is that hunched up person dragging her arms on the floor in the video?

Gait Just what is Bonnie doing with her feet? Try walking at different speeds with Bonnie while your husband films you. Experiment with taking smaller or larger steps. A video recording will show you how your strides are affecting hers.

Timing How good is it? Did you want Bonnie to jump through your arms on that beat? Was she late because you still had your arms by your side when you gave the command to leap? You will be able to answer that question and many others when you see the video.

Tone of voice If you rely on verbal commands, assess your voice. Does it sound at a show as it does in training? Listen to your video recordings. Do you sound desperate and pleading or authoritative and confident? Are you speaking too much or too little? If you don't recognise yourself, neither will Bonnie.

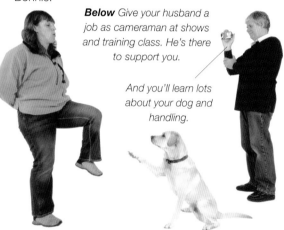

Below Give your husband a job as cameraman at shows and training class. He's there to support you.

And you'll learn lots about your dog and handling.

The unexpected Why did Bonnie lose the plot in that corner? Look at the video and you will see a dog in the front row giving her the eye. Why did Bonnie exit the ring limping? Watch the video and you can see her stub her toe on a pivot turn.

Training v competition Your dog is fantastic in training, but lacklustre at shows. Study your videos of both and compare them. Are you smiling or grimacing in pain as the music starts. What else are you doing differently? All will be revealed on tape.

Video recordings from your training classes and competitions will help you to evaluate your performances and chart progress. Your instructor can tell you, your friends can tell you and your husband can tell you, but you won't believe them until you see it with your own eyes on play back. And look – you never should have worn that wig for the clown routine!

PART TWO

6

FIT FOR
THE RING

Keep your dog and yourself in tip-top condition and you
will enjoy a long-lasting working relationship. Build
stamina and suppleness to improve performance and
reduce the risk of injury. And when teaching new skills to
your dog, monitor progress carefully. If you see signs of
stress or discomfort, play safe and consult your vet.

A Spoonful Too Many

Q *I am doing a dance routine to Mary Poppin's "A Spoonful of Sugar" with my Labrador Retriever, Groucho. Groucho is a true hound and will eat anything. I thought I could fill a glass bottle with some water flavoured with sugar and coloured with red food dye and drip the stuff into his mouth during the chorus. What do you think?*

A I think that this tune from the famous Walt Disney movie will make a great routine for you and Groucho. You could create a motif move that can be repeated each time Mary sings those famous lines, "Just a spoonful of sugar helps the medicine go down". However, I think you are taking the idea too literally and there are a number of reasons why I would encourage you to think again.

Sugar sweet Sugar is not good for your teeth and it is not good for Groucho's. A sweetener will certainly make plain tap water appetising, but what tastes yummy is not necessarily the best thing for you. And you will be practising "helping the medicine go down" several times a day. This is definitely not the best medicine if Groucho is a diabetic or on a special diet. Given the choice, he would probably prefer something flavoured with chicken or cheese.

Food dye Red food dye is reputed to make children hyperactive – goodness knows what a daily spoonful would do to a dog. And, as you have a retriever that is probably prone to throwing his slobber around, watch out if any gets on your clothes – it could stain. More problematic, how will you know if Groucho has bitten his lip and made it bleed? He could be teasing you by frothing coloured saliva and blowing red bubbles!

Choking risk If you drop anything from a height into Groucho's mouth, even water, it could accidentally go down his windpipe and he could choke. If he chokes, Groucho will be immobilised and so busy trying to catch his breath that he won't be able to do any dance steps. You will be skipping alone to the music.

Glass Drop your glass bottle and it could break. Tiny slivers of glass will cover the dance floor for Groucho and the competitors that follow him to step on. What's wrong with clear plastic?

Treat Lastly, your bottle of red sugar water could be construed as a food treat rather than a prop. You would actually be pouring it into Groucho's mouth. Food treats are not permitted in the ring during a competition.

Always consider the health and safety issues of any props you chose. Remember that your dog will not just be using them once in the ring, but over and over again if you practise on a daily basis. In this case, you would be better off miming the action. Teach Groucho to sit and look up at you as you go through the motions of getting his medicine ready. Play make believe. Or better yet, teach Groucho to hold the spoon and you can pretend to empty a bottle into it.

TIP
Become a mime artist if you want to illustrate the words of a song. You can pretend to sail a ship, drive a car or fly to the Moon! Just let your imagination take over.

Because my handler is sitting on the ground, these jumps aren't too high for my little legs. Perfectly safe!

Is that really my medicine or something much more tasty?

Health And Safety

Consider safety issues when you pick a prop and assess risk factors when you choose a dance move. Ensure your routine can be performed without injuring you, your dog or other competitors.

Or is the spoon a clever cue for "Sit pretty"?

This is a safe landing pad and not too far if I fall.

Hold that umbrella firmly or it might drop on my head!

Warming Up

Q *My daughter is fifteen and hopes to become a professional ballerina. She spends a great proportion of each lesson doing warm-up exercises before starting any dance sequences. Should I be doing the same thing with my dancing beagle, Bertie, or is this just something we humans do?*

A Bertie is a ballet dancer of sorts and if you want him to have an injury-free and long dancing career, incorporating warming-up exercises into your training sessions is a must. If Bertie's engine is warm, he will be less likely to pull a muscle or tear a tendon while giving you a twirl. In addition, he will be prepped to give you his optimum performance. He'll be able to jump higher, hold a pose for longer or circle faster. Muscles will be supple, oxygen utilisation will be improved and blood flow will be increased.

Static Learn how to give Bertie a massage. Rub his muscles warm, knead away knots and enhance your bond of friendship by so doing. However, a massage does not simply involve random patting of your dog, so get some expert advice on how to go about it from a professional canine massage practitioner.

Dynamic Warming your dog up on the move is fun and can be done in partnership. Start by walking your dog on the left, then the right. Progress to a gentle trot on both sides. And finally a jog. You don't need to go miles or beat any times. You are simply aiming to go up a notch, not win a race. You'll be nicely warm after this too.

Ladder A ladder or row of small hurdles is another way to get Bertie ready for action without tiring him out. Put a ladder on the ground and walk Bertie through. He must put one paw at a time in each gap (bunny hops are not allowed) and keep looking straight ahead (not at you). Don't let him cheat and try and jump over all the poles to get to the end! Start slowly, so that Bertie can master the technique. As he gains competency, he can walk faster. Make sure to work both the left and right side. This exercise will get Bertie warm and increase his proprioception (awareness of the relative position of parts of his body). A good dancer need to know where his paws are at all times.

Walking The Ladder
Check that your dog is looking straight ahead and putting one leg at a time between the rungs of the ladder.

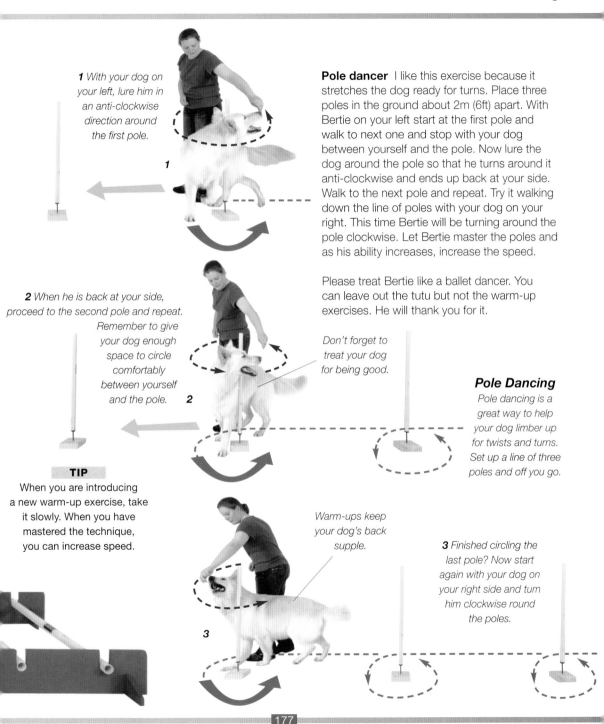

1 With your dog on your left, lure him in an anti-clockwise direction around the first pole.

1

Pole dancer I like this exercise because it stretches the dog ready for turns. Place three poles in the ground about 2m (6ft) apart. With Bertie on your left start at the first pole and walk to next one and stop with your dog between yourself and the pole. Now lure the dog around the pole so that he turns around it anti-clockwise and ends up back at your side. Walk to the next pole and repeat. Try it walking down the line of poles with your dog on your right. This time Bertie will be turning around the pole clockwise. Let Bertie master the poles and as his ability increases, increase the speed.

Please treat Bertie like a ballet dancer. You can leave out the tutu but not the warm-up exercises. He will thank you for it.

2 When he is back at your side, proceed to the second pole and repeat. Remember to give your dog enough space to circle comfortably between yourself and the pole.

2

Don't forget to treat your dog for being good.

Pole Dancing
Pole dancing is a great way to help your dog limber up for twists and turns. Set up a line of three poles and off you go.

TIP
When you are introducing a new warm-up exercise, take it slowly. When you have mastered the technique, you can increase speed.

Warm-ups keep your dog's back supple.

3 Finished circling the last pole? Now start again with your dog on your right side and turn him clockwise round the poles.

3

Fingers And Thumbs

Q *I would like to clicker-train my Shetland Sheepdog, Ely, who loves treats. I'm past my best. A stroke has left me quite weak on one side and my hands are arthritic. I have to hold the clicker and treats all in the same hand and I just don't seem to be strong enough or coordinated enough to do it. Can you help me train Ely?*

A Many handlers find clicking and treating a little daunting at first and are all fingers and thumbs. You have to juggle the treats and the clicker as well as watch the dog. Don't give up. I hope these tips will be helpful.

Choice of clicker Shop around for a clicker that you can hold and operate easily. It might be a good idea to have more than one type of clicker for different types of clicking actions. There is a target stick that you can load with a treat at its end. The clicker is fixed to the handle and delivers the treat for you when you click. This could be perfect for you.

Armchair clicking This is my favourite way to click and just right for winter evenings when it's too cold to train outside. I get comfortable in an armchair and place a button clicker under one foot. On the coffee table I put a couple of biscuits for me and a couple of biscuits for my dog and get training. With my free hands, I can treat whichever one of us deserves it most. With practice, I have developed a great aim and can throw a cube of cheese right into my dog's mouth at ten paces.

Phone a friend Get your friends and family involved. It's a good way to help them understand what clicker training is all about. Explain clearly what you are trying to achieve and ask one of them to click for you so that you can treat Ely. Work as a team and you'll both be proud of the result.

Be ready Make sure that your treats are easily accessible and you don't have to fiddle about to get at them. Do you have trouble opening your bum

bag? Does the zip or the drawstring always gets stuck? Can you get your hand in and out of your pocket quickly? And do you end up with an old penny when you thought you were pulling out a titbit? How about putting your treats in a bowl on a table by your side when training so that they are ready to pop into Ely's mouth? Ely will know they are there and probably will try to help himself – however, he will quickly learn that is not a self-service restaurant. The fastest way to get a treat is by a trick.

The clicker is an important tool, but not the only one. If you find another method of training easier to handle that gets you the results you want, go with that. However, you may find that with patience, your clicking improves so don't give up too soon.

Above *Button clickers work in your hand or under a foot. Try it!*
Right *Tape your clicker and target stick together for ease of use.*

Tummy Trouble

Q *My Samoyed, Snowy, has Inflammatory Bowel Disease (IBD) and is on a strict elimination diet. No treats! No titbits! If he deviates from his dry prescription food diet, Snowy gets diarrhoea. How am I going to click and treat a dog like him?*

A I am sorry to hear that Snowy has been diagnosed with Inflammatory Bowel Disease but Snowy is lucky that his symptoms, namely diarrhoea, can be controlled by dietary management. You will just have to train him without treats or titbits.

Permitted foods Reward Snowy with the food that he is allowed to eat. Measure out Snowy's daily food allowance and put a portion to one side for training. Snowy will still be finding a meal each day in his bowl but the rest of his food he will be earning from you every time you click. You can lure, treat and jackpot with his prescription kibble. Although his permitted food will probably not be as attractive to him as your classmate's forbidden frankfurter, Snowy will eventually grasp that some kibble is better than no kibble at all. He will jump to attention in anticipation of food, even if it is the same old stuff he eats day in, day out.

Toys can help Is there something that Snowy likes to do besides eat? Reward him with a game of fetch with his favourite ball or a game of tug with a rope toy. Some dogs just love making a squeaky plastic bone squeak. Many trainers take steps to ensure that their dogs are just as happy to work for a toy as they are for cubes of cheese or pepperoni. Their dogs will "Sit" just as enthusiastically for a ragger as they will for a piece of chicken. Click and play.

Activities as rewards Don't forget that Snowy can be rewarded with a walk, a paddle in a puddle, or an invitation to sit with you on the settee. If Snowy likes water, click and let him run under the garden sprinkler. Draw the line at the fish pond!

Touch My dogs will do anything for a tummy tickle. How about yours? Does Snowy prefer to have his head scratched or maybe he goes gaga if you stroke his ears? A dog that is tactile will love to be rewarded with your touch. Click and pet. You can grade your cuddles. Good – pat on the head. Very good – caress both ears. Very, very good – all over smooch.

Voice power Use your voice to make Snowy wag his tail in ecstasy. Experiment with pitch, tone and volume so that you can praise him when he is a good boy and give him encouragement when he is trying hard to understand what you want. Many dogs live to make their owners laugh. Click and have a giggle.

Food treats, especially if they are appetising, will immediately open a superhighway channel of communication to your dog. But if you can't use treats because your dog has special dietary needs, it's not the end of the world. Use your dry kibble, switch Snowy on to his toys, give him a cuddle and don't forget to tell him he is a "Good boy". You will be able to teach him all he needs to know to be a dance star without risking an attack of diarrhoea. And you'll never have to clean treat crumbs from your pocket!

Preparing To Stand On Two Legs

Q *My labradoodle Shirley is an amazing acrobat. She can walk on her back legs. I want to incorporate this move into my next freestyle routine as it would look so flashy. However, I am aware that dogs have four paws for a reason and I don't want Shirley to hurt herself. How can I use this move in a routine?*

A You are a very responsible dog owner to think of how different moves will impact on Shirley's immediate and long-term health. Like gymnastic training, you must ensure that your doggy dancing routine develops gradually alongside strengthening and stretching exercises. Nadia Comaneci was the first gymnast to perform an aerial flight series of cartwheel and handsprings on the balance beam, but it took preparation. So you must prepare Shirley for any tricks that entail extra physical demands.

Warm up Get Shirley moving on four legs first. Start with her walking by your side, then a trot and then a gallop. Throw a toy for her to chase or do a few recalls and send aways to get her blood pumping.

Support Shirley probably stands on her hind legs to see if there are any crumbs on the kitchen counter. My dogs do. You are not asking Shirley to do anything outside her natural repertoire but she will need to improve her balance and body tension to hold an upright position for any length of time. Help her. You can support Shirley by allowing her to place her front legs on your arm, the back of a chair (make sure it's not going to topple) or a wall. If you use a cane in your routine, she can lean on this. As Shirley becomes stronger, she will need your help

less. Don't ask her to walk on her hind legs before she can stand on them. And don't expect her to walk the length of your garden on her first attempt. A step at a time is the way to go.

Duration Don't leave Shirley balancing on her hind legs while you go and make a cup of coffee. That's way too long! Build up duration in seconds, not minutes.

Practice You want to maintain back strength with short practice sessions. Overdoing it will only result in injury. I don't think Nadia Comaneci did 50 cartwheels everyday on her way to the gym – just half a dozen good ones when she got there.

Safety Be sensible. Your kitchen floor is slippery and your garden may be full of holes and depressions where your puppy has been excavating for worms in the lawn. Find a surface that is going to give Shirley secure footing as she will be standing on only two of her four feet.

Monitor Whatever tricks you teach Shirley, you must monitor her progress. If at anytime you think she looks uncomfortable or in pain, stop. If she seems reluctant to perform there is probably a reason and it's advisable to see your vet who will be able to get to the bottom of her discomfort.

> **TIP**
> Warm your dog up before asking him to perform any trick like the "High" that requires much more physical effort and co-ordination than usual.

Lots of support here. Not only a paw rest but somewhere to lean.

I'm gonna fall! Increase duration slowly.

Perfect balance. This dog is in control and moving.

Good Preparation

Build technique slowly. Don't be afraid to give your dog support and assistance until he can maintain a pose independently. Monitor his progress carefully.

Double trouble! Two dogs delivering a standing ovation.

Bionic Dog

Q *Last year my collie, Tank, fell off the A-frame in agility and has had a full arthrodesis in his right fore leg. The wrist joint is immobilized with a steel plate. It took a while but Tank has fully recovered from his operation. Unless you knew what to look for, you wouldn't notice that his gait is a little bit different to most dogs. He runs and jumps and chases his Frisbee. Can he dance too?*

A I am so glad to learn that Tank has made a full recovery from his accident and is now ready for some new challenges. Collies become bored easily and love to be active. So, although a return to agility is probably out, I don't see why you shouldn't have a go at doggy dancing provided you call the tune and discuss your plans with your vet.

I've a bad paw but with your love I'll soon recover.

What is it? An arthrodesis is fashioned out of a metal plate and bone grafts and results in the two adjoining bones in a joint fusing together so that there is no movement between them. The joint is very strong but doesn't bend. The majority of dogs adapt very well and their disability is hardly discernible, especially when the rest of the dog is in perfect working order.

Moves Tanks's arthrodesis will limit your choice of moves. Avoid leaps and jumps as they would put too much stress on Tank's wrist joints – the higher he jumped, the greater the impact on his joint in landing and greater the risk that he would hurt himself again. Concentrate on moves that demand all four feet on the ground and keep his weight as evenly distributed as possible. Keep the tricks within Tank's capabilities and he will have a long career strutting his stuff for friends, family and show judges

Symmetry I would lower some criteria. You'll never get his front paws symmetric. For example, Tank will not be able to tuck both his paws underneath his

chest, only one. And when he sits up and begs one paw will be straight out while the other one curls down. I don't think this really matters and a move can still look good while being lop-sided. Lop-sided can be terribly cute!

Gait You certainly won't be marked down for an unusual gait just as you will not be marked for your dog having spots or having one ear bigger than the other. Tank has an imperceptible limp that is mechanical and not painful. Moreover, the dip in his gait is regular and predictable so you will still be able to march him in time to the music.

Monitor carefully It is important to monitor Tank's progress. Don't put Tank in a position where he is trying so hard to please you that he compromises his arthrodesis. Don't ask more than he can physically give you. If he looks uncomfortable after a training session, let him rest. And as soon as you notice any problems, contact your vet for a check-up.

Choreograph a routine that showcases Tank's star qualities and the judges won't notice the fact that he walks with a limp.

Jumping Up And Down

Q *I have an amazing jumping collie cross called Tango. We are competent agility competitors and I want to widen our horizons by trying canine freestyle. I am sure Tango's leaps in the air will astound the judges. Jumping over a fence is just like jumping over my back or an arm or a leg, isn't it?*

A No, it's not.
Because Tango is already a fit agility dog and you know the importance of conditioning and warm-up exercises, you'll be starting your dancing career with an advantage. However, Tango will need to modify and adjust his basic jumping skills when he steps on to the dance floor. He can jump, leap, spring or bounce. Consider some of the following.

Relative heights Hold your arm out straight from your shoulder. It will be a lot higher than a 61cm (2ft) agility jump. Tango can still probably clear it, but a waist-high jump would be just as flashy and easier to achieve. Always think about how height will affect take-offs and landings. Too high and Tango will be adding a parachute to his Christmas list!

Gauging the jump Agility jumps do not move around the ring. People make poor hurdles. They rarely stand perfectly still and have a tendency to wave their limbs in the air. This can make it more difficult for Tango to aim his leap. And in agility, the pole falls out of the cups if the dog knocks it. If Tango knocks you with any force, you'll both end up in a heap on the floor with bruises.

Context In agility, Tango is running from one jump to the next. He has the speed and momentum to gently arc over the pole. This is not always the case in doggy dancing. His jump may be made on the spot or embedded in a round of heelwork. Tango will need to learn to spring in the air with different degrees of acceleration and to time his landings to match his music.

Check the surface In agility, you check the course for mole hills and puddles. You will need to check your surfaces in doggy dancing, too. If you are practising in a village hall, how slippery is the floor? Is it carpeted? If the floor is concrete, Tango might want you to buy him a pair of shock absorbers to protect his shins.

Injury risk Whatever canine sport you participate in, there is always a risk of accident or injury and you should always consult a vet if your dog is hurt or in pain. Doggy dancing is no exception. There will be different sets of stresses and strains to take into account even though Tango is a healthy agility dog. However, most potential injuries can be avoided altogether with sensible preparation and training. Jumps, especially high ones, always get an "Oooh" from the crowd. But it is your responsibility to decide if you are going to jump, adjust the height of your jumps, do fewer of them or none at all when you get to the show. Use your common sense and you and Tango should have a long jumping career together.

Command and use your hand signal.

Hold the umbrella steady.

Above *Where's the next jump? Send your dog round your back and he can return and do this one again.*

Canine Coughs And Sneezes

Q *My bearded collie, Yogi, stared coughing five days ago. At first I thought he had something stuck in his throat, but I now suspect him of sneaking a cigarette when my back is turned! The cough is usually worse in the mornings but is getting better. Yogi is bright in himself and it certainly hasn't affected his appetite. I've a show this weekend and, although I'm sure Yogi is fit enough to attend, I'm worried he might cough in the middle of his heelwork. How will this be marked?*

A Don't worry about the judges or marking. Worry about the competitors who will want to lynch you for bringing a dog to a show with what sounds from your description like kennel cough.

Kennel cough or infectious tracheobronchitis is a highly contagious inflammation of the respiratory system caused by viral or bacterial infections. It will spread quickly in any environment where dogs mix socially or rub shoulders, such as kennels, grooming parlours, dog training clubs or heelwork to music competitions. Severity of symptoms vary. It's a bit like human flu. Some of us are so ill that we simply cannot get out of bed and others just get a few sniffles and go about their business. It is often the old and the young that seem to suffer the most and in animals that are immuno-suppressed, the disease can progress and sometimes be fatal. Coughing can last from a few days to several weeks. And you should be aware that even after your dog has stopped coughing, he can remain infectious for up to three months.

Vet check It would be a good idea to get Yogi checked by a vet. I am only guessing that Yogi has kennel cough. His symptoms may be signs of something else that needs investigation. But if my suspicions are confirmed, your vet may prescribe antibiotics or cough suppressants. He will probably suggest a rest from training too as Yogi may look OK but feel a bit under the weather. In addition, your vet can also give you information on kennel cough vaccinations. Prevention is always better than cure.

Entry form declarations

When you enter a Kennel Club heelwork to music show, you are asked to sign a declaration that says you will "not bring to the Competition any dog, which has contracted or been knowingly exposed to any infectious or contagious disease during 21 days prior to the day of the competition". So in addition to the indignation of all your friends and fellow competitors who will be fuming at you for exposing their dogs to kennel cough, you risk incurring the wrath of the Kennel Club and subsequent disqualification.

It is always better to be safe than sorry. It is unfair on your dog to ask him to give you his best at a competition if he is feeling below par. And your friends will treat you like a leper if they hear your dog cough. Get Yogi checked by your vet.

Above *Dogs can't cover their mouths when they cough or sneeze. Germs can easily spread from one dog to another.*

Managing Fits

Q *My dog Sal is epileptic. She is a Golden Retriever with a high stepping gait and I would love to do some freestyle with her but I'm not sure if this type of training would trigger fits. She is on medication and fit-free at the moment, but I don't want to rock the boat. What do you think?*

A Many dogs with epilepsy live full and active lives. With the right medication and regular check-ups at their vets, they chase rabbits over the fields and sneak up on the settee when no-one is looking just like any other dog. I'm glad to learn that Sal's fits are under control.

Fitting Fits or seizures can occur in your dog for different reasons and they can vary in severity. Your dog will usually become unconscious and may fall over. She may cry out, paddle her feet, salivate excessively and she could empty her bladder and bowels. It can be very frightening and distressing to watch your dog lose control in this way, even for the few minutes that a fit normally lasts.

Epilepsy tests Your vet will carry out tests to determine if your dog is fitting because of epilepsy or some other cause. Epilepsy is the result of abnormal brain activity and the first signs usually come to light when the dog is between one and five years of age. It is important to remember that a diagnosis of epilepsy is not the end of the world as medication can greatly reduce the frequency and severity of fits and your dog can go about his doggy business just like any other dog.

Occurrence Fits usually occur when your dog is nicely relaxed; often in the evening or at night. Or they can be triggered by stressful situations like moving house or specific events like Bonfire Night. Observe Sal carefully and you might be able to spot a pattern that will allow you to predict when a fit is likely

to happen and then take steps to reduce any environmental stimuli that will prolong it. If you have other dogs, move them out of the room. Turn off the TV and turn down the lights until your dog has recovered.

Below *Your vet is best placed to help and advise you.*

Your veterinary professional
I think you should have a chat with your vet. He is best placed to advise you and I am sure you have already developed a good rapport with him during check-ups. Discuss potential risks and if you need to take any specific precautions. If your vet gives you his blessing, you can start polishing your heelwork tomorrow. And don't forget to take a video of your dance routine to your next appointment – he's bound to be impressed!

If you later discover that Sal gets very stressed in classes or that the loud music at shows precipitates a fit, you will need to update your vet. It may be that you will have to increase Sal's tablets or take the decision to continue training but discontinue competing. So keep in touch. By working with your vet, you will ensure that Sal can enjoy a great life on and off the dance floor.

Licky Dogs

Q My sandy coloured dog Trinket is a lovable crossbreed with a licking habit. She licks the knuckles on her front legs till they are wet with saliva and discolored. She looks like she is wearing little brown boots! How do I get the stain out? We both want to look our best when we start competing.

A Licking *(below)*, like smoking, can be a hard habit to give up. The first step is to find out why Trinket is licking her paws so persistently.

Medical reasons There are many medical reasons for a dog to lick, so consult your vet. Maybe Trinket has been worrying a little wart or cyst on her paw and that could be easily removed by surgery. Fleas, mites and fungal infections can also make a dog's feet itchy and cause licking and nibbling. And so can an allergy to something in the environment or certain types of food. Your vet will treat any trauma to the skin caused by Trinket's licking and he may order blood tests, perform skin scrapes or biopsies to get to the underlying cause. Treatment may include special shampoos, a course of tablets or an exclusion diet. When Trinket stops licking, the stain will go away.

Behavioural influences Licking can be a bit like biting your nails – a stress-busting activity that is strangely comforting. For a dog that likes to lick, anything from moving house to a spell in hospital can be a good excuse to indulge. Has something in your life changed recently that would cause Trinket concern? In addition, some dogs lick out of boredom. Leave them at home all day and instead of chewing the furniture, they go to work on their feet. Perhaps you could ask a friend to walk Trinket if you are going to be out? Or leave her an interactive toy to keep her occupied. It can take time and patience to eradicate paw licking if it is behaviourally based. In the short term, you could fit Trinket with a muzzle to help break the habit or try spraying her feet with bitter apple spray. Be watchful and distract her from her paws with toys or treats if you think she is going to start licking.

Stain removal Visit your local pet shop or grooming parlour and buy a stain remover. There are a number on the market that vary in price and mode of application. How successful they are depends on how badly Trinket's feet are stained. Repeated treatments may be recommend in order to restore natural hair colour.

Marking practice The judge will not mark you down for any discoloration of your dog's paws, especially if Trinket is otherwise impeccably groomed. However, if Trinket's performance is interrupted when she stops mid-twist and sets about licking her feet, you will lose points. Is she stressed or has the itchiness become too distracting?

Don't rely on stain removers if Trinket is an obsessive licker. There could be an underlying medical or behavioural issue that needs investigation and could be easily resolved.

Motherhood And Puppies

Q *I have a Miniature Australian Collie called Mouse. I can't go anywhere without people stopping to admire her and asking where they can get a puppy just like her. I'd have no trouble finding homes for her babies and I'm considering breeding from her. Only problem is that she loves training. Would I have to stop and for how long?*

A Ooh! Puppies! They make me go all gooey and I can never get enough of them.

Consultation with your vet If you are going to breed from Mouse, make an appointment with your vet for a chat about her care during pregnancy. There is more to it than the simple act of mating. Your vet will be happy to give you information on whelping and weaning. Motherhood can be an expensive and time-consuming business. Choose Mouse's husband carefully and take steps to make sure that their offspring are happy and healthy.

Pregnancy Just because Mouse is pregnant doesn't mean you have to stop all training at once, especially if she is accustomed to spending lots of quality time with you on the dance floor. However, her changing size, condition and shape will be deciding

factors. It can be hard to keep your balance with a fat belly. Observe her carefully. Some moves may become more risky and some more uncomfortable. Avoid high energy, high impact exercises and choose something less stressful and gentle. Let Mouse pick the pace. As she becomes big and heavy with puppies, she'll tire easily and will probably be happiest sunbathing in the garden. Why don't you have a break too, and join her?

And after Again, let Mouse be your guide. She may not want to leave her babies and they will need lots of feeds. When the puppies have been weaned and gone to their new homes, you can start to gradually rebuild Mouse's fitness. Don't ask her to do hours of heelwork at fast pace to make up for lost training time. She won't thank you. Keep training exercises short and simple. Every dog is different. Some bitches make a remarkably quick comeback and others take a little longer to regain condition.

Let your dog training take a back seat during Mouse's pregnancy. Your primary concern should be Mouse's health and that of the puppies. There are lots of things you can do without Mouse. Listen to the radio and add pieces of music to your play list. Take an afternoon out to scour the second-hand shops for props or costumes. Plan new routines on paper while Mouse lounges in her basket. Enjoy the break together. There will be plenty of time later to work together and win rosettes at shows.

Mouse won't forget her doggy dancing moves if she has a break to have puppies. Give her time off during her pregnancy and while she is nursing her pups. Don't rush her recovery. Relax and enjoy this special time together.

Above *If you want to keep dancing, cut out any moves that could put your bitch and her unborn puppies at risk.*

To Neuter Or Not

Q *I have never neutered any of my dogs before and I've had both dogs and bitches. I don't see why they should have to have surgery unless there is a good medical reason for it. Also, I think it may change their personalities and I like my dogs to be real workers in training, not couch potatoes. What do you think?*

A To neuter or not to neuter? Some people hold very strong views on whether they will spay or castrate their pet. It is worth chatting to your vet and weighing up the pros and cons before making a decision as you will have to live with the consequences permanently.

Spaying If you want puppies, don't spay your bitch. But remember that you will have to contend with her seasons, which usually come round every six months and miss a few training classes and shows. Male dogs quickly become canine Romeos around a bitch in season and you don't want an accidental mating. When your girl is pregnant, she will need extra care. As she becomes big and heavy with pups, she will tire easily and the last thing on her mind will be dancing the fandango with you. Once the litter is born, you will have to let her have some quality time with her pups and when they have been weaned and gone to their new homes, you'll have to build up her fitness. Every bitch is different. Some make a quick comeback and others take a little more time to get back into condition.

On the other hand, if you don't want puppies, you can have your bitch spayed as early as six months. She will need time off to recover from the op, but early spaying can reduce the risk of mammary cancer, uterine cancer, false pregnancies

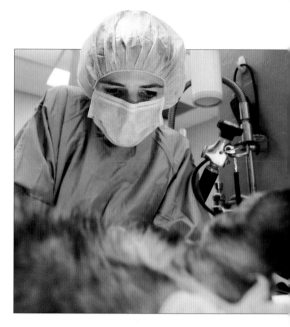

Above Are you thinking of having your pet spayed or castrated? Your vet will be happy to offer advice and discuss the surgical procedure with you.

and pyometra (infection of the womb). Some handlers report that their spayed bitches are less hormonal and more even-keeled and therefore easier to train. The downside of spaying is that there are a few bitches that develop urinary incontinence as a result but this is easily treated with medication. And the coats of some dogs get a little more fluffy.

Castration Castration is the surgical removal of the testicles, the main source of the male hormone testosterone. As a dog matures, this hormone starts to be released and triggers male behaviours. The boys just can't help it! They will looking far and wide for attractive bitches with a view to rampant sex. In addition, male dogs will start cocking their leg to mark their territory with urine to say "I was here!". And some get very macho declaring "I am king of the playground – don't mess with me or I'll show you my teeth!" These male attributes are not always pleasant to live with and no wonder many handlers argue that their male dogs are less distracted and sexually frustrated after castration and therefore more focused workers.

But there are no guarantees. The earlier you castrate your dog, the less likely he will be to develop prostatic disease or testicular cancer in the future and the greater your chances of eliminating some of the more undesirable male behaviours before they become a habit. But if your dog has spent years as a ladies' man, castration is unlikely to change him. Once your dog has had the snip, he will need a bit of time to recover from surgery and some owners complain that their dog piles on the pounds after castration. However, if you monitor your pet's diet and make sure he gets plenty of exercise, there is no reason to expect him to put on extra weight.

Above *Many dog owners report that castration eliminates undesirable male behaviours like scent-marking their possessions and territory with urine.*

Weighing up the pros and cons I don't think neutering will necessarily change your dog's personality. If your dog is a bouncy active dog before neutering, he or she will be a bouncy active dog after it. If your dog is showing real potential in the show ring strutting his or her stuff before the op, that trend will continue. However, neutering can change how other dogs react to your pet. For example, other male dogs are less likely to see a castrated male dog as a threat or rival. And neutering can certainly make it easier for your dog to live in our world. Do you want your miniature poodle to be at the mercy of your neighbour's Rottweiler every time she comes into season? And what about the Labrador that is roaming the neighbourhood looking for a date. Love is blind and he could be hit by a car.

Talk to other handlers at shows and training. I think you will discover that many of the stars of heelwork to music and canine freestyle have been neutered, but their desire for work and training has remained intact.

Left *When your bitch has puppies, give her time to enjoy and care for them. Dancing will be the last thing on her mind.*

Hearing Handicap

Q *I have a wonderful border crossbreed called Bonnie. I know she would love heelwork to music, but I'm not sure how much of a handicap my hearing would be. I am completely deaf in one ear but I do have some residual hearing in the other. I manage fine at home and at work, but how would I manage training with music?*

A You won't know until you try. Remaining in time with the music will be more difficult for you but not impossible. How much of the music you can hear will depend on the amount of residual hearing you have, the type of hearing loss (high or low frequency) and the music (bass or treble note dominated). Just as there are conversational markers in speech that keep you on track, there are musical cues that you can look for that will help you keep on the beat.

One, two and three! All dancers must learn to count in order to keep in time to the music and the more often they practise a routine, the more deeply the rhythm becomes embedded into the depths of their souls. Aim for an inner sense of timing. Here are some visual aids that will help you to develop the rhythm and timing you will need for your chosen piece of music.

- **A metronome** Metronomes *(right)* have been used by musicians to measure beats per minute for centuries and they vary in sophistication. The traditional type can be adjusted by moving a weight on a rod to increase or decrease the tempo. The rod swings back and forth making a click at the end of each swing. More modern metronomes are electronic and some are as small as a wristwatch. Keep your eye on the display.
- **A drummer** Get someone to be your drummer and watch the rise and fall of his sticks. Unlike a metronome, your drummer will be able to reflect sudden changes of tempo. His face will be a picture of musical interpretation.

- **A classmate** Find someone to walk in time to your music. Copying their arm and leg movements will give you a muscle memory of the timing of the movement. It is just like having a dancer or keep fit instructor in front of the class and following their lead.

Sound system Use a high quality sound system when you practise and place the speakers to your advantage. Check sound systems at shows when you reconnoitre the ring before the performance begins.

Hearing aids Make sure your hearing aid fits well. You don't want to lose it in the middle of your routine.

Vibration You could put your CD player on the floor and feel the music vibrating through the floor boards, but this isn't very practical for a dancer who leaps, jumps and spins with a dog.

Have you ever played this game? You are asked to sing along to a song and suddenly the volume is turned down and you have to keep singing. When the volume is turned up, does your singing match the singer on the recording? It's that inner sense of timing that counts. Practise your routine assiduously and you too won't need to hear the music to keep in time.

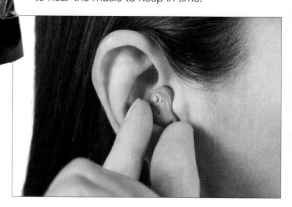

Above *Check that your hearing aid fits snugly and try to develop an inner sense of rhythm and musical timing.*

Failing Eye Sight

Q *Hope you can help. My miniature poodle, Lenny, has been diagnosed with Progressive Retinal Atrophy (PRA). He can see all right at the minute but I've been warned by the vet that his eyesight will get progressively worse and that he will eventually become blind. Should I retire him now or keep dancing?*

A If he can see, keep dancing!

Progressive Retinal Atrophy (PRA) Progressive Retinal Atrophy (PRA) is an inheritable disease which affects your dog's retina. Although PRA is not painful, there is no treatment or cure and all dogs diagnosed with this disease will eventually go blind *(right)*.

Grieving Many owners mourn their pet's loss of vision, but it is important to realise that dogs with PRA carry on as usual. They don't hurt and they are not suffering. Because their visual deterioration is slow and gradual, they have lots of time to adjust. For them, life is still a bowl of biscuits and they just have to rely on their other senses a little bit more.

Routine You will be surprised how much a dog with limited vision can do. Many owners are shocked to learn that their dogs have been losing their sight for some time before diagnosis and they haven't noticed. So, don't suddenly change your dance routines in anticipation of blindness. If you have always thrown a ball for Lenny on your walks, keep throwing it. He'll find it! Just because he is going to lose his sight, doesn't mean you should stop giving him mental stimulation and exercise.

Keep dancing If you and Lenny enjoy dancing together, keep dancing while you can. Be on the look-out for any problems that might be caused by poor vision, but don't let your concern for his well-being evolve into an all-purpose excuse. Did Lenny miss that cue because he couldn't see it or because he wasn't looking? Give him extra help as and when he needs it. Reinforce your verbal cues and make your body language bigger so it's easier to see. Decrease the amount of distance work in your routine and concentrate on moves that keep him close to you. Teach Lenny to touch your leg with his head in heelwork. Will he hold one end of your sash in his mouth while you hold the other? Stay out of the shadows if he has trouble adjusting to bright lights. If he can hear your voice, he'll know you are close by.

The right time to retire I would never give a bow and arrow to a blind archer but I would always try to provide my dogs with fun and interesting things to do. The time to retire Lenny is when doggy dancing isn't fun anymore. If he is struggling to find you when you enter the ring or if he looks vulnerable because he can't see where the barking dogs are sitting, it's time to give up competition. But that doesn't mean you have to halt training classes or performing tricks at home. Monitor and assess Lenny but don't write him off while he still has potential. I think he will amaze you with his adaptability and keep dancing for a long time yet. He'll still be able to smell a treat at a hundred paces even if he can't see it!

Wearing Spectacles

Q *Please don't laugh at me. I wear glasses and can't see a thing without them – even my Pomeranian, Speckles, blends into the carpet. Can I wear my glasses when I compete in heelwork to music?*

A Of course you can! I don't want you to mistake a judge for the ring steward or trip and fall over Speckles. So keep your specs on.

Safety Remember, you don't want your glasses falling off your nose. If you are wearing glasses and are participating in an activity that involves getting on your feet and jumping around, it's a good idea to make sure your glasses are firmly secured. Check that the arms of your spectacles are tightened so they don't slip off your face and think about buying a securing strap to keep them in place. And if they do fly off during a spectacular pirouette, are your lenses shatterproof?

Fashion accessory Glasses can be very individual and expressive. They certainly aren't boring! You can select from a variety of vibrant colours and exciting styles so choose a pair that will match your lipstick, your hair style and your personality. You will not only be able to see where you are going but you will look very trendy and up to date. More importantly, very you!

Costume accessory Your glasses can also be an integral part of your costume. Glasses can turn you into someone else if you want to escape from yourself. Dare I suggest a BIG pair of glasses if you are doing an Elton John number? Or (if it's appropriate) you could wear small frames that give you a demure schoolmistress/ librarian look. Have you tried a monocle? How about prescription goggles for an underwater number?

A ready-made prop You could use your glasses as a prop. I am thinking of those spectacles on a stick called lorgnettes that elderly ladies would grandly raise to their faces and look down their noses at their companions. If you could make something like that, it would be a great target stick. However, if Speckles is an enthusiastic grabber of target sticks, take care she doesn't knock them off the end. The resulting breakage would be difficult to explain to your optician.

Alternatives If you hate your glasses, what about contact lenses? You would never again have to worry about your glasses falling off when you peered over a balcony. You could go out in the rain and never worry about rain drops spoiling your view. Soft lenses, gas permeable lenses or once a month lenses. There are plenty of options available these days to discuss with your optician. Or you could consider laser surgery to correct your vision problems. A bigger step, of course, but one lots of people are taking these days with no regrets.

Mix and match Or you could mix and match. If you were up all night and your eyes are tired, wear your glasses and give your contacts a rest. Many handlers train in their glasses, but keep their contacts for "best", competitions and displays.

Whatever you do, please make sure you can see where you are going and don't step on Speckles!

Left Wear your glasses with pride. Your specs should be a fashion accessory that makes you feel individual and special.

Dizzy Spells

Q *I recently had an inflammation of my inner ear, labyrinthitis which has affected my balance. For the first few days, I felt like I had either had one gin and tonic too many or I was seasick! Although much better now, I still get an occasional dizzy spell. My Weimaraner, Shadow, and I have a show at the weekend. Can you help?*

A I am glad to hear that the symptoms of labyrinthitis are subsiding and that you are feeling better. Although I can't promise to stop you getting dizzy and falling over in the ring, I can offer you some advice.

Withdraw This is the simplest solution. If you are not feeling 100 per cent, you will not be able to give your best performance and neither will Shadow. Instead of concentrating on what moves come next, you will be anticipating another dizzy spell. Dogs are sensitive creatures and Shadow will know that your confidence has taken a knock. He could react by either working more hesitantly – for example, lagging behind in heelwork. Or he could step up to take over your routine and start barking orders. Why create problems for yourself. There will be other dog shows when you will be firing on all cylinders and able to stay in charge.

Cut and paste If you do decide to give it a go, cut out of your routine any moves that might literally tip your balance. Subtract the spins and twirls and add a static pose like a "beg" or a "wave". Go for heelwork in straight lines rather than in circles. Simplify your routine. Lower your performance criteria. Stick to what Shadow can do easily and well and cut out the things that he finds difficult. You can always up the ante at another show.

Rest and recuperate Be honest with yourself. Are you fully recovered? Shadow will never hold it against you if you take some time off sick but he might not be so forgiving if you lose your balance and step on his toes. He won't forget all that you have taught him or stop loving you just because you have a few more days in bed. If your symptoms are not disappearing as quickly as they should, consider making an appointment to see your doctor. It is not worth rushing your recovery just for a dog show.

Left *If you are in pain, leave doggy dancing for another day when you feel better and can smile again.*
Below *If you are feeling dizzy and nauseous, bending over your dog is likely to see you on the floor!*

Knee Pain

Q *I have a knee problem. I've seen my doctor who suspects cartilage damage and has offered me an arthroscopy to investigate the pain I have in my joint. I'm happy to put off surgery, wear a knee support and pop a painkiller. A bit of creaking isn't going to stop me and my Vizsla, Red, from training and dancing at shows. Will I be penalised for wearing a knee support?*

A You can hide a knee support under your costume. The judges won't know you are wearing one and wouldn't mark you down for doing so if they did. But they might get agitated if your knees creak so loudly they can't hear the music. And you won't be able to hide your discomfort if you hobble about gritting your teeth rather than floating across the floor with a smile on your face.

Pain with a message Only you know how much your knee hurts. Does the pain get worse with exercise? Does it lessen with rest? Pain is an indication that something is not right. How bad will it have to get before you call it a day and go back to your doctor?

Pain with a purpose Pain nags like an old woman. You will take more time and care when placing your feet and may avoid certain movements. Instead of a big step, you'll take a small one. You might decide against a move because you'll risk tripping and falling over. In place of a leap, you'll substitute an arm move. If your aches and pains are uppermost in your mind, you won't be giving Red your full attention and you'll be setting limits on what you can do with him.

Surgery If you go ahead with your arthroscopy, any damaged ligament or cartilage can be repaired or removed. Of course, you would have to be sensible during your recuperation and your return to normal exercise would be dependent on the type and degree of your knee injury. Some people bounce back quickly and others take a bit more time. However

long a break you take from training and competition, it is not the end of the world. Red will not forget everything you have taught him in the meantime and, if you follow the doctor's orders, you will be firing on all cylinders, pain free.

I do admire your commitment to dog dancing and I do understand how you want to keep going at all costs. However, I do think those costs are too high. You shouldn't have to take painkillers to have fun and enjoy training your dog and you risk further damage to your knee by soldiering on. Talk to your doctor again. You owe it to yourself and to Red to get your knee fixed. Your training and competition career will be temporarily interrupted, but it will be worth it if you are eventually able to move with greater ease. You'll probably wonder why you put it off for so long.

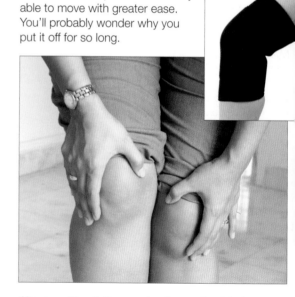

Above and inset *Knees get quite a work-out in doggy dancing. You can easily hide a knee support under your costume but it is more difficult to hide the pain.*

Feeling The Heat

Q *Everyone looks forward to summer except me. I have a Rottweiler called Betty and she hates the heat. Instead of being all feisty and keen to work, Betty droops, drools and lags behind in everything. What can I do to keep her cool?*

A You can't blame Betty for feeling the heat. Dogs have a few sweat glands on their feet but rely on panting to regulate their body temperature. It can be a pretty inefficient system for dogs that are overweight, have short muzzles or carry big double coats of fur. Help Betty to keep herself cool at shows so she can give you her best performance.

Avoid dehydration Make sure that Betty's water bowl is full so she won't dehydrate. Add a few ice cubes to it to keep it nice and cold. Or you can freeze a bowl of water the night before to take with you.

Stay in the shade Keep Betty out of direct sunlight as much as possible. You'll find shade by the side of your car, the back of the marquee or under a tree. Make a little tent out of reflective sheeting and get underneath it with her. You'll both stay cool.

Provide some water You don't want to take Betty into the ring looking like a drowned rat so swimming in the stream that runs through the showground is out. But you could buy a water pistol and squirt her tummy, feet and tongue to cool her down. She'll love it but not if she has been squirted in the past for being naughty! Try using a plant mister instead which is a little more gentle but just as effective.

Summer accessories For Betty's travelling kennel, you can buy a battery-operated fan as well as a cool bed and pillow to keep her body temperature down. How would Betty look in a bonnet, bandana or sun shades? Would she toss them off in disgust or allow them to shield her from the sun rays? What about a reflective coat or wet towelling jacket (these can dry quickly on a warm day, but the doggy smell lingers on). And don't forget the sun screen for those areas of exposed skin that may burn.

Not so great expectations Even if you take all these steps, Betty still may be too hot to give you her best. You will need to lower your expectations. She will probably think a bit slower, move a bit slower and pant a lot more (and so will you). If your class is at the beginning or end of the day, you're lucky. It will be a bit cooler than at midday when the sun is at its maximum strength. I know you have probably travelled a long distance and paid entry fees to compete, but if you think that your dog will not be up to scratch and you will be disappointed in her, why not do a training round or scratch from the competition? Remember that while you have the option of discarding your costume's jacket on a warm day, Betty can't take off hers!

Right *Joe Cool is not going to get too hot while he's waiting on a summer day for his class to start.*

Why Won't He Play?

Q *Glory is a glorious Westie who can't understand what all the fuss is about when I bring out a tennis ball or tug rope. The dogs around her go bananas while she just sits and looks at her toenails. I'd like to use a toy in training, but Glory just is not interested. Can you help?*

A It's hard not to draw comparisons when you see dogs having fun with whatever their handlers pull out of their training bags. Especially if your own dog regards canines that put balls in their mouths as plain bonkers.

Won't play There are many reasons why a dog won't play. A pup will learn to stay away from toys if an older dog in the household says "Those are mine. Touch one and you die." Or maybe the pup has been scolded for picking up something he shouldn't and has applied this lesson to his toys. Sometimes a puppy has been teased with a toy but never given the chance to get hold of it so he gives up trying. Toys – yuck! If you want Glory to play with a ball or tug, you'll have to work hard to make them interesting.

Movement There is nothing more boring than a static toy. Drag it along the floor in a zig zag. Make the toy's movement mimic an injured bird and Glory might rouse herself to chase it. Praise Glory for any interest. Tell her she is a "good girl" for looking or watching. Next time she might take a swipe at it with her paw.

The art of noise Toys that make a noise will attract Glory's attention and she will want to investigate. The squeak will sound like a small furry creature that is about to crawl away to die and Glory might surprise you by diving in to put it out of its misery. Join in and praise. Glory may become adept at killing squeaky toys. Don't complain. Keep buying replacements and invest in some ear plugs.

Find the food Hiding food in a toy makes it smell delicious! Some toys are manufactured specially with little pockets for secreting a piece of sausage or biscuit inside. Or make one yourself. Take an old sock and stuff it with titbits. Glory will be keen to find out what smells so good. If she sniffs the sock, give her a taste of what's inside. Cheer her on if she starts to disembowel it.

You become the game Be a playmate. Push Glory away from you. Does she bounce back? Run up the garden. Does Glory chase after you? Have a toy in your hand ready to add to the fun of the game.

Favourites Be prepared to play with anything, no matter how odd or embarrassing. Glory may fall in love with an old brassiere. If she starts goofing around with the toilet brush, praise her!

Toys are an important tool in dog training because they are great motivators and can really pep up an exercise, but they are not the only ones. Glory may prefer food rewards to a ball and if that is what gets you the results you want, keep using them!

Left Hide a tasty treat in a toy to arouse your dog's interest.

How long it takes to get out!

Wheelchair Dancing

Q *My husband took me to a heelwork to music display last weekend. We both love dogs. I was surprised to see a handler working her dog to the music from a wheelchair. It was a beautiful routine and brought tears to my eyes. I, too, am a wheelchair user and I've a little crossbreed bitch called Teflon who's already done some basic obedience classes. I've chosen my music and am keen to start. Any advice?*

A There is always one routine that stands out in a crowd and this one did for you. I'm so glad that you are keen to train Teflon further and try your luck at doggy dancing. You will have lots of fun and be amazed at what you can accomplish together.

The sky's the limit Like every team on the dance floor, you will have your strengths and weaknesses but your routine will have to be choreographed to take into account your wheelchair. I've seen some very imaginative moves from wheelchair users – dogs resting their front feet on the foot or armrests to push their handlers backwards or in circles. The great thing about doggy dancing is that inventiveness is encouraged and rewarded, so the sky's the limit.

Training techniques If you've done some basic obedience, you're ahead of the game. And if you have clicker-trained Teflon, you already have the tools to teach her new tricks and sequences. There may be times when you need a little extra help from a trainer or classmate, but don't we all? Find a training club that is friendly, supportive and has an accessible meeting place. Never be afraid to experiment and develop your own ideas so look for an instructor whom you like and who is open minded.

Wheelchair power Don't immediately rush out and buy a new one. You are familiar with

what you've got and you will have enough on your plate teaching Teflon how to twist and spin. Later, when you have more experience of choreographing routines, you may decide to upgrade to a wheelchair with greater manoeuvrability and power.

Check the surfaces How much is your mobility affected by flooring? Get into the habit of checking out training and show venues. If you are expected to dance on the village green on a wet day, would one of your wheels get stuck in the mud just when your music begs you to accelerate forward? If the surface is not suitable or safe, you can always withdraw. You won't be the only one who won't dance in the rain.

Take the initiative Dog agility has a Disabled Handlers Association that helps puts people in touch with one another to discuss training and mobility challenges in their canine discipline. Perhaps you and Teflon could start something similar for heelwork to music? There are a growing number of doggy dancers out there with a range of different disabilities and sometimes just talking to someone with a similar problem makes all the difference to finding a solution.

So take the plunge and make a start. I look forward to seeing you and Teflon at a show sometime soon.

Right *Wheelchair users and their dogs love doggy dancing too! If you run a club or host a show, makes sure it is accessible to all.*

RESOURCES AND INDEX

Where can I buy a clicker? Where can I find a heelwork
to music class? Do you know the name of a good
trainer? The more places you look, the more answers
you are likely to find. And the more questions you
will want to ask. Here is a list of useful resources to
get you started in the hunt for further information.

Resources

Governing Body

The Kennel Club is currently the only organisation sanctioning heelwork to music shows in Britain and to participate your dog must be on either its Breed or Activity Register. The first Kennel Club Heelwork to Music Show was held in 2003 and gained many new supporters. Good news spreads fast and the Kennel Club responded by setting up a working party in 2005 to refine and develop the rules and regulations governing the sport. They hold the Heelwork to Music, Freestyle and International finals at Crufts each year and launched the Young Kennel Club Heelwork to Music Finals in 2008. In addition, the Kennel Club promotes a number of other activities (obedience, agility and flyball)and events (Scruffs and Discover Dogs) as well as providing additional services and information to dog owners.

The Kennel Club
1 Clarges Street
London W1J 8AB
Telephone: 0870 606 6750
www.the-kennel-club.org.uk

National Clubs and Associations

The two main dog dancing clubs in Great Britain are Canine Freestyle GB and the Paws 'n' Music Association. Both hold shows throughout the year which include Crufts semi-finals as well as Young Kennel Club Qualifiers. Join their membership and you will not only benefit from reduced show entry fees but can keep in touch with your friends through newsletters and email groups.

Canine Freestyle GB
Telephone: 07759909101
Email: cfgb@caninefreestyle.com
www.caninefreestylegb.com

Paws 'n' Music
Pen Yr Orsedd
Gwalchmai,
Holyhead
Anglesey LL65 4RB
Email: enq@paws-n-music.co.uk
www.paws-n-music.co.uk

The International Scene

Looking beyond these shores? There are a number of international organisations that aim to advance the sport of dog dancing. These include the Canine Freestyle Federation (www.canine-freestyle.org), the Musical Dog Sport Association (www.musicaldogsport.org) and World Canine Freestyle Federation (www.worldcaninefreestyle.org). Different countries boast their own homegrown stars and leading lights. Their websites are well worth visiting for training tips and videos. Cross the Atlantic and you find Sandra Davis (www.dancingdogs.net) and Carolyn Scott (www.caninefreestylemagicmatch.com). And on the other side of the Atlantic, keep an eye open for Emmy Simonsen from Denmark (www.hazyland.dk) and Marleen van Hess from Belgium (users.skynet.be/dogdancing). The introduction of pet passports has meant that many people are combining a holiday in Europe with a heelwork to music show. And Britain is likewise receiving its share of overseas visitors.

UK Dancing Celebrities

These are the stars that really twinkle. Choose any one to be a role model. And they aren't just pretty faces. They all work hard to promote dog dancing through judging, workshops and training material like clickers, training bags, DVDs and books.

Richard Curtis
Richard Curtis is one of the UK's leading heelwork to music and canine freestyle handlers and he proved that the "other" breeds can beat the collies when his Portuguese Water Spaniel, Disco, won at Crufts in 2006 with his clown routine.
Email: richard@k9freestyle.co.uk
www.k9freestyle.co.uk

Tina Humphrey

Tina is one of our most experienced trainers and competitors and she won the first heat of the BBC show *When Will I Be Famous* with her dog Chandi proving that dog dancing is an act that can top the popularity polls. No rosettes this time, but a cash prize of £10,000!

www.bluecroft.co.uk

Mary Ray

Mary is a down-to-earth dancing diva! She is not only responsible for starting the sport in the United Kingdom in the 1990s but she is the dancing star of each year's closing ceremony at Crufts. Her dogs excel at whatever they put their paws to and that includes agility and obedience. I loved her Glenn Miller and River Dance routines.

Telephone: 01788 561253
Email: *maryanddaveray@aol.com*
www.maryray.co.uk

Dr. Attila Szkukalek

Attila is a competitor, international judge and freestyle tutor. Attila and his Border Collie, Fly, pioneered freestyle with their innovative moves shown in their "Carmen", "Charlie Chaplin" and "Gladiator" routines.

83 Stafford Street
Norwich
NR2 3BG
Telephone: 01603 611184
Email: *attila@dogdance.net*
www.dogdance.net

Top Lodge Dancing Dogs

Top Lodge comprises a trio of top dancers – Kath Hardman, Karen Sykes and Lesley Neville. They have all been Crufts winners and travel throughout the UK and abroad performing at many events, judging and training others in the sport.

Telephone: 07759909101
Email: *cabaret@dancingdogs.co.uk*
www.dancingdogs.co.uk

Quality Trainers

The Association of Pet Dog Trainers, founded in 1995 by John Fisher, seeks to ensure that dog training classes are run on fair, kind and effective principles. Look at their list of APDT-assessed trainers to find one near you offering classes in doggy dancing.

APDT (Association of Pet Dog Trainers)

PO Box 17
Kempsford GL7 4WZ
Telephone: 01285 810811
Email: *apdtoffice@aol.com*
www.apdt.co.uk

The Perfect Gift For You and Your Dog

You can find everything you ever wanted at Training Lines. They sell clickers, books, treats, beds, grooming tools, toys and lots, lots more. Whether you are looking for a training accessory or a Christmas present for your pooch, make Training Lines your first stop by shopping there online.

Training Lines: Unique Dog Products

Smithy Croft
Strichen
Fraserburgh AB43 6SL
Telephone: 0845 644 2397
Email: *info@traininglines.co.uk*
Website: www.traininglines.co.uk

In The Frame

If you have worked hard to look good on the dance floor, why not buy a photo or video to mark the event? Whether it was a winning routine or your youngster's debut, you won't want to forget the occasion. And a recording or picture is the perfect gift.

Allan Brown Photography

Allan is a member of the Top Lodge Dancing Dogs team and has developed his skills at taking superb action dog dancing photographs that capture the athletic quality of routines at shows and demonstrations.

Visit his blog to view his work.

Telephone: 01773 820731
Email: allan.m.brown@live.co.uk
http://allanbrown.blogspot.com

Rivergate Photography

Andrew Cartlidge is a consulting structural engineer who describes himself as a keen amateur photographer. If you expect all his photographs to be of buildings, you would be disappointed. His pictures of animals, people and country events are great and he is on the scene for the most of the dog dancing competitions in the UK. Check his website to see if you were caught on camera and perhaps buy a print to celebrate.

Unit 7b Northbrook Industrial Estate
Vincent Avenue
Shirley
Southampton
Hampshire SO16 6PB
Telephone: 023 8098 8020
Fax: 07092 373850
Mobile: 07971 206059
Email: mail@rivergate.org.uk
www.rivergate.org.uk

Lincolnshire Lions

Lincolnshire Lions are a section of the Louth and District Dog Club. They offer videos of selected shows during the year at reasonable rates. This gives handlers the opportunity to self-assess their routines and to understand what makes a successful team.

Alan Eves
Telephone: 01507 327612
Email: alan.eves@btinternet.com

Further Education

If you want to polish your clicker training skills or participate in a clicker challenge, this is the place to go. In fact, just go to Kay Laurence's Wag More Barn and learn some more about your dog.

Learning About Dogs

Kay Laurence has been a key figure in dog training for many years and in 2000 opened the doors of Learning About Dogs. She's never looked back. Her team of instructors come from a variety of fields of canine sports and specialisms. They aim to inspire and educate you at workshops and seminars held at Wag More Barn. And they do!

PO Box 13
Chipping Campden, GL55 6WX
Telephone: 01386 430189
www.learningaboutdogs.com

Keeping Fit

Improve your fitness and performance with DAQ (Dynamic, Agile & Quick). DAQ is a progressive training system of low impact exercises used to produce good movement and balance. And it's great fun!

DAQ (Dynamic, Agile and Quick)

Steve and Yvonne Croxford
Shade Cottage
Coventry Road
Wigston Parva
Leicestershire, LE10 3AP
Telephone: 01455 220245
www.pace-agility.org
www.daqinternational.com

And Looking Good

What to wear for your routine? Want a red wig to feel like Ginger Rogers? With luck you will find just what you are looking for at a jumble sale or charity shop. If you are good with a needle and thread, you can make your own costume. But if you're not, you'll love The British Costume Association (BCA). It is the organisation for fancy dress and theatrical costume supplies. It has a store directory so that you can find a shop near you to visit and it has a costume request service.

The British Costume Association (BCA)
PO Box 136
Ashington
NE62 5ZX
Telephone: 0845 2300515
www.incostume.co.uk

Hands-on Therapies
A massage for you or your dog can be a luxurious
bit of pampering – perfect after a hard day's training.
Or it may be part of a remedial therapy after an injury.
However, it is advisable to check with your doctor or
vet before booking an appointment for any hands-on
treatment.

ACAT (The Association of Complementary Animal Therapists)
Members agree to abide by a strict code of practice
and ethics. You can find your nearest practitioner via
their website.
P.O. Box 31
Chudleigh
Devon TQ13 0ZQ
www.theacat.co.uk

Galen Therapy Centre
The Centre offers massage treatments at their
clinic as well as a range of training
workshops and courses.
Julia Robertson
Galen Therapy Centre
Mill House
Coolham
West Sussex RH13 8GR
Telephone: 0845 3751767
Mobile: 0781 0600329
Email: *mail@caninetherapy.co.uk*
www.galentherapycentre.co.uk
www.caninetherapy.co.uk

(ICAT) The Institute of Complementary Animal Therapies
ICAT provides practitioner Diploma courses in Canine

Remedial Massage as well as
workshops covering complementary
animal therapies.
Julie Boxall
Principal
PO Box 299
Chudleigh
Devon TQ13 0ZQ
Telephone: 01626 852485
Mobile: 07977 359347
info@theicat.co.uk
www.theicat.co.uk

McTimoney Chiropractic Association (MCA)
McTimoney chiropractors are qualified to treat both
humans and animals. They seek to promote good
health and alleviate the causes of aches and pains.
Crowmarsh Gifford
Wallingford
Oxfordshire OX10 8DJ
Telephone: 01491 829211
www.mctimoney-chiropractic.org

Tellington Touch
The Tellington TTouch team uses massage and
ground exercises to help animals improve overall
athletic ability while at the same time enriching
the bond between pet and owner.
Sarah Fisher
UK Team Centre
Tilley Farm
Timsbury Road
Farmborough
Nr Bath
Somerset BA2 0AB
Telephone: 01761 471182
www.ttouchteam.co.uk
www.tilleyfarm.co.uk

Index

Picture Credits

Unless otherwise credited below, all the photographs that appear in this book were taken by Mark Burch and are © Interpet Publishing Ltd.

Jane Burton, Warren Photographic: 120 both, 182.

Crestock.com
Eric Isselée: 26 top.

Dreamstime.com
Scott Griessel: 188. Dan Hughes: 125. Erik Lam: 181 top centre. Juriah Mosin: 194 bottom. Tina Rencelj: 178. Lakatos Sandor: 18 top. Saniphoto: 134. Showface: 131. Anke van Wyk: 184. Ivonne Wierink: 156.

Fotolia.com
Andy An: 26 bottom. Jeffrey Banke: 173, 185. CPJ Photography: 189 bottom. Diefotomacher: 29 left. Dixi: 149 top left. Jose Manuel Gelpi: 19 centre left. Fenghua He: 190 centre. Eric Isselée: 31 bottom, 160 top, 191. Kerioak: 142 top. Lennynt: 160 bottom. Steve Luker: 192. Jaroslaw Miszczak: 30 bottom. Perrush: 24 top. Pavel Timofeev: 138. Tomasz Wojnarowicz: 139. Simone van den Berg: 7 bottom centre, 28 bottom, 152 bottom right.

Interpet Archive: 30 top, 40, 64, 106-7, 118, 149 top right, 154, 158, 197.

iStockphoto.com
Zuzana Buranova: 108. Brian Chase: 194 inset. Mike Chatwin: 186. Anne Clark: 153. Dirkr: 152 bottom centre. Arthur Fatykhov: 18 left. Brian Goodman: 193 bottom right. Eric Isselée: 20 top, 124, 194 top. Denise Kappa: 195. Erik Lam: 7 top, 187 top, 199. Gloria-Leigh Logan: 170. Macatack: 189 top. Jackie McDermott: 23 top. Narvikk: 25 top. Michael Pettigrew: 23 centre left. Fanelie Rosier: 157. Richard Scherzinger: 181 top right. Ron Sumners: 193 centre. Rolf Weschke: 190 bottom right. Annette Wiechmann: 187 bottom. Zootzims: 163.

Shutterstock.com
AleksKo: 126 left. Jaimie Duplass: 144. Michael C. Gray: 140. Ivanpavlisko: 132. Somer McCain: 121. Lakatos Sandor: 129. Anna Utekhina: 12 right.

Acknowledgements

This book is for Tam, my Border Collie, who was my first dancing partner and always kept perfect time. I miss you!

I would still be writing this book with a pen if Murray Peake hadn't bought me the Ladybird Book *The Computer: How it Works* many years ago. Thank you for freeing me from the grip of Tippex and getting me off that first page. I love the delete button.

Others whom I wouldn't be without are editor, Philip de Ste. Croix, and production manager, Malcolm Little, who have read every word I've written and laughed in all the right places. I am waiting for you to get and train your own dogs.

And, of course, Kim Blundell whose cartoons say what words can't. And Mark Burch who makes all my friends and their dogs feel relaxed in front of the camera. Everyone at the photoshoot proved that Britain really does have talent. Thank you to everyone who strutted their stuff for the camera: Trudi Bament and Zed; Margaret Challans and Blue; Gina Graham and Ember, Cassie, and Dizzy; Kimberley Hampsheir and Ding; Louise Ince and Barney, Mylo and Jodi; Lara Inglott and Daisy; Bridget Jamieson and Bailey; Mindy Kerr and Chip and Sunny; Amanda Leek and George and Whispa; Annette Leslie and Dennis and Freddie; Louise Leverton and Danny; Karen McCarthy and Vienna; Chris Mancini and Taggie; Carol Mortimer and Inky; Issy Nicholls and Phoebe and Freya; Janice Philpott and Toby; Sarah Reed and Seven and Tally; Sally Turner and Race and March; Carol Wallace and Compo, Tilly and Molly; Lesley Wells and Barney; Tricia Whitehill and Daisy; Shannon Wyllie and Toddy.

I must thank, too, my colleagues at Vets-Now Emergency Service (Northampton) for again sharing my excitement for the project and holding my hand when I was flagging. You guys are great!

And it is impossible to forget the many people who have helped me problem-solve and train my own dogs in a variety of canine sports. Mary Ray stands out amongst them as an all-round training goddess who is never short of words of encouragement. And she is so much fun! As is Carol Wallace who has endured my poodles with great stoicism and good humour.

Lastly, where would I be without my own students and their dogs? You are my inspiration and I hope you look forward to classes as much as I do.